Paris: The 'New Rome' of Napoleon I

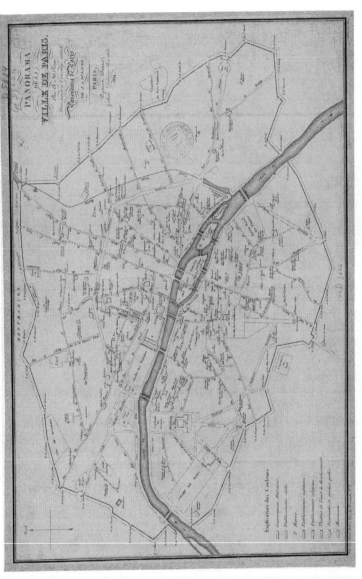

Figure 1 Perrot, A. M. *Panorama of Paris*, 1824. Engraving, BnF, Cartes et Plans, inv. GE D-5604. Photo: BnF, Paris. While this map shows the names of streets, squares and structures of note, it also gives an idea of the topographical relationship between the Roman city's *decumanus* and *cardo*, and Paris' 'new' road network.

Paris: The 'New Rome' of Napoleon I

Diana Rowell

BLOOMSBURY
LONDON • NEW DELHI • NEW YORK • SYDNEY

Bloomsbury Academic
An imprint of Bloomsbury Publishing Plc

50 Bedford Square	1385 Broadway
London	New York
WC1B 3DP	NY 10018
UK	USA

www.bloomsbury.com

Bloomsbury is a registered trade mark of Bloomsbury Publishing Plc

First published 2012
Reprinted 2012, 2013
Paperback Edition first published 2014

© Diana Rowell, 2012

Diana Rowell has asserted her right under the Copyright, Designs and Patents Act, 1988, to be identified as Author of this work.

All rights reserved. No part of this publication may be reproduced or transmitted in any form or by any means, electronic or mechanical, including photocopying, recording, or any information storage or retrieval system, without prior permission in writing from the publishers.

No responsibility for loss caused to any individual or organization acting on or refraining from action as a result of the material in this publication can be accepted by Bloomsbury or the author.

British Library Cataloguing-in-Publication Data
A catalogue record for this book is available from the British Library.

ISBN: HB: 978-1-4411-3518-6
PB: 978-1-4725-2529-1

Library of Congress Cataloging-in-Publication Data
A catalog record for this book is available from the Library of Congress.

Typeset by Newgen Imaging Systems, Pvt Ltd, Chennai, India
Printed and bound in Great Britain

Contents

List of Figures   vii
List of Abbreviations   ix
Acknowledgements   x

Introduction – Paris: The 'New Rome' of Napoleon I   1

1 Paris: A 'New Rome'   11
    The lure of Roman antiquity   12
    Roman Gaul and the language of power   15
    On the road to domination   19
    'Rome' reigns in Republican Paris   23
    The cultivation of Napoleon's image and the creation of
        the Napoleonic myth   26
    Projection and reception: Place and space   33

2 The Monument and the Monumental Axis   37
    Napoleon's Arc de Triomphe de l'Étoile   38
    Napoleon's Arc de Triomphe du Carrousel   47
    The western section of Napoleon's *voie triomphale*
        and the Rue de Rivoli   55
    Napoleon's Vendôme Column   57
    The eastern section of Napoleon's *voie triomphale*
        and the visionary Rue Impérial   65
    The monument and the monumental axis in perspective   69

3 The Impact and Implications of the Sun-King's 'New Rome(s)'   89
    The role of antiquity in the Sun-King's new monarchy   91
    The projection of the Sun-King's capital as a new
        and a superior 'Rome'   100
    The Sun-King's 'parallel Romes'   105
    The reception of the Sun-King and his 'new Rome(s)'   109
    Napoleon's publicists and the Sun-King's Paris   114
    From the Sun-King's Paris to Napoleon's 'new Rome'   115

4	The 'Roman' Triumph and the Language of Power	124
	The Roman Triumph: Evidence and conceptions	125
	The Triumph of the Caesars and the *entrée royale* of the kings	130
	The 'Triumphs' of the Republic	136
	The staging of power: A tale of two 'Triumphs'	147

Conclusion — 156

Appendices — 167
Glossary — 171
Notes — 177
Select Bibliography — 206
Index — 229

List of Figures

1	Perrot, A. M. *Panorama of Paris*, 1824	ii
2	Berthault, P.-G. Detail of the *Entrée triomphale des monuments des sciences et arts en France (9–10 Thermidor, An VI)*, 1802	72
3	David, J.-L. *The Coronation of the Emperor Napoléon I and the Crowning of the Empress Joséphine in Notre-Dame Cathedral on 2 December, 1804*, c.1806–7	72
4	Anon. *Entrée of Napoléon I and Marie-Louise of Austria as they near the Avenue des Champs-Élysées (2 April, 1810)*, c.1810	73
5	The Arc de Triomphe de l'Étoile	73
6	The Arch of Titus	74
7	The Arc du Carrousel	74
8	The Arch of Septimius Severus	75
9	The Arch of Constantine	75
10	Testard, A. *A 'bird's-eye view' of Paris*, 1860	76
11	Anon. *Map of Paris (including the city's fauxbourgs)*, c.1720	77
12	The Vendôme Column (Colonne de la Grande Armée)	78
13	Trajan's Column	79
14	Friedrich. *The demolition of Louis XIV's equestrian statue in 1792 (Place Vendôme)*, 1793	80
15	Detail of the Vendôme Column's pedestal	80
16	Detail of the Trajanic column's pedestal	81
17	A view of the Vendôme Column from the Rue de Rivoli	81
18	The Louvre's glass pyramid	82
19	The Grande Arche de la Défense	82

20	Anon. *Inauguration Ceremony (13 August, 1699) for the erection of Louis XIV's equestrian statue in the (then) Place des Conquêtes, c.*1700	83
21	The Porte Saint-Denis	84
22	The Porte Saint-Martin	84
23	Callet, A. F. *Allegory of the Surrender of Ulm, 20 October, 1805*	85
24	Werner, J. *Triumph of King Louis XIV of France driving the Chariot of the Sun preceded by Aurora, c.*1662–7	86
25	Lepautre, J. *Detail of the temporary obelisk-topped triumphal arch erected in the Place Dauphine for the 1660 Entrée triomphale, c.*1662	87
26	Lepautre, J. *Detail of the temporary triumphal arch erected on the Pont Notre-Dame for the 1660 Entrée triomphale, c.*1662	88

List of Abbreviations

BnF   Bibliothèque nationale de France
BnF, Cartes et Plans Bibliothèque nationale de France, Département des Cartes et Plans
BnF, Estampes   Bibliothèque nationale de France, Département des Estampes et de la Photographie
Moniteur Universel *Gazzette Nationale ou Le Moniteur Universel*

Acknowledgements

My interest in Napoleon's appropriation of the Roman world began some years ago when I first lived in Paris and visiting friends had set their sights on a guided tour of this wonderful city. On reaching the Place Vendôme, they were eager for a detailed explanation of the square's eye-catching centrepiece. I could answer only that this towering structure crowned by an effigy of Napoleon I reminded me of antique Rome's famed Trajanic column. I would therefore like to thank Leigh and Marion Pollinger for fuelling my curiosity and my ongoing fascination with the 'Roman' landscape(s) of Napoleonic Paris.

This study owes much to the support and encouragement of a number of people, none of whom is responsible for any error I may have made in my research of this vast, exciting and at times, daunting topic. I would like to express my warmest thanks to Ray Laurence, Amy Smith, Phiroze Vasunia and Catharine Edwards. Others whose suggestions and support over the years have been greatly appreciated include Andrew Wallace-Hadrill, Maria Wyke and also Jean Tulard, who took the time to recommend a variety of French works on Napoleonic rule. For the most part, my periods of research were divided between the British Library and Parisian institutions, not least the Bibliothèque nationale de France. I wish to thank collectively those who answered my deluge of questions and helped in making my library-based research a most rewarding experience. Similarly, my thanks go to Michael Greenwood at Continuum; the Classics Department at the University of Reading; Valerie Scott, Maria Pia Malvezzi and the rest of the staff at the British School at Rome. Others who have contributed in so many and such a variety of ways include my mother, Lambaire, Gwen, Michael, Barbara, Julie, Saras, Lou, Ellie, Anne and also my equally dear friends, Gwen and Djamel Amriou. I dedicate this book to Frank, without whom it would not have been possible.

Introduction – Paris: The 'New Rome' of Napoleon I

If I were master of France, I would make Paris not only the most beautiful city to exist and the most beautiful city to have existed, but also the most beautiful city that could exist.[1]

Classical Rome played a pivotal role in the grandiose visions of Napoleon Bonaparte to transform Paris into an imperial metropolis that would eclipse all other cities in the past, in the present and in the future. The capital's new monumental landscape became a visual paradigm of Napoleon's rule as emperor (1804–14 and 1815) and a potent vehicle through which to display his unparalleled authority. The practice of defining a new beginning in this way was not unprecedented: it was a phenomenon that was bound to the evolution of Paris' Roman character, its ritual and architecture and to the long history of power relations in France (and other European states). This book investigates how Napoleonic Paris may be understood as a 'new Rome', in which the Napoleonic era was presented as surpassing all recreations of Rome from the past, particularly that of Louis XIV (1643–1715).

Why should Napoleon have focussed upon the 'new Rome' of Louis XIV? French monarchs such as François I, Henri II and Henri IV, after all, had translated the antique into an array of media that might have resulted in their having a significant impact upon Napoleon and his imperial capital. Although it is important not to overlook the implications of Napoleon's affiliation with the Frankish king and Holy Roman Emperor, Charlemagne (c.742–814),[2] this book shows how the multifaceted legacy of Louis XIV had a more profound impact upon the Roman character of Napoleonic Paris than that of any other French sovereign. While recognizing that the manipulation of Republican Rome during the French Revolution (c.1789–99) also shaped Napoleon's exploitation of antiquity, we should not isolate the Napoleonic era from pre-revolutionary receptions of Rome in Paris. What I shall explore in this study is not a dialectic between Napoleon and antiquity but rather, a three-way ('tripartite') relationship between antiquity, Napoleon and earlier reinventions of classical Rome.

The reinvention of classical Rome's triumphal architecture and its associated symbolism, imagery and ritual were central to this relationship. The triumph in antiquity encapsulated the notion of conquest and domination. In essence, it was ritual whereby a victorious general, having been granted the right by the Senate to enter Rome, rode in procession from the *porta triumphalis* to the Temple of Jupiter (the Capitol), sacred site and heart of the mighty Roman Empire.[3] Once the Republic gave way to the Imperial period, a triumph was celebrated only by the emperor (and his family). Although aspects of the triumph and the passage of the *triumphator* along a triumphal arch-studded route to the Capitol remain unclear, the tradition was linked intricately to the display of power and, above all, to the *triumphator*'s entrance-*ritus* – his symbolic and physical entrance into power.[4] The comment by the eminent French historian and philosopher, Montesquieu (1689–1755), that the custom of triumphs contributed so much to Rome's greatness, underlines further the symbolic and the political appeal of the Roman triumph.[5]

Montesquieu's perception of Rome's triumphs would have been governed not only by his knowledge of antiquity but also by secondary sources and elaborate re-enactments of the triumph, which still were an intrinsic part of the political arena in eighteenth-century Europe. Today's historian is becoming increasingly aware that the lens through which the ancient past and post-antique receptions of antiquity are interpreted, is coloured inevitably by the preconceptions of the day. There is a fine line between history (the past) and historiography (man's subjective interpretation and application of the past).[6] We must therefore account for exaggerations, omissions and selectivity, and consider both the contextual and the temporal setting of the sources from which we draw. Equally, we may turn these potential hazards around and see them in a positive light. Historical enquiry may be used as an effective tool with which to gauge interpretations of the past; these interpretations (or receptions) are invaluable to the study of the past (also the present) and over time they, too, become part of that past. For example, in this book we will see how our conception of Napoleon's relationship with antiquity is incomplete without a full investigation of the diverse and the controversial receptions of Louis XIV. The reception of this king from the past was linked to the projection of Napoleonic Paris as a 'new Rome'. This relationship was shaped not so much by history but rather by the various interpretations of the past and, within this relationship, the sociopolitical climate of the present. I intend to demonstrate how we may enhance our understanding of Napoleon's relationship with antiquity and aspects relating to the changing nature of his rule, his image, his triumphal spectacle and above all, Paris in its new role as the nucleus of the Napoleonic Empire.

By taking this approach, this study engages with and contributes to the subject area of reception, a field of enquiry that has taken an increasingly interdisciplinary approach that enables the investigator to explore exciting areas that stretch beyond the traditional foci of the classical tradition. A notable example is the collection of papers, *Roman Presences: Receptions of Rome in European Culture, 1789–1945* (1999) that considers how the image of ancient Rome was appropriated (and misappropriated) by leaders such as Napoleon, Hitler and Mussolini in the establishment and the dissemination of power. For example, in her enlightening investigation of the relationship forged between Napoleon and the first Roman emperor, Augustus (27 BCE–14 CE), Huet traces Napoleon's exploitation of the Augustan 'myth' and the creation of his own myth through the use of imagery and propaganda.[7] Emphasis is placed on the precarious post-revolutionary climate; Napoleon's need to legitimise his position, and the subsequent call for change and modernity. She underlines the portrayal of Napoleon as a modern hero and yet a 'true reincarnation of a Roman emperor': an Augustus capable of maintaining peace in the aftermath of turmoil – but an Augustus with a distinctly modern persona, a 'new Augustus'.[8] No reference is made to pre-1789 appropriations of Augustan imagery, however, not least the image(s) of Louis XIV as an improved Augustus and as a saviour of his people after the devastation wrought upon France by a series of internal rebellions (*la Fronde*). Of particular relevance is a link between Augustus as Patron of the Arts and the presentation of Paris as cultural capital of the world under both Louis XIV and Napoleon. To comprehend the exploitation of Augustus under Napoleon, we must therefore take into account both the very same call for modernity and change that had contributed to the (albeit complex) presentation of Louis as new Augustus, and also how the projection and the reception of these parallels influenced Napoleon and his capital.

It needs to be recognized that there is a still wider pattern of reception in France, as can be seen with reference to the reign of France's first Bourbon monarch, Henri IV (1589–1610). The King had been compared to Augustus, and his urban projects resulted in his being praised for modernizing Paris as Augustus had transformed Rome.[9] This demonstrates how the Augustan legacy had already been translated into an extensive programme of urban beautification and renewal, where Paris, as the symbolic centre of power, was portrayed as a new and an improved Imperial Rome. Equally, it shows how we cannot comprehend fully the reinvention of the antique under Napoleon, Louis XIV or indeed any French ruler or regime, without consideration of the wider contextual and historical setting.

The image of Julius Caesar (100–44 BCE) also found its place in Paris. This introduces the relevance of a stimulating collection of essays, *Julius Caesar in Western Culture* (2006), in which the multitudinous receptions of Caesar from antiquity through to the twenty-first century are analysed within their respective sociopolitical and temporal contexts.[10] Of particular note is Hemmerle's *Crossing the Rubicon into Paris: Caesarian Comparisons from Napoleon to de Gaulle*. Although the title suggests that the investigation begins with the Napoleonic era, it is clear that '1789' is seen as an appropriate date to start and that the revolutionaries' vilification of the Caesarian legacy is very much a part of this relationship. This is paramount to understanding the ambiguous treatment of Caesar by Napoleon. What we also see here, however, is an example of a phenomenon that appears to permeate works on Napoleon's exploitation of the antique – simply put, emphasis is placed upon the links between antiquity, the Revolution and Napoleon, while the implications of pre-1789 receptions of ancient Rome and how they influenced this relationship remain surprisingly hazy.[11] This is alluded to indirectly by Hemmerle when he briefly mentions Louis XIV but adds that this is 'another story'.[12] These observations bring into focus the question of historical periodization and the view held by scholars such as Hobsbawm that revolutions break with the past and as a result, that there is a distinction in France between pre- and post-1789.[13] An evaluation in this book of the interrelationship between Napoleon, Louis XIV and the sovereigns' respective 'new Romes', demonstrates that the 1789 'cut-off' date is too neat a division.[14]

The revolutionaries had labelled Louis XIV their archetypal despot and, as a violent and politically charged symbolic statement against absolute rule, they also stripped Paris of imagery associated with the monarchy. How, therefore, can we begin to comprehend Napoleon's changing persona from heroic saviour of the Revolution to imperial sovereign, whose rule and 'new Rome', in ways, were not dissimilar to those of Louis XIV? No less important is an understanding of the Emperor's efforts to surpass the Sun-King, the man Horne aptly refers to as his 'great predecessor and rival in *la gloire*'.[15] The convoluted nature of Napoleon's reign is typified by Adolphe Thiers in his authoritative twenty-volume *Histoire du Consulat et de l'Empire* (1845–62). Thiers was a true champion of Napoleon's *légende dorée* and yet even he envisaged a distinct divide between the republican and monarchical phases of Napoleonic rule. He saw Napoleon's Coronation as a turning point from dictatorship to despotism, characterized by the evolution of a glorious republican liberator into a sovereign, whose vanity and obsessive thirst for conquest would sow the seeds for his ultimate downfall.[16]

We might recall the brief allusion by Hemmerle to the link between antiquity, Louis XIV and Napoleon as 'another story'. It is my aim to investigate the other 'story' and to demonstrate how we might bridge the gap between scholarly compartmentalizations that tend to focus upon either the reception of antiquity under Louis XIV and the French monarchy *or* the interrelationship between antiquity, the Revolution and Napoleon. This is achieved by examining how antiquity's literary sources, architecture, imagery, coins and other forms of visual stimuli, were employed by Napoleon and his predecessors in their respective manipulations of classical Rome. Attention is also given to post-antique material, such as Andrea Mantegna's series of Renaissance paintings of *The Triumphs of Caesar*. We shall see how this, too, influenced interpretations of antiquity and the diverse recreations of the Roman triumph in Europe and France, that later would play a pivotal role in the presentation of Napoleonic Paris as a new and a superior Rome.

This study utilizes a wide range of primary French sources from the reign of Louis XIV to the Napoleonic era (and beyond). While visual stimuli such as paintings, medals and architectural imagery are used, as are literary works including histories and guidebooks, sections of this book differ to a number of studies by drawing on material published in newspapers. Newspapers serve not only as a valuable lens through which to gauge the 'new Romes' of Louis XIV and of Napoleon, but they also allow us additional insight into the differences in presentation and in audience within a pre-revolutionary, a revolutionary and a post-revolutionary context. Although theatre and opera were efficient modes of transmission under Napoleon, the press was employed as a particularly potent form of state-controlled propaganda to influence and to control public opinion. This reinforces the benefits of the newspaper as a source through which to trace the ways Napoleon and his publicists reinvented Rome to disseminate a new political agenda and the Emperor's power.

This book also draws from a spectrum of spatially orientated analyses such as those by Lefebvre (1991 and 2003), Etlin (1994) and MacDonald (1986). This is especially important as cities evolve over time and are redefined continually. For example, the Rome of the Caesars and their 'pagan' deities gave way to a new city that was characterized by the Papacy and Catholicism – Rome is a city of many diverse 'pasts', and these pasts (or layers) exist on both a physical and on a cognitive level.[17] Paris, too, is a city of many pasts and conflicting layers. An analysis in this study of the multidimensional language of Paris' monuments and the spaces they occupied demonstrates how we can clarify the trialectic relationship between antiquity, Napoleon and what went before during the

Revolution and under Louis XIV. Lefebvre's discussion of the contradictory nature of 'the monument' helps articulate aspects of this complex relationship. It also underpins the power of monuments and why, from antiquity, 'the monument' played (and continues to play) such a central role in the political arena and the transmission of messages:

> *Against the monument.* The monument is essentially repressive. It is the seat of an institution (the church, the state, the university). Any space that is organized around the monument is colonized and oppressed. The great monuments have been raised to glorify conquerors and the powerful . . . The misfortune of architecture is that it wanted to construct monuments, but the idea of *habiting* them was either conceived in terms of those monuments or neglected entirely . . . Monumental space is formal. And although the monument is always laden with symbols, it presents them to social awareness and contemplation (passive) just when those symbols, already outdated, are beginning to lose their meaning, such as the symbols of the revolution on the Napoleonic Arc de Triomphe.
>
> *For the monument.* It is the only conceivable or imaginable site of collective (social) life. It controls people, yes, but does so to bring them together. Beauty and monumentality go hand in hand . . . Monuments project onto the land a conception of the world, whereas the city projected (and continues to project) social life (globality). In their very essence, and sometimes at the very heart of a space in which the characteristics of a society are most recognizable and commonplace, monuments embody a sense of transcendence, a sense of being *elsewhere*. They have always been u-topic. Throughout their height and depth, along a dimension that was alien to urban trajectories, they proclaim duty, power, knowledge, joy, hope.[18]

Aspects of Lefebvre's 'monument' recall the opening quotation to this book, in which Napoleon (Bonaparte) expressed his desire to control France and to transform Paris into the most beautiful city to exist in the present, the past and the future. These factors emphasize the potential of considering the multidimensional nature of Lefebvre's 'monument', and how this may be applied to Napoleon's new Roman architecture and his exploitation of Paris' existing symbolic landscape(s). It also helps conceptualize how the emperor Napoleon oppresses and stamps his image across Paris in the mode of Louis XIV (*Against the monument*), though enables thought and idealism to be seen through the lens of the Revolution (*For the monument*). Antiquity may be used as the underlying and the unifying language of 'the monument' that embodies power, but which also allows for hope and the joy of a new superior age.

Before embarking upon this fascinating journey, it is necessary to go back to Paris' early years and consider the fundamental role the Roman occupation itself played in shaping the city's subsequent layers. The very character of Paris and its evolution from insignificant Celtic settlement to monumental metropolis, owes an immeasurable amount to Roman influence, the origins of which can be traced to 121 BCE with the crossing of the Alps and the creation of Latin *provincia* (a part of which forms modern-day Provence). It was, nonetheless, only with the advent and aftermath of Julius Caesar's Gallic Wars, that 'France' became subordinate to Roman control. It was, moreover, the Celtic settlement on the River Seine (*Lutetia Parisiorum*) – that popular legend envisaged as being founded by Helen of Troy's lover, Paris – in which Caesar established his headquarters in c.53 BCE. Once the original settlement had become subject to Caesar's army, the Romans set to work and before long, Lutetia had spread beyond the Île de la Cité to the Left bank.

Jacques-Guillaume Legrand and Charles-Paul Landon's *Description de Paris et de ses édifices* typifies the importance Napoleonic contemporaries attached to Caesar's occupation and to the impact of Roman rule. The first of the two volumes begins with a description of the Roman occupation which, according to the authors, lasted 530 years.[19] Although a substantial amount of the Roman city's physical remains were no longer extant by the Napoleonic era, some still were visible, and the guide provides an invaluable insight into the degree of knowledge at this time. The nature of Gallo-Roman remains such as the Aquéduc d'Arcueil and the Palais des Thermes is addressed.[20] Since the early 1840s, these impressive *thermae* – including a *frigidarium* and the partial remains of a *tepidarium*, *caldarium* and *palaestra* – have been incorporated into the modern city's Musée de Cluny.

Napoleon's visions of transforming Paris were linked to a palpable exploitation of antique Rome which, as *caput mundi*, had embodied the concept of military supremacy and power. Lutetia's place as a prosperous and an influential extension of this empire, combined with the weight Napoleon's propagandists attached to the antique city's achievements and monumental character, bring into play how we might compare Roman and Napoleonic Paris. As a prelude to a detailed study in this book of Napoleon's conscious emulation of antique Rome itself, these comparisons also underline how the myth of Paris' Roman past (and that of Rome) was every bit as important as the reality of the physical remains.

Napoleonic Paris, like Roman Lutetia, acted as a sociopolitical, cultural, religious and monumental locus. By building roads and bridges to improve communication, villas and palaces to impress; temples to worship their deities;

law-courts to diffuse their laws; *fora* to spread their politics and educate; and amphitheatres, theatres, *thermae* and public fountains for the populace, the Romans, in effect, had recreated a mini Rome on Gallic soil. As the heart of Napoleon's omnipotent empire, Paris, however, was far more than a mini Rome. Given the city's importance as a mirror of Napoleon's rule, it is necessary to consider how the fundamental language of Napoleonic Paris located parallels with that of the Roman metropolis which once had occupied a similar space.

The Palais Bourbon and the Emperor's Temple de la Gloire (the famous church, La Madeleine), for instance, underwent a monumental face-lift, and it is unlikely that their classical façades would have looked unduly incongruous alongside the illustrious law-courts and temples that Lutetia once boasted. The space now occupied by the Louvre-Tuileries complex was to be remodelled as a veritable Napoleonic forum, functioning as the political core of the Emperor's grandiose capital. His 'forum', like its Roman counterparts, was multifunctional, and the presence of a victorious army parading around such a space would have evoked the military superiority of the Roman Empire's majestic past. Given the Palais du Louvre's salient role as a museum displaying Napoleon's *spolia*, I will also consider the parallels between this and ancient Roman temples and *fora* which, as Stirling notes, acted as 'didactic museums or art galleries of Roman conquest'.[21] The Palais des Tuileries – a building which, like the Louvre, evinced Napoleon's power – also served as his official residence. In light of the Emperor's 'Romanisation' of the area as a whole, the palace would have simultaneously recalled the forcible legacy of Lutetia's Palais des Césars.

Further examples include the sociopolitical implications inherent in Roman and Napoleonic exploitations of urban space as a means of entertaining and serving the populace. Napoleon held elaborate spectacles and he improved Paris' infrastructure. Where the latter is concerned, we might compare the efficacy of Lutetia and Paris' increased water supplies as demonstrations both of technological expertise and of humanitarianism. Though no *thermae* were built, the benefits and impressive character of the Emperor's Canal de l'Ourcq, as well as the many additional projects increasing the supply of water to the capital, would have found parallels with Roman Lutetia's aqueduct and Strabo's 'veritable rivers'.[22] Although the monumental core of post-antique Paris was centred mainly on the Right Bank, thus occupying space not associated directly with Lutetia's nucleus, there was a topographical relationship between the new road network and the Roman city (Figure 1). How Lutetia's *cardo* (north-south axis) and its *decumanus* (east-west axis) influenced the topographical and ritualistic character of the city's subsequent layers is explored in this study, as is the role these multidimensional layers were to play in Napoleon's visions to recreate a new and a singularly magnificent 'Rome'.

Plan of the book

The first chapter outlines how classical Rome and the multifarious receptions of Rome over the centuries shaped the nature of Paris. It is also shown how Roman antiquity and the diverse re-appropriations of Rome in France influenced Napoleon from his youth through to his rule as emperor. Within this relationship, I will trace the evolution and promotion of Napoleon's imagery, and investigate the impact this had upon Napoleonic Paris and its role as the 'first city' of the Napoleonic Empire. Chapter 2 explores the presentation of Napoleonic Paris as a 'new Rome' in greater depth with reference, in particular, to the power of 'the monument' and the visions Napoleon harboured for an immense processional way that would trace Paris' east-west axis. Emphasis is placed on the structures (either constructed or transformed under Napoleon) associated with the axis, and how their form, imagery and topographical location helped in selectively reinventing the triumphal landscape of both classical Rome and post-antique Paris. By evaluating the complex language of Napoleon's monuments and that of the symbolic spaces they occupied, the chapter also serves as a building block upon which to base my arguments in Chapter 3. Here, the influence of Paris' 'Roman' landscape upon Napoleon and his capital is developed through an examination of the impact and implications of the 'new Rome(s)' established under Louis XIV. The King's architecture and ubiquitous imagery in Paris and at Versailles coloured both the nature of Napoleon's 'new Rome' and the ways in which it and the Emperor's Roman imagery were disseminated. With this in mind, I will examine the two sovereigns' respective systems of representation and the differences in the presentation of their imagery in relation to the King's divine right to kingship, as opposed to Napoleon's post-revolutionary rule. Arguments developed provide a basis upon which to explore, in the final chapter, the nature of the post-antique 'triumph', and how these diverse re-enactments of Rome's triumphal ritual influenced the evolution of the Napolconic 'triumph'. We shall see how the Emperor's 'triumphs' became increasingly distanced from those re-enacted during the French Republic, and also explore the links between triumphal spectacle in Napoleon's 'new Rome' and the Paris of Louis XIV.

I have deliberated long and hard about how best to present a study that delves into so many temporal periods and such a volume of subject matter – although my narrative flits inevitably from one era to another (and back again), only a thematic structure provides the scope with which to argue with clarity Napoleon's presentation of Paris as a 'new Rome'. This book concerns Napoleon and Napoleonic Paris only in as much as they serve to illustrate the influence of classical Rome upon subsequent generations, and how antiquity and receptions of antiquity are exploited to suit contemporary needs. The nature of Napoleon's achievements, rule, imagery and his architecture, therefore, is addressed only when it serves to explain a relevant point. This basic methodology also applies to my analysis of Louis XIV, the revolutionary era and any other regime (or individual) I discuss in my study. This said, I hope that students of French history, the history of architecture, art or urban geography, and those who are already expert in these areas, find something here. I would be equally delighted if this book were to whet the appetite of those who simply want to know more, as well as those who have a keen interest in the link(s) between political leaders, the past and the present.

1

Paris: A 'New Rome'

In a few simple but evocative words, the chorus of a song composed for the *Entrée triomphale des monuments des sciences et arts* (1798) epitomizes the essence of this chapter:

Rome is no longer in Rome, it is all in Paris.[1]

The song demonstrates how Rome was integral to the presentation of Paris as a powerful and an impressive metropolis. During the 1500s, under the reign of François I, 'Rome' had found its place in France, as it had under the reign of Henri IV and those of other French monarchs. Later, the Paris of Louis XIV was hailed a 'new Rome' and, only a short while before the outbreak of the French Revolution in 1789, Louis-Sébastian Mercier had asserted that 'Rome is no longer in Rome, it is where I am'.[2] The widely publicized song from 1798, however, reveals how the entrance of Roman and Italian spoils into the French Republic's capital was intended to take France's reinvention of *Romanitas* to new and unparalleled heights.

Napoleon (Bonaparte) was instrumental both in the acquisition of the treasures and the subsequent staging of their entrance into Paris in 1798 (Figure 2). Though a decisive step in the evolution of the republican general's quest for personal glory, the procession, nonetheless, was still a tool of revolutionary propaganda. Moreover, it would be remiss to consider the 1798 *entrée* unaffected by the French monarchy's earlier re-enactments of the Roman triumph. The wording of the song's chorus and the presence of such a spectacle in the capital, prior to its transformation into Napoleon's imperial nucleus, underlines how his exploitation of classical Rome develops from earlier perceptions of Paris as a 'new Rome'. In order to contextualize this relationship and quite simply, to set the scene, this chapter begins with a review of aspects relating to the appeal of Roman antiquity in France (and Europe) and the degree to which its image was pursued, interpreted and diffused in the intervening years.

The lure of Roman antiquity

Petrarch's renewal of the classical tradition in the twelfth century was followed by influential developments such as the discovery in 1506 of the *Laocoön* which, importantly, was to play a role in the 1798 entrance of spoils into Republican Paris.[3] Additional examples embrace the French translation of Suetonius' 'Twelve Caesars' by Guillaume Michel (1520) and, by 1553, the compilation of Pirro Ligorio's illustrated anthology of antiquities in forty volumes. Andrea Palladio's revival of classical architecture in Italy is also indicative of a new-found enthusiasm for antiquity. His acclaimed theoretical work, *Quattro Libri dell'Architettura* (1570), was translated into French in its entirety in 1650 and continued to be a major reference in France and throughout much of Europe.

The post-Renaissance era witnessed what was probably the most influential development in the history of France's own 'creative imitation' of Roman architecture.[4] The implications of the founding of the *Académie de France à Rome* and the creation of the *Prix de Rome* under Louis XIV were central to this relationship and as such, they receive a detailed analysis in Chapter 3. Giovanni Battista Piranesi, a champion of anything Roman, though not the first to be fascinated by Rome's classical landscape, also did much to rekindle the city's image as a living testimony to the grandeur of ancient Rome. His detailed engravings of its monuments and vistas – *Le vedute di Roma* (1748–78) – stand as a testimony to this. That many of his most diligent pupils were French, suggests a rather special bond between Piranesi and France. Further, before the Academy's relocation to Rome's Villa Medici by Napoleon, its offices were in the Palazzo Mancini: a focal point for artists and architects, located next to Piranesi's engravings shop. The commercial nature of the engravings (they were mass-produced and thus relatively inexpensive) and the shop's location on the busy via del Corso, also suggest that many a Piranesi print would have found its way back to France as a souvenir. These developments underline the importance attached to the diffusion of the image of Roman antiquity abroad prior to Napoleonic rule. Giovanni Paolo Panini's celebrated *vetute* and architectural fantasies (*capricci*) of the antique city act as a further case in point. He worked for a period as Professor of Perspective at Rome's French Academy and his most acclaimed *capriccio*, an oil painting undertaken in c.1755 (*Roma Antica*), superimposes a selection of Rome's monuments and antiquities, including structures that later were to play a central role in the presentation of Napoleonic Paris as a 'new Rome'.

The 'reawakening' of Herculaneum (1738) and Pompeii (1748) had also generated interest in the ancient world's architecture, antiquities and art.

Initially, however, the discoveries were kept quiet and the looting of treasure took precedence over systematic excavation. The ancient cities at this stage appear generally to have incited greed and curiosity, more than a realization that their study could revolutionize man's ever-limited understanding of antiquity.[5]

Johann Joachim Winckelmann (1717–68) – advocate of the superior role of ancient Greece – was fully aware of Herculaneum and Pompeii's importance as invaluable sources of material culture, and even he had fallen under the spell of their antique townscapes and artefacts. He not only had first-hand knowledge of the sites (as well as those of Stabia, Paestum *and* Rome), but he had also written about his finds in various letters and works, an edition of which was published in a French translation in 1784.[6] Equally significant are the views of the French writer and diplomat, François-René de Chateaubriand (1768–1848). His *Voyage en Italie* provides insight both into the state of the sites and the excavations undertaken by the French. We see here his respect for the ancient cities and his disillusionment with the manner in which they were being treated.[7] Like Winckelmann, he was infuriated that the archaeologists had not thought to leave Pompeii's treasures in situ, and instead were transporting them to the museum at Portici. His vision for the site to be transformed into a living museum also reveals great foresight for an individual who had little or no archaeological grounding. Interestingly and as we shall see, not insignificantly, Antoine-Chrysostome Quatremère de Quincy harboured similar views: he scorned the 'decontextualization' of in situ artefacts in general, and later was to envisage the city of Rome itself as a living museum.[8]

The frenzy of French archaeological activity (reaching its peak between 1806 and 1815) not only suggests how the earlier reawakening of the antique sites was to influence Napoleon, but also how he and his regime intended to improve upon former resurrections of the classical world.[9] This is reinforced by the publication in France of François Mazois' four-volume *Les ruines de Pompéi* from 1812 onwards, in which were details of the excavations, illustrations and ground plans, and also the presentation of Pompeii as a whole city.[10] Neither is it without significance that the houses and decoration of Herculaneum and Pompeii were to influence the 'le style Empire' of the Napoleonic epoch.

Although Rome had been the focus of what is known as Europe's Grand Tour (France's *Voyage d'Italie*), Herculaneum and Pompeii had acted as compulsory stops on the tourists' itineraries. These tourists were known to have made sketches of the sites, and it was common place to purchase and bring home mementoes such as in situ artefacts and, on occasion, even fragmentary frescoes.[11] This reveals a popular appreciation of the Roman world (amongst the elite and the bourgeoisie) and also the extent to which the image of antiquity was diffused in France only a while before Napoleonic rule.

Guidebooks had long provided the French with accessible, uncomplicated literature (and visual aids) relating to Rome, its monuments, history and also other Italian attractions. The twelfth-century *Mirabilia Urbis Romae* and Master Gregorius' *De mirabilibus urbis Romae* were succeeded by a variety of guides such as a French edition of Richard Lassels' *Voyage of Italy* (1670), François Misson's *Voyage d'Italie* (1691); François Deseine's *L'ancienne Rome* (1713) and Charles Cochin's *Voyage d'Italie* (1758). Equally notable is Giuseppe Vasi's *Le magnificenze di Roma* (1763), within which was many a famous illustration. Moreover, in its revised form, the *Itinerario istruttivo di Roma* (1791) was translated into French and became the period's primary guidebook. For those unable to travel abroad, certain guides would have been on sale in France, and additional stimuli available in the guise of antiquarian collections shipped over from Rome and its environs.

Fascination with Rome's cityscape as home to antiquity's great Caesars was complemented by splendid collections of antiquities in the Capitoline Museum and the Museo Pio-Clementino. The relevance of this is underpinned with the symbolic transfer of many of these treasures to Republican Paris in 1798 and later, the role they played in the diffusion of Napoleonic Paris as a new and superior Rome. Works by tourists such as the letters of the French magistrate, Charles de Brosses who, having arrived in Rome in 1739, wrote that it was the most beautiful city in the world, underline the interest the Eternal City generated in France.[12] His choice of the adjective 'beautiful' recalls Bonaparte's later assertion that if he were master of France, he would transform Paris into the most beautiful city ever to have existed (as cited in my introduction). The travels of the French mathematician and astronomer, Jérôme-Lefrançois de Lalande, took him to Rome. In his *Voyage d'Italie* which was first published in 1769, he also sought to demonstrate France's superior knowledge of ancient culture via Roman antiquity's history and archaeology.[13] Edward Gibbon's *The History of the Decline and Fall of the Roman Empire* (1776–88) is not only notable for the mine of information he accumulated and employed on his visit to Rome in 1764, but also because his masterpiece had been translated into French (1795) and thus would have reached a French readership. An edition was also published in 1805: the preface by the translator (Monsieur Briand) brims with detail including reference to additional post-antique histories of Rome by celebrated figures such as Niccolò Machiavelli. Ironically, the trauma of the Napoleonic wars in the

1790s and the turbulent relations between Republican France and Rome marked the end of France's *Voyage d'Italie* and the golden age of travel in Europe.[14]

Roman Gaul and the language of power

The accessibility of Roman Gaul's structures, in terms both of their relative proximity to Paris and state of preservation already suggests that there was a certain preference for drawing on antique monuments from France. While these monuments acted as poignant reminders of Gaul's past subjection to the Roman Empire, by virtue of their presence on French soil, they also formed an integral part of France's own heritage. Louis XIV, for instance, is said to have remarked that the immense façade of Orange's Roman theatre was the most beautiful wall of his kingdom. The powerful language of these eye-catching structures would have influenced Paris' changing 'Roman' landscape. Indeed, their tangibility and didactic nature rendered the structures valuable media through which to recreate Napoleonic Paris as a new and an improved hub of imperial power. Their durable presence, moreover, would have had a part to play in Napoleon's quest to create equally permanent epitaphs to his own empire. This empire, of course, was to include much of Italy and as we shall see, even Rome itself.

The Maison Carrée – a beautifully conserved first-century BCE temple situated in the forum of Roman Nîmes – served as a model for Napoleonic Paris' monumental Temple de la Gloire (La Madeleine).[15] The sequence of restorations the Maison Carrée underwent between 1670 and 1691 (in which Louis XIV had taken a personal interest), reinforces the long-standing interest the building had generated.[16] Equally, the single-*fornix* honorary Arch of *Glanum* (today's Saint-Rémy-de-Provence), though now in a state of disrepair, inspired various projects for the Emperor's Arc de Triomphe de l'Étoile.[17] While Napoleon's triumphal Vendôme Column was consciously modelled on Rome's Column of Trajan, there are also similarities between the pediment of the Napoleonic structure and that of the largely intact Mausoleum of the Julii (*c.*30–20 BCE) of *Glanum*, especially in relation to the general form of the bases and aspects of their iconography.

This last example brings into focus how Napoleon – and his predecessors – borrowed and personalized the architectural form of the Roman column as part of their 'language of power'.[18] Though the triumphal column is recognized as a forceful symbol of Roman *and* post-antique imperialism, one must also bear in mind the evolution of the arch into ancient Rome's most conspicuous triumphal monument – the free-standing arch. Both column and arch, moreover, celebrated and displayed, in a highly visual manner, the ideology of victory and dynastic authority. This was translated into a post-Roman and a universal context; and the didactic language of these monuments was expressed invariably by way of location, form, size, height, inscriptions and iconography.[19]

MacDonald demonstrates the elevated status of monumental arches by remarking that by the Roman Empire they had become 'symbols both of Roman rule and of Roman cities'; he then emphasizes the prominent role of the free-standing imperial arch and its part as 'a primary urban instrument'.[20] The interrelated function of the arch as a vehicle of connection and division, and thus entrance, passage, transition and view-framing[21] was translated into a Napoleonic idiom which will be investigated in Chapter 2 of this book. Triumphal arches initially were simple temporary structures, probably erected in timber, to accommodate triumphs (it would appear that by the early second-century BCE they had become a common enough feature of Rome's cityscape). The stone form we equate with the Empire was then built in its place to actually commemorate the triumph. In essence, such structures celebrated the triumph of a victorious general after battle, and during the Empire they became increasingly elaborate monuments erected by the *Senatus Populusque* to honour and glorify the exploits of the emperor.

Though there is generally a need for the modern scholar to distinguish between the city gate, the boundary marker, the triumphal arch and its honorary counterpart, the complexities of these categories appear not to have concerned Napoleon's architects.[22] Louis-François Joseph de Bausset, a prefect of the Emperor's Imperial Palace, reveals how elements from the various categories were used selectively to create Napoleonic arches.[23] He also focuses on the role of the triumphal arch as a tool of propaganda, and with this he reinforces the close relationship between the triumphal arch, triumphal ritual and the display of power.[24] For example, the arch in Orange (*Arausio*) – like its less conspicuous Gallo-Roman counterparts – clearly has no topographical relationship with the route(s) the *triumphator* once followed in antique Rome, with which the existing triumphal arches of Constantine, Septimius Severus and Titus are associated.[25] However, as one of Roman Gaul's most celebrated epitaphs and symbols of power, the Arc d'Orange was important to the Napoleonic regime. This is underlined by the sketches made of this arch by the co-architect of the Emperor's Arc du Carrousel, Charles Percier, on his journey back from Rome. Napoleon's triumphal Arc du Carrousel, while based on those of Septimius Severus and Constantine, also finds parallels with the triple-bayed honorary Arc d'Orange. The resemblance encompasses the general form, as well as the iconography and language of the Parisian structure and its Gallo-Roman counterpart. The Arc du Carrousel's depictions of the glorious deeds of the *Grande Armée*, for instance, appear both to evoke and translate into a Napoleonic idiom, the images of the Roman legions' heroic actions on the Arc d'Orange. The erection of the antique structure on French soil renders it all the more interesting in this respect. The similarities, moreover, may be viewed on two different, but also interrelated levels, as they reinforce the influential role of the Arc d'Orange as a 'speaking' monument and as such, one of the many media used by Napoleon to disseminate his own powerful rhetoric. On the one hand, there appears to be a tangible role reversal at work: the depictions of the victorious Romans and vanquished Gauls of the Arc d'Orange are reversed on the Arc du Carrousel, where naturally it is Napoleon and his army who are portrayed as the heroic victors. The similarities, however, also suggest an equivalence between the Roman legions' subjugation of the 'barbarians' and the Napoleonic troops' equally masterful triumph over less civilized (and non-French) contemporary nations.

The enduring presence of additional symbols of Roman ingenuity and rule such as the Pont du Gard, the theatres in Arles and Orange, and La Turbie's victory monument (Le Trophée des Alpes) are also relevant. As demonstration of the influential nature of the structures, we might compare the fundamental language of the Trophée des Alpes (*c*.7–6 BCE) with that of Napoleon's Colonne de la Grande Armée at Wimille (Boulogne). Not only were the two structures essentially triumphal in character, but their height and visually dominating positions, still are such that they may be seen from the land and the sea.[26] Both the Trophée des Alpes and the other Gallo-Roman structures discussed here share an additional trait as they were constructed under Augustan rule. Significantly, Augustus – like Caesar – had played a prominent role in the post-antique theatre of power and later he, too, was exploited by Napoleon's propagandists.[27] The fragmentary inscription of La Turbie's victory monument reveals that it was dedicated to Augustus by the Senate and the Roman People as a celebration of the Emperor's imperial power.[28]

There would seem to be a connection between an emphasis on the appearance of urban centres *en masse* by Napoleon, and Suetonius' celebrated appraisal of Augustan Rome:

> Aware that the city was architecturally unworthy of her position as capital of the Roman Empire . . . Augustus so improved her appearance that he could justifiably boast: 'I found Rome built of bricks; I leave her clothed in marble.'[29]

Both the presentation of Paris as the nucleus of Napoleon's empire and his personalization of the city's monumental character were likened to the famous transformation of Rome under Augustus.[30] While I shall argue in due course that aspects of this relationship were ambiguous, Napoleon's occupation of Rome as conqueror finds parallels with Augustus *and* Caesar's former conquests and 'transformations' of Gallo-Roman towns such as Orange and Paris respectively.

Given the close temporal link between Bonaparte's rise to power and the Grand Tour, the route taken by tourists from Paris and the north, to Rome and other Italian attractions, also needs to be considered. While travelling southwards through France, the tourists would have had the opportunity to take in many of the impressive landmarks left by the conquering Romans. On a hypothetical level, individuals without a basic knowledge of the ancient Roman world would not have readily understood the implications of monumental structures such as the Arc d'Orange. The antiquities and structures the traveller witnessed once he actually reached Rome would also need to have been viewed within a similar interpretive framework. The very fact that the splendours of Rome and its empire were so appealing to so many, however, already speaks volumes about the general lure of the classical world in late eighteenth-century Europe. This also tells us something about a Grand Tourist's potential capacity to decode the powerful language of architecture. Even though certain tourists, no doubt, came along simply because these cultural voyages were in vogue, many would have communicated their experiences on their return. An individual's potential ability to understand antique structures and in consequence, his appreciation of the language of Napoleon's Rome inspired monuments, is emphasized as learning and education were important elements of the tours.[31] Similarly, the monuments, as well as the route from Paris, which followed to an extent, the original communication network linking Gallo-Roman towns, would surely have impressed upon the traveller the Romans' innovation and force, and indeed the wonders of France's own Roman heritage. Interestingly, Napoleon created a military route that re-traced sections of the Augustan *voie Julia* - a once much used road that had linked towns such as *Cemenelum* (Cimiez) and *Albintimilium* (Ventimiglia) *and* was related topographically to the Trophée des Alpes. While bearing these factors in mind, it would appear that by transforming Paris into a 'new Rome', Napoleon and his architects of power were also planning to create a new way of viewing the antique world. The reference point for understanding antiquity therefore would now be located in the present, and be bound inextricably to the Napoleonic capital's magnificent structures and the outstanding actions of the Emperor Napoleon. This underscores the importance of exploring both how antiquity – and post-antique receptions of antiquity – influenced Napoleon and the ways in which he selectively appropriated the past. The remaining pages of this chapter begin to unravel this relationship, and also serve as a basis upon which to gain a rather deeper understanding of Napoleonic Paris in its role as a 'new Rome'.

On the road to domination

Bonaparte's involvement in a conspiracy to overthrow the Directory resulted in the formation of the Consulate and his seizure of power in November 1799 (the *coup* of 18–19 *Brumaire*). In order to contextualize both this and his subsequent rise from Consul to First Consul for Life (1802) and finally Emperor in 1804, however, we must go back to the climate into which he was born and within which he was immersed as a student and later, as a young soldier.

'Napoleone di Buonaparte' was born on Corsica in 1769 – ironically not as an Italian, but a Frenchman, and in consequence a subject of Louis XV (the island had only ceased to be under Genoese control in 1768). Instrumental in forming Bonaparte's personality were his visions as a youth to liberate Corsica from the clutches of the French and thus succeed where his idol, Pascal Paoli (leader of the Corsican independence movement), had failed. Dwyer notes that Bonaparte had already cast himself in an 'heroic mould', similar to that of Paoli, and thereafter would manipulate an idealized image of himself to suit the climate of the moment.[32] Bound intricately to this was the emphasis in schools in eighteenth-century mainland France on the teaching of the moral integrity, courage and military prowess of antiquity's heroic exemplars. A number of classical works were mandatory components of the educational curriculum. The histories of Plutarch, Livy and Tacitus were studied, as well as literary pieces such as Cicero's *Orations*, Ovid's *Metamorphoses* and Virgil's *Aeneid*.[33] Coming from a family of good Corsican lineage, Bonaparte (aged 9) had been in a position to receive his secondary education on the mainland. After a brief spell of study at the college in Autun, he was sent to the royal military school at Brienne. Bonaparte's education here was to have a considerable influence upon the formation of his personality. Indeed, the establishment's stringent rules also helps us to formulate an image of this ambitious 'outsider' whose strange Corsican accent, it would seem, alienated him further from his classmates.[34] It was during these early years that a somewhat aloof and insular Bonaparte immersed himself in the lives and glorious conquests of antiquity's great exemplars, not least Julius Caesar. The distance that separated

Bonaparte from his beloved Corsica, and his insatiable appetite for study and the reading of ancient works, notably Plutarch's *Lives*, nurtured further his visions of fighting heroically for the liberty of his people.[35] The dream of becoming his own Plutarchian hero was thus in the making, and a little nearer being realized when, some 5 years later in 1784, he gained a scholarship to the prestigious Parisian *École Militaire*. This marked the beginning of Bonaparte's training as a professional soldier: at 16, he had already graduated and attained the status of sub-lieutenant of artillery. By the early 1790s, the talented young soldier had managed (eventually) to return to his homeland between postings to military establishments such as the esteemed artillery school at Auxonne. It was during this period, too, that he focussed on political thought and the works of figures whose philosophies had been instrumental in shaping French revolutionary ideology. Particularly noteworthy was Bonaparte's continuing interest in the person and *oeuvres* of Jean-Jacques Rousseau who, like the young Bonaparte, had had a special affinity with Corsica.

Equally significant was Bonaparte's love for writing which, beginning in his youth with works focussing mainly on Rousseau and Corsica (and even designs for a monumental history of the island), in various guises spanned his life. Bonaparte's fascination with history also materialized in the form of detailed notes he made of historical works such as Gabriel Bonnot de Mably's *Observations sur l'histoire de France* and Charles Rollin's *Histoire ancienne*.[36] An underlying preoccupation in many of his notes with the despotic nature of monarchical rule, as Tulard affirms, reveals the extent to which the young Corsican was influenced by Rousseau and other 'philosophes révolutionnaires'.[37]

Due also to the French belief that Corsican nobility was somehow inferior to their own but, in main, to his ability to be on whichever side was on top, Bonaparte was not labelled an aristocrat after the outbreak of the Revolution in 1789. This, combined with his aptitude, charisma and thirst for personal conquest, resulted in a speedy advancement and his involvement in numerous offensive manoeuvres. By 1792, he had joined the French army in Italy and, several promotions and 4 years later, Bonaparte – whose decisive hand in defeating royalist rebels in 1795 had earned him the reputation of saviour of the Republic – was named the commander-in-chief of the French Republic's Army of Italy.[38]

Examples of this 'Italian connection' include the victories of Lodi and Arcole (1796); the Treaty of Campo-Formio in 1797; Bonaparte's declaration of war on the Papal States (1797); the battle of Marengo (1800); Napoleon's crowning as King of Italy in 1805 and, the following year, the appointment of his brother,

Joseph Bonaparte, as King of Naples.³⁹ This not only illustrates how French aggression towards the Italian states increased substantially once the Army of Italy was under Bonaparte's control, but also just how widespread French domination was. In a relatively short period, France controlled the principal centres of the Italian States: Milan, Naples and Rome.

The implications of the ongoing and fractious relationship between Republican and then Napoleonic France with contemporary Rome cannot be overstated. The Eternal City was subject to French rule, not once, but twice, and on both occasions policy was aggressive and the majority of Romans were vehemently opposed to the oppressive presence of their new rulers. The first occupation (1798–9) was short-lived and, for the most part, unsuccessful. The second occupation (1809–14) took place when France was under Napoleonic control and, in theory at least, it was to embody the Emperor's ultimate display of superiority over both the antique and the modern world.

In true Napoleonic fashion, press reports reaching Paris regaled the occupation's successes, conveniently omitting anything that might spoil their leader's glorious image as universal conqueror.⁴⁰ The reality, nonetheless, was somewhat different. The regime's unpopularity was heightened by the economic and social destruction wrought by the confiscation of monasteries and convents, the deportation of clergy who refused to sign the oath of loyalty; the imposition of conscription and above all, the expulsion of Pope Pius VII, which not only increased hostility towards the French in the Papal States, but also shocked Europe, turning the Pope into a veritable martyr.⁴¹

The Napoleonic interlude appears incredibly bleak from this angle. The French, however, in main under the guidance of the Napoleonic city's civil head, Camille De Tournon, managed still to achieve a considerable amount. Examples embrace a number of improvements to the modern city and the reorganization of the educational, medical and penal systems. Tournon arrived in Rome in November 1809 and his *Études statistiques sur Rome et la partie occidentale des états Romains* (first published in 1831) serve as an invaluable source of information from a contemporary perspective. When addressing the differences between the French Republic's occupation and that of Napoleon, Tournon highlights how the former's spoliation of Rome's treasures contrasted markedly with the many positive aspects of Napoleonic rule, in particular, the restoration of the ancient Roman city.⁴² Though fraught with difficulties, one of the regime's most noteworthy achievements was the beautification of the northern entry into Rome.⁴³ The refashioned area (including the Piazza del Popolo and the Pincian hill) was to be named the Jardin du Grand César. The garden's name, of course, would have recalled the glories and splendour of antique Rome. It is possible that the Napoleonic gardens were to evoke the concept of 'country in town' which was especially reminiscent of the imperial Roman city's impressive *horti*.[44] Inscriptions, frescoes and literary works would have served as reminders of the ancient city's green areas and the urban gardens incorporated into the Horti Maecenatis and Horti Lolliani (to name but two of these sometimes elusive testaments to Rome's former beauty).

Archaeological activity under Napoleon concentrated on structures such as the Pantheon, Trajan's Column (and Forum), the Colosseum and the Arch of Constantine. The isolation of the arches of Septimius Severus and Titus, and certain additional structures in what Tournon calls 'le noble Forum romain', also reveal more positive aspects of the Napoleonic presence.[45] Positive in one respect, yes, as the restorations, clearings and embellishments revived the city's ancient core, but also worrying, as demonstrated by Antonio Canova's warning to Tournon in 1810 that the isolation of the Arch of Titus from its surrounding structures had resulted in the monument being in serious danger of total collapse. The more negative aspects of Napoleonic intervention here are underscored by Johns who asserts that the French had seriously underestimated the extent to which the arch had relied upon the surrounding layers of earth, and also the protection provided by the adjoining medieval structures, now destroyed in the desire to isolate the monument.[46] It was only in 1818 (after the Napoleonic interlude) that work was undertaken to stabilize the arch.[47] Grandiose, costly and unrealistic visions of a *passaggiata pubblica* in the archaeological zone, encompassing the area in and around the Forum, also fall into the 'worrying' category. This colossal *passaggiata* (or Jardin du Capitole) would have incorporated not only the Forum and Capitoline but also the Colosseum, Palatine, the Baths of Titus, as well as structures extending towards the Tiber such as the temples of Vesta and of Fortuna Virile, and the Arch of Janus.[48]

This said, it would be a serious error to underestimate the relevance of Napoleonic activity in Rome, especially given Napoleon's immense interest in the city's resurrection, maintenance and beautification and, linked inexorably to this, the projection of Rome's new role as the Empire's 'second city' (Paris, of course, being the 'first').[49] Inescapable, moreover, is the symbolic intent explicit in Tournon's allusion to the immortalization of Rome's great figures through the construction of monuments.[50] This, as we shall see in the following chapter, had a major role to play in the construction in the Emperor's 'first city' of his own Rome inspired triumphal arches and the monumental Vendôme Column.

Napoleon had every intention of visiting Rome, the city that was so much a part of his propaganda. His constant military campaigns and enforced abdication in 1814, however, ensured absolutely that he was never to see Rome with his own eyes. His abdication, following so swiftly on the heels of the cessation of Napoleonic rule in Rome, resulted in a double blow.[51] The two most potent tools with which the Emperor had projected his force and superiority were now lost: Paris, the imperial nucleus and showpiece of his own empire; and Rome, cultural capital and home to the great Caesars of the classical past.

'Rome' reigns in Republican Paris

The French Revolution was not a singular event which simultaneously changed France's infrastructure, but rather, a sequence of incidents, uprisings and, to an extent, homogeneous phases punctuated by varying revolutionary regimes, spanning a decade or more.[52] Though France was not proclaimed a republic until 21 September 1792, the storming of the Bastille (14 July 1789) marked the historical and symbolic beginning of the Revolution. Interestingly, the storming of the prison was the result of a misunderstanding on the part of its governor; in reality, very few people were harmed, and it was only after the episode had been sensationalized and turned into a veritable example of the people's victory over tyranny that the fortress was torn down (a task finished by commercial companies).[53] This acts as a pertinent example of how the manipulation of fact had already become a forceful political tool. It also exemplifies how revolutionary propaganda was to influence Napoleon's equally elaborate falsification of fact to serve political ends.

In essence, the Revolution's *raison d'être* – hence its adoption of the egalitarian ideals of the Roman Republic – was to promote a new symbolic order; an improved non-hierarchical society, in total contrast to the absolutist and despotic ideology of the monarchy, and the decadence associated both with it and with Imperial Rome. The irony of this is typified by the Revolution's constant call upon ancient Rome, and yet the establishment of a new calendar in 1793 which, set to date from the founding of the Republic just over a year previously, changed the time span and original names of the months stemming from the Roman world. Importantly, the definition of 'new' was changing constantly. Given the didactic nature of visual stimuli and the rapid political changes, architects and artists were under immense pressure to keep up with demand – as a result, many works were either unfinished or unable to keep pace with the changing climate.[54]

The projection of *la nouvelle ère* was manifest in a profusion of media ranging from the reinvention of Republican Rome's figures, symbols, spectacle, ritual and political terms, to Rome inspired art, sculpture and *architecture parlante* (the prolific use of the latter enabled the powers-that-be to 'speak' to the citizen through words, symbols and images).[55] A suitable point of reference lies with Jacques-Louis David (1748–1825), the influential French artist whose 'neo-classical' works materialized during the *ancien régime* and spanned both the revolutionary and the Napoleonic periods.[56] Masterpieces such as David's *Oath of the Horatii* (1784) and *Brutus* (1789) not only act as examples of the influence antiquity – and post-antique adaptations of *Romanitas* – exerted prior to the Napoleonic epoch, but their popularity as expressions of revolutionary fervour may also be used to highlight the emphasis placed on the ideals of Republican Rome. A degree of caution is required, however, for although David's *Oath of the Horatii* had become a poignant symbol of revolutionary propaganda by the 1790s, the relationship between the French Revolution and the Horatii brothers swearing they would 'win or die for liberty' was not as explicit as many have argued.[57] In 1785 the painting was exhibited and received as a pro-monarchical piece; in 1791 the canvas was returned to the Salon and hailed instead as a forceful revolutionary emblem.[58] This speaks volumes about the political subcontext of art during the revolutionary years (in relation both to its creation and reception) and also about the dexterity with which the antique was manipulated to serve (conflicting) contemporary rhetoric.

The fact that constitutional terms from the Roman world, such as Consul, Senate and Tribune were even used, also says much about the influence of the antique. Revolutionary symbols were equally reminiscent of classical Rome: examples include the Roman lictor's axe and *fasces* (or 'rods'). Likewise, Roman deities such as Minerva and the demi-god Hercules were reinvented. Figures such as the Gracchi, Cato, Cicero and the Brutuses were appropriated; their actions and political affiliations praised and also used to furnish the Revolution's new rhetoric.[59] The significance of Enlightenment thinkers, and Rousseau in particular, resurfaces, for he had long reiterated the critiques of antiquity's moralists that luxury and virtue were incongruous, and that the former as a tool of despotism also corrupted and undermined the state and its citizenry. Rousseau's *Discours sur les sciences et les arts* (1750) and his *Discours sur l'origine et les fondements de l'inégalité parmi les hommes* (1755) are recognized as especially influential in relation to the changing perceptions among intellectuals.[60] In his 1750 work, Rousseau implied that the development of luxury and absolute government in France were synonymous, and that the former 'rendered men servile'.[61] Cato the

Elder was seen by the revolutionaries as a model of the antique Roman, whose *virtus* and patriotism were traits that every citizen was encouraged to respect. Significantly, the American colonists who struggled to overthrow England in the American War of Independence (1775–83) had also called upon Republican Rome in their quest to advocate a new beginning (France had even played a role in helping the colonists). Plutarchian exemplars such as Junius Brutus, Cato the Elder and Cicero were subsequently adopted, and used as forceful expressions of American liberty and *virtus*.[62] Alternatively, Caesar was perceived as the antithesis of everything that revolutionary America stood for: the dictator epitomized England; his image seen to encapsulate tyranny and the corruption of the nation's moral fabric.[63] In revolutionary France, Caesar was to be received in a similar manner, except that here he typified the despotic monarchs of the country's absolutist past. The influence of revolutionary America might also help qualify the initially paradoxical fusion between France's quest to project a new beginning and its simultaneous exploitation of Republican Rome's rhetoric. Here, however, the manipulation of *Romanitas* was taken to unprecedented heights. Maximilien Robespierre – whose name was (and is still) synonymous with the atrocities of 'The Terror' – was responsible for the creation of France's Republic of Virtue and he was known simply as 'the Roman'.[64]

As the Revolution evolved and the appeal of prototypes such as Cato began to wane, a less radical Republican France sought inspiration from a slightly different angle and adopted an additional dimension, that of Augustus. Such a choice was far from coincidental and most apt, as Augustus' potentially precarious position as successor to the assassinated Caesar was cleverly manipulated to the new leader's advantage by his forming the Principate, a new form of rule which continued to recognize republican ideals.[65]

If then we consider Bonaparte's continuation, but modification of revolutionary ideals (his crowning as Emperor, and not as King after the consulship), it is possible to appreciate how influential both the Revolution and the antique past were in shaping his constitutional position. Furthermore, the hugely fragile post-revolutionary climate, as the chaos wrought upon Rome after Caesar's assassination, resulted in both Paris and Rome being ready for the changes 'Octavian' and 'Bonaparte' had in store. Equally noteworthy is Octavian's name-change to Augustus (27 BCE); Bonaparte's adoption of the title Napoleon and with this, the sovereign's respective metamorphoses from Consul to Emperor.[66] It is vital, however, that we recall earlier transformations of Paris within an Augustan context, as shown by a bust of Louis XIV with the accompanying inscription, *Augusto Augustior* 'more august than Augustus'.[67]

This is not to say that the link created between the King and Augustus was either straightforward or static. As Apostolidès cautions, we should not see Louis XIV simply as a modern reincarnation of the Emperor but, as his reign evolved, more a new Augustan figure in his own right whose impressive achievements would combine the present with the past, and myth with history.[68] As a French monarch whose absolutist rule contrasted markedly with the egalitarian language of the Revolution, these considerations underpin the value of exploring later in this book, both how revolutionary *and* pre-revolutionary appropriations of ancient Rome were to influence Napoleon and the character of his imperial capital. Further, within this (or these) relationship(s), it is important to recognize that the complex association of Louis XIV with Augustus also finds certain parallels with Napoleon's reception of the same legacy and those of other figures from the antique past.[69]

The cultivation of Napoleon's image and the creation of the Napoleonic myth

A myth is not necessarily created after the existence of the individual(s) in question. Indeed, the Napoleonic myth was developing and evolving while Napoleon was still alive, and it was to have an enormous impact upon the later creation of what may be termed his legend. A distinction between the Napoleonic myth and legend has been developed by scholars in more recent years. Hazareesingh, for instance, sees the former as being instigated by Napoleon to control his public image(s), starting with the early Italian campaigns through to the publication of the *Mémorial*, while the latter was 'a much broader and more heterogeneous phenomenon, which developed spontaneously in France after 1815'.[70] Equally insightful is the author's comment that although the legend was inevitably influenced by the myth, Napoleon had no direct control over the former, whereas the latter was linked to the cultivation and dissemination of media to serve Napoleonic politics.[71] These observations reinforce the potential of investigating how the ancient past and the post-antique reception of this past shaped the nature of Napoleon's image(s), and also the ways in which he and his propagandists projected his imagery.

We have seen already how Bonaparte's early military career as an individual fighting for the revolutionary cause had helped him put his Enlightenment ideals into practice and use to his advantage. He was influenced by figures such as the seventeenth-century dramatist Pierre Corneille, whose works stressed the duty and destiny of classical heroes and, as noted earlier, by Rousseau's ubiquitous *œuvres*.⁷² The philosopher's consideration of antiquity's *hommes illustres* pointed to Plutarch as a model; his *Lives*, in turn, were devoured by Bonaparte, who continued to read and learn from them throughout his life. Although the popularity of the Plutarchian legacy had undergone its peaks and troughs, its lure on an international level cannot be overstated. Its multifaceted appeal extended back to the Renaissance (and earlier). Plutarch's portraits of antiquity's great figures were also manifest in a variety of eighteenth-century works such as Turpin's *La France illustre ou le Plutarch Française* (1775–80), all of which drew upon the ancient biographer to create their own 'lives' of illustrious Frenchmen.⁷³ The combined influence of Plutarch's *Lives* and those undertaken by the French in relation to the projection of Bonaparte as a modern classical hero and the creation of the Napoleonic myth, therefore, is of the utmost importance.

The concept of using the past to assist the present, of course, stretches back to antiquity. Augustus, for instance, had manipulated Rome's traditional foundation myths and figures to legitimize his position, just as he and his publicists had created the Augustan myth. Although the major exemplar of what is known as the Napoleonic myth was Napoleon himself, he not only actively exploited the antique past and its legendary figures, but also borrowed from that world similar tactics to maintain and elevate his own reputation. These considerations call to mind Napoleon's accounts of his personal achievements and those of Augustus in his *Res Gestae Divi Augusti* (discovered in Ankara in 1555) – this, however, is *not* to say that the ex-emperor on St. Helena sought deliberately to create an association between his legacy and that of Augustus. On a similarly generalized level, we might also consider Augustus' role as a 'divine' inheritor through his adoptive father Caesar, and the similarities here with the links forged between Napoleon and Charlemagne who, as Holy Roman Emperor and successor of Rome's emperors, as Huet remarks, was 'responsible for the formation – and the idea – of France'.⁷⁴

Like his predecessors, Napoleon drew inspiration from several historical figures, rather than a single exemplary figure from the past. In Louis-Pierre Baltard's 1802 edition of *Paris et ses monumens*, Amaury-Duval refers to 'Napoléon Bonaparte' as a 'nouveau Periclès'.⁷⁵ Pericles (*c.*495–429 BCE) would have served as a suitable model, not only for his reputation as champion of Athenian democracy, but also because his name was synonymous with the building of the Parthenon; Athens' imperial might and its Golden Age. Additional Plutarchian figures such as Alexander the Great (356–323 BCE) and Hannibal (247–182 BCE) were indisputably influential. Similarly noteworthy is the Roman Emperor Trajan (53–117 CE) in his role as empire and imperial builder. We might note Lesueur's opera *Le Triomphe de Trajan* which, as Tulard remarks, in reality, was 'le triomphe de Napoléon'.[76] A classical prototype whose presence was exploited more publicly than any other and whose name surfaced continually, both in contemporary propaganda and from Napoleon's own hand, however, was Caesar. Though positive allusions to Caesar only materialized once the shadow of the Revolution was a little more distant,[77] it would appear that Napoleon harboured far more of a personal affinity with Caesar than he did with Augustus. His fascination with Caesar's *commentarii* and the creation of his own *Précis des guerres de Jules César* – a collection of notes on Caesar's Gallic campaigns first published in Paris (1836) – would already suggest this were the case. The introduction to Napoleon III's incomplete second volume of his own *Histoire de Jules César* (1866) serves as a demonstration of the long-standing interest in France (and elsewhere) in Caesar's *commentarii* – also the *de bello Gallico* and *de bello civili*.[78] Moreover, while furnishing his readers with the names of sovereigns involved in the publication of these works, he places special emphasis on his famous uncle's *Précis* and its important contribution to the Caesarian tradition.[79]

Wintjes describes the *Précis* as a 'remarkable' work which though critical of Caesar's tactics and a reflection of Napoleon's stance that modern warfare was infinitely superior to that of antiquity, reveals his unquestionable respect for Caesar as one of the great commanders of military history.[80] Napoleon created his *Précis* in exile on St. Helena; and it was during this period that the ex-emperor of France set to work dictating a number of additional works in which Caesar surfaced.[81] When it came to Napoleon's views regarding Caesarian rule in general they, too, were both critical and complimentary – a pertinent example of the latter lies with his praise for Caesar's qualities as a champion of the people.[82] As always, however, the restatement of the antique was selective: Napoleon's misgivings regarding certain aspects of the Caesarian legacy appear not to have deterred an emphasis during his reign on Caesar's talent as a military leader. Indeed, it was this, above all, which prompted the dissemination of the many analogies between the two great conquerors. The relevance of Napoleon's familiarity with Plutarch's *Lives* resurfaces, not least with the ancient biographer's reference to Caesar's merits as a figure of unparalleled military prowess:

> Nay, if one compare him with such men as Fabius and Scipio and Metellus, and with the men of his own time or a little before him, like Sulla, Marius, the two Luculli, or even Pompey himself, whose fame for every sort of military

excellence was at this time flowering out and reaching to the skies, Caesar will be found to surpass them all in his achievements.[83]

A pamphlet, *Parallèle entre César, Cromwell, Monck et Bonaparte* (1800), drew explicit parallels between Bonaparte and Caesar. The pamphlet not only reiterates how influential Caesar was as a military prototype, but it also demonstrates how he was employed as an overtly political tool.[84] Reference is made to Caesar's favourable relationship with the people and his power as First Consul; and one can but recognize a distinct comparison with the (then) *Premier Consul*, Bonaparte, whose popular image was engineered to appeal to the masses. Caesar, too, was known for his dealings with Africa; and once again a parallel with Bonaparte surfaces, as his victories in Africa were instrumental in moulding his image as a military hero. Similarly, the pamphlet points to the immortalization of Caesar through his exploits in Gaul and Italy. Here, we return to the Caesar who originally conquered Gaul and laid the foundations for the transformation of Roman Lutetia which, in the distant future, would become the nucleus of the Napoleonic Empire.

Tellingly, Antoine Claire Thibaudeau's contemporary assessment of the momentous Marengo victory (1800) hints at a telling role reversal between Caesar's subjugation of Gaul and Bonaparte's decisive victories over modern Italy:

> Never have we seen such a rapid, brilliant or a decisive campaign as this. Covered in laurels, the First Consul sped across Italy ... and returned to Paris, able to claim, like Caesar: *veni, vedi, vici*.[85]

Thibaudeau was one of many to recount the euphoria that went hand in hand with the victory of Marengo. The whole of Paris, we are told, turned out *en masse* with cries of 'Vive le Premier Consul' in celebration of Bonaparte's triumphant return after his heroic Italian campaign.[86] The *fêtes*, ceremonies, fireworks, banquets and games all contributed to an event which, as Jacques Marquet de Norvins confirms, was seen as marking a new era in French history.[87] Norvins (a participant of the celebrations) explains later that there had even been talk of holding a *Jeux olympiques*, but that it was not sufficiently Roman.[88] His stipulation that he and the rest of the French populace resembled Romans rather than Greeks and that *César* was there in person, reinforces how the projection of Bonaparte's heroic image was linked intricately to that of antique Rome and its great military genius, Caesar. The *veni, vidi, vici* motto attributed to Caesar was also translated into a Napoleonic idiom in Pierre-Nolasque Bergeret's *Allégorie de la Bataille d'Austerlitz* (1806), in which France's triumphant hero and emperor sported a shield bearing the inscription.

The Romans, of course, had recognized the benefits of diffusing an effective and a durable image of their influential figures.[89] The Napoleonic machine of power was similarly aware of the value of manipulating and disseminating a suitably appropriate and forceful image of Napoleon. Moreover, the antique was used as a potent medium of propaganda, at a time when France was growing increasingly stronger as a world power and demonstrating her hegemony over Italy, in particular. Its diffusion came in many guises and embraced not only crowd generating events, press propaganda and censorship; salons and *brasseries*, but also literature, poetry; a variety of art forms, theatre, opera; medals; coins; architecture and sculpture – all of these elements played a vital part in exaggerating Napoleon's successes, both elevating him above the realms of a mere mortal and transforming him a legendary hero. Napoleon recognized the advantages of an influential entourage of broadcasters; he was a master of propaganda and later in his career, also a master of self-publicity.[90]

This may be shown by the ideological and political role of art as an image-diffusing and an image-manipulating medium from Bonaparte's earlier career as a republican general to his later rule as emperor. Scholars tend generally to equate the birth of the Napoleonic myth with the first Italian campaign (1796–7).[91] This is encapsulated in Antoine-Jean Gros' embroidered portrayal of *Bonaparte on the Bridge of Arcole* (*c*.1797), which glorified and immortalized the Republican general's exploits at the Battle of Arcole in 1796.[92] The extent to which this (and other paintings) falsified fact is widely acknowledged within scholarly circles. Dwyer, for instance, remarks that in reality Bonaparte did not get within fifty paces of the 'disappointingly small' bridge, and that his victory was markedly less magnificent than the press and other modes of transmission had the populace believe.[93] More elaborate still was David's *Bonaparte Crossing the St. Bernard Pass* (1800–1), in which our undying hero astride a magnificent white steed recalls not only Charlemagne (alias Karolus Magnus), but also the Carthaginian general, Hannibal, who famously had crossed the Alps and inflicted a number of defeats on the Romans – the names of these earlier transalpine conquerors (with that of Bonaparte) are inscribed on the boulders beneath the horse.[94] The work also has a certain Caesarian quality and unsurprisingly, it has been viewed as an artistic rendition of Bonaparte surpassing his antique counterpart(s).[95] Although David's famous painting had his audience believe that it portrayed the heroic and decisive part played by the nation's saviour at the Battle of Marengo, in reality, Bonaparte would have been defeated had it not been for the intervention of one of his generals, General Desaix.[96] Additional hyperbole in this painting, typified by David's portrayal of Bonaparte astride a glorious white stallion, when in reality he was led across the Alps on a mule, reinforce the crucial role of art – and the exploitation of the antique – as a political tool.[97]

As Napoleon consolidated his power, so his propaganda, if possible, became more elaborate and grandiose, ironic as this may appear, given that his far from static image was also governed by the ever-present necessity to legitimize his position in a precariously changeable post-revolutionary climate. The mixture of Roman and medieval imagery in Ingres' *Napoleon on his Imperial Throne* (1806) stands as a testament to this,[98] as do David's imperial portraits, which were no less influential once he became the Emperor's official painter in 1804, than they had been during the Republic. Commissioned by Napoleon, works such as the *Coronation of Napoleon and Josephine* (c.1806–7) and the *Distribution of the Eagles* (1810) re-emphasize how part of the symbolism employed to propagate the Emperor's image found parallels with the ancient Roman world (Figure 3).[99] Long gone was the youthful hero who had aligned himself with Republican Rome and the person and *oeuvres* of Rousseau.[100] Although it would be a mistake to assume that Napoleon had rejected all Plutarchian concepts of virtue, the imagery inherent in these works illustrates how his thirst for personal glory and imperial grandeur evolved as his rule became increasingly autocratic. Examples include depictions of Napoleon crowned by a laurel wreath which, as Ellis notes, 'now symbolized the return of glory under a new Caesar'.[101] Equally notable is the replacement of the French Republic's Roman symbols, not least, the axe and *fasces*, with the eagle as an emblem, once Napoleon had advanced from First Consul to Emperor. The importance of the eagle – which became Napoleon's battle-standard and symbol of empire – is seen in associations with Charlemagne and also with the concept of force manifest in the exploitation of Imperial Roman symbolism. This is exemplified by an address that the recently crowned Emperor Napoleon gave in 1804, in which he made explicit the relationship between empire, power, the 'French' eagle and its antique Roman counterpart.[102]

The appropriation of the antique went further still, as it played a similarly intrinsic role in Napoleonic legislation. The *Code Napoléon* (1804) was regarded by the Emperor himself as one of his principle achievements. As the 'restorer of laws', a life-sized sculpture was placed in the middle of the assembly room in the Palais Bourbon; it should perhaps come as no surprise that Napoleon was dressed as a Caesar. Of equal note is the relief ensemble by Jean-Guillaume Moitte on the west wall of the Louvre's Cour Carré: '*History Inscribing upon Her*

Tablet the Names of Napoleon the Great and the Legislators Moses, Numa, and Lycurgus' (*c.*1805–7). Significantly, it is Plutarch who is our source for Numa as a peaceful and pious king (Rome's second) and a propagator of laws.[103] Plutarch is also our main source for Lycurgus. His reputation as the founder of ancient Sparta's constitution and strict military regime would have placed him as a suitable model for the disciplined nature of Napoleonic institutions, not least the *École Spéciale Militaire* and the newly established *lycées* set up under Napoleon's stringent educational reforms. Similarly noteworthy is David's portrayal of *Napoleon in his Study* (1812), in which the presence of a sword and the rolled *Code Napoléon* symbolize the Emperor's achievements as empire-builder and lawmaker.[104] Lyons observes the inclusion of a half-burnt candle: this he likens to the burning candle of Benito Mussolini, thus portrayed as a diligent leader working into the night for the good of his people while they slept.[105] Tellingly, the painting also depicts a volume of Plutarch's *Lives* near the feet of a modern Napoleon. It is possible this would have reinforced his image as a virtuous legislator whose legendary attributes, while resembling those of Numa and Lycurgus, were both unquestionably influential and thoroughly modern in their own right. By the same token, the juxtaposition of imagery evoking legislative prowess and imperial power brings to mind the Emperor's multifaceted accomplishments. The language of such imagery would have contributed to the projection of Napoleon as an exceptional figure, thus magnifying his image and later, his own legacy as a legendary *homme illustre*.

Linked intricately to what we perceive today as Napoleon's legacy, was also the circulation of material during his exile and then later after his death.[106] Given the wide-ranging manipulation of *Romanitas* when Napoleon was at the helm, it was inevitable that the antique should again play an intrinsic role in the Napoleonic legend. The manifestation of the Napoleonic legend came in numerous guises and unsurprisingly it encompassed both positive and negative perceptions of Napoleon's rule. We see Napoleon both as the heroic saviour of the Revolution and as the omnipotent sovereign who had augmented France's culture, arts and sciences as never before. *La légende dorée* also reveals the military genius, the simple family man; the father and protector of his people; the peaceful legislator; the demi-god and even the reincarnation of Christ. Opposing factions have ensured that this be accompanied by *la légende noire*, which portrays Napoleon as a tyrannical despot, a murderer; a luxury-loving hypocrite; an ogre; a demon and even the incarnation of an antichrist.[107] Given the pivotal role antiquity had played throughout his life and the place attributed to Las Cases' *Mémorial* as Napoleon's most enduring and pertinent epitaph, this section closes with Nicolas-Toussaint

Charlet's frontispiece for the 1842 edition of the work.[108] In this engraving, the dominating presence of a mostly Roman Napoleon as a conquering warrior is accentuated by his crown of laurels, a hovering eagle above, and also a globe beneath both him and his rearing horse. This work encapsulates how the Emperor himself would surely have presented two of the most potent facets to his rule – that of military force and universal dominion.

Projection and reception: Place and space

Today, spectacles are relayed to the masses by television, internet, radio, photography and the press. If we are not present, several of these media afford us a clearer impression of the spectacle and the principal players than if we had been there in person. The News, whether in print or broadcast on the television, radio or internet, is also a rapid and an effortless means of keeping abreast with current events and figures in the Public Eye. Familiarity, in the wider sense of the word, facilitates patriotism and pride: if a sovereign or political leader is never seen (or heard), the nation is unable to relate to their image, and their popularity and authority, in consequence, may wane.

Without such a variety of media, our forebears had to work differently at projecting a suitable image of their influential figures (it stands that the nature of the image an individual wishes to project has changed over time). The ancient sources reveal the importance given to the 'see and be seen' concept that underpinned the display and diffusion of imperial authority.[109] The triumph serves as a pertinent example as it exhibited in a most symbolic manner, both the force of the *triumphator* and the might of Rome and its empire. Although we must not overlook the fundamental role of the triumph as a ritualistic ceremony that signalled a *triumphator*'s entrance-*ritus* into the city of Rome, Gregory notes that an additional aspect of 'that quintessential Roman institution' lay with its interrelated importance both as an essential mode of visual communication and as a 'multi-media event' in a society where literacy, in main, was limited to the intellectual and social elite.[110] This is exemplified by Plutarch's remark that the triumphal procession of Marcellus 'produced a superb spectacle such as has seldom been seen in Rome'.[111] While in no way must this suggest that the triumph was simply a public relations exercise, these observations reinforce the advantages of the ceremony as an efficient vehicle of transmission.

This may be demonstrated further by imagining how the movement and fluidity associated with the triumphal procession would have maximized the space available both for the crowds and the strategically placed architecture along the route. After the triumph was over, it is possible the didactic and symbolic nature of the architecture would have been imbued with additional meaning as the place through which the *triumphator* had passed. Processions were effective, too, as they were able not only to pass through areas already laden with meaning, but could also exploit symbolic space at the beginning and at the end of a route. Equally, the transitory nature of the procession enabled the *triumphator* potentially to be more visible than if he had occupied static space. He thus became a palpable figure with whom the spectators might feel they could relate more easily; and even if he were absent, his 'presence' would be manifest with the lavish imagery and triumphal architecture celebrating his glory. Further, the pomp of the spectacle and the exultation of the *triumphator's* glorious feats would have generated admiration, thus ensuring he be regarded as an extraordinary being and an heroic exemplar. Music – trumpet blasts and the chanting of songs – would increase the electric atmosphere, as would the cheers of the excited crowd, and also the clatter of the horses, parading troops and booty-laden chariots as they passed by. The impact of the procession upon the human senses would also have come in the guise of the vibrant colours and impressive nature of visual stimuli – much of which would have a marked effect upon the audience who, no doubt, would magnify the event and the tangible force of the *triumphator* (and Rome) at a later stage.[112]

For centuries, elaborate recreations of the Roman triumph had been an intrinsic part of the political and symbolic landscape(s) of Paris and other urban centres in France and further afield. The above considerations not only underscore the many advantages of the post-antique 'triumph' both as a power- and as an image-diffusing medium, but they also underline why, as *the* showpiece and nucleus of the Napoleonic Empire, Paris became an ideal stage upon which to project the Emperor's own form of power and his military supremacy.

From 1631 the French possessed an additional mode of transmission – the newspaper. Under Louis XIV, the press flourished and became increasingly powerful as a vehicle through which to diffuse the King's image.[113] New papers were created, and *La Gazette* – France's first newspaper and the Crown's major political tool – now appeared twice, rather than once, a week. Due to the Revolution's accent on the liberty of the press, as many as 150 daily newspapers began to circulate in Paris alone. Numbers then diminished dramatically once journalists lost their lives to the guillotine under 'The Terror'.[114] As a measure of the degree to which censorship continued once Bonaparte became First Consul, we see that papers circulating in Paris were reduced from 72 to 13. Significantly, Bonaparte's increasing authority and his transformation into Napoleon, went hand in hand with the implementation of truly Draconian measures: during the First Empire, the circulation of newspapers plummeted from thirteen to a mere 4.

The above outline reinforces the power of the French press as a political weapon, and also how it was manipulated to project a decidedly subjective view of events.[115] Mazedier's comment that censorship was still more marked under Napoleon than it had been during the *ancien régime*,[116] reiterates the degrees to which he went to manipulate information to his own advantage. Napoleon himself was not beyond contributing personally (though often under a pseudonym) to newspapers such as *Le Moniteur Universel*. These observations bring into focus two important and far from unrelated points. They demonstrate how contemporary newspapers enable today's researcher to gain valuable insight into the projection of Napoleonic propaganda and Napoleon's image. They also exemplify how newspapers act as an invaluable means of establishing how the notion of the triumph was used by Napoleon (and France's respective powers) to disseminate contemporary authority.

As accessible, as well as relatively inexpensive commodities (both for the producer and the consumer), newspapers became effective pre- and post-event instruments through which to form and control public opinion in Paris, the provinces and abroad. Although vehicles of transmission such as art and architecture were more durable than spectacle, the newspaper served as an instant, a vivid and detailed means of recording and magnifying events. Its role as a 'mass' medium of transmission would have played an important part in immortalizing the creation of Napoleon's exemplary and heroic image, not only for those who attended his events in person (and those who did not), but also for posterity. Papers tend to have placed as much (and at times more) emphasis on forthcoming events as they did on post-event descriptions. They were therefore an efficient means of advertising festivals and attracting as large a crowd as possible (details could also be passed onto the illiterate). *Le Moniteur Universel*, for instance, supplies descriptions of the ceremonial route Napoleon and his new empress, Marie-Louise, were to follow for their *entrée* into Paris in 1810. Information is supplied relating to the location and nature of the monuments the *cortège* would pass, as well as details of the times and locations of the ceremonies and attractions laid on for the citizenry. Equally, the paper stipulates the designated spaces set aside for the crowd who, of course, were to witness first-hand, Napoleon's spectacular adaptation of the Roman triumph.[117]

The *Journal de l'Empire* provides details of the forthcoming *entrée* and alludes to the didactic role of the associated architecture.[118] Particular attention is paid to the (unfinished) Arc de Triomphe de l'Étoile that was decorated temporarily for the imperial couple's entrance into Paris (Figure 4). An emphasis is placed on the description and interpretation of the iconography, since there were to be no inscriptions to explain its meaning on the arch.[119] The paper also stipulates where the public could purchase leaflets providing further descriptions of the monument's imagery.[120] A *trompe-l'oeil* bas-relief under the title *Prospérité de l'Empire* is described: it includes a depiction of the imperial couple in a triumphal chariot, and another of the Empress and Napoleon representing their contribution to the *Beaux-Arts* and to agriculture.[121] The description of a further bas-relief depicting Napoleon, again in his imperial dress *à la romaine*, reveals the Emperor as the French peoples' legislator (specific reference is made to his civil and penal codes).[122] Equally telling is the description of 'Napoleon' with soldiers who deposit arms at his feet – the symbolism is explained by the Emperor's clemency and his ability to pardon his defeated enemies.[123] We see here a juxtaposition of the modern and antique, in which both ancient Rome and the symbolism of the triumph were reinvented to display different facets of Napoleon's exceptional rule. Such examples demonstrate how the Emperor's publicists manipulated the triumph to disseminate a most contemporary version of *Romanitas* whereby the omnipresent Napoleon, as always, was projected as the '*triumphator*' par excellence. The lavish Rome inspired backdrops; the very presence of the Emperor in his capital, combined with the spectacular pre- and post-event media coverage of the spectacle, moreover, would have contributed to the projection of Napoleonic Paris as a singularly magnificent 'new Rome'.

2

The Monument and the Monumental Axis

In the 1802 edition of *Paris et ses monuments*, Amaury-Duval stated that 'of all the arts, the most useful is architecture'.[1] This is indicative of the ways in which architecture under Napoleon was to become the focus of discussion in the media and how, via the discussion of the capital's new architecture, the media were to enhance the standing of the Emperor as its creator. These observations underscore the pivotal role of Paris' 'Roman' monuments both as forceful didactic media and as visual statements encoded with the politics of the Napoleonic regime.

Napoleon harboured grandiose visions to transform the path of Paris' east-west axis into a triumphal route that would bisect the city. By exploring the projection of his monuments, and their visual and symbolic links with the axis, this chapter also reinforces the potential of using spatial theory to gain valuable insight into the relationship between antiquity, architecture, Napoleon and the dissemination of power. It is shown how the three-way link between the Emperor, the classical world *and* Paris' former recreations of *Romanitas* has advantages as an analytical framework for the study of Napoleon and the reception of antiquity. With the implications of this tripartite relationship in mind, the following pages build upon existing scholarly discussion of Napoleonic monumentalization of Paris.[2] Three works are of particular significance: Etlin, *Symbolic Space* (1994); Leith, *Space and Revolution* (1991); and Marrinan, *Romantic Paris: Histories of a Cultural Landscape, 1800–1850* (2009). The authors examine the implications of the capital's 'layers' of space, and also focus on the image of a city that Etlin locates within the interplay between 'physical appearance and mental construct'.[3] We will see within the development of Napoleon's projected *voie triomphale* the interrelationship of antiquity, the French Republic's former visions for the east-west axis and the earlier manipulation of the same axis under Louis XIV. Underpinning this analysis is Lefebvre's understanding of 'the monument':

> A monumental work, like a musical one, does not have a 'signified' (or 'signifieds'); rather, it has a *horizon of meaning*: a specific or indefinite multiplicity of

meanings, a shifting hierarchy in which now one, now another meaning comes momentarily to the fore, by means of – and for the sake of – a particular action. The social and political operation of a monumental work traverses the various 'systems' and 'subsystems', or codes and subcodes, which constitute and found the society concerned. But it also surpasses such codes and subcodes, and implies a 'supercoding', in that it tends towards the all-embracing presence of the totality.[4]

By applying Lefebvre's incisive definition of encoded meaning in monuments, we may approach the Napoleonic monuments of Paris as having a 'supercoding' that embraces the 'subcodes' of the Revolution, the *ancien régime* and antiquity. The Emperor's new monuments therefore had an horizon of meaning that embraced all things. This underlines why one requires insight into the 'subcodes' of the Revolution and the French monarchy – especially Louis XIV – to understand the Napoleonic capital's image as a 'new Rome'.

Discussion will focus on structures associated with Napoleon and the path of the east-west axis: these include the Arc de Triomphe de l'Étoile, the Arc du Carrousel, the Vendôme Column, the Fontaine de la Victoire and the elephant fountain. Since the Avenue des Champs-Élysées, the Place de la Concorde, the Palais des Tuileries, the Palais du Louvre, the Place de la Bastille and Place de la Nation already had physical links with this axis, and occupied space either considered or reinvented by the architects of Napoleon's imperial city, these landmarks, too, are explored. The chapter, in main, follows the topographical course of the axis from west to east and as a result, space associated with the western limits of Napoleonic Paris is examined first.

Napoleon's Arc de Triomphe de l'Étoile

A leaflet available to the modern visitor to the Arc de Triomphe opens with reference to the pertinent links between the monument and antique Rome:

> In 1806, just after the Battle of Austerlitz, Napoleon I declared to his soldiers, 'you will march home through arches of victory'. The monument was to dominate Paris and indulge the Emperor's liking for Ancient Rome.[5]

Despite the number of works on the Arc de Triomphe, there appears to be no detailed analysis of its relationship with the Roman world. Given that one of the monument's key functions was to accommodate triumphal activity,[6] the paucity of detailed scholarly attention in this respect is all the more surprising.

This may be due to the fact that Napoleon was never to parade beneath the finished structure. It may also be a result of the ambiguity inherent in the Napoleonic references to its role as a triumphal arch[7] and that it might appear initially to be less 'Roman' than the Emperor's Arc du Carrousel. Equally notable are negative receptions both of the Arc de Triomphe and of its benefactor by scholars such as Lyons, whose condemnation of the monument as 'hideous and expensive' is combined with a reference to the Napoleonic 'ego'.[8] Paradoxically, there is a resemblance between Suetonius' allusions to Domitian's megalomanic construction of triumphal arches and Lyon's criticism of Napoleon's Arc de Triomphe:

> He raised so many and such enormous arcades and arches, decorated with chariots and triumphal insignia, in various city districts, that someone scribbled '*arci*', meaning 'arches' on one of them – but used Greek characters, and spelled out the Greek word for 'Enough!'[9]

The imposing size of Napoleon's arch and his plans in 1806 to construct four permanent Parisian triumphal arches, of course, did not imply a deliberate recreation of Domitian's Rome. Instead, what we see in the linkage is a means of using an example from antiquity to condemn the actions of Napoleon as exemplified by the construction of triumphal arches.

The Arc de Triomphe stands on elevated ground at the western end of the Avenue des Champs-Élysées.[10] Dwarfing any of ancient Rome's extant triumphal arches, it remains one of the largest in the world.[11] As much a personal project of Napoleon's, as of its principal architect, Jean-François-Thérèse Chalgrin, the arch was to mirror the Emperor's admiration for colossal monuments. Indeed, it was said that the destruction of men and the construction of monuments were central to Napoleon, and that his passion for vast structures almost equalled that of his love for war.[12]

The first stone of the Arc de Triomphe was laid on Napoleon's birthday – 15 August 1806, and although it was only completed in 1836, the structure is probably the Emperor's most acclaimed personal epitaph; testament to his military feats and symbol of his empire's power.[13] At the time of its construction, however, the arch was projected as a tribute to the exploits of the *Grande Armée*. Given the fairly recent Revolution, the deliberate disguise of one of the monument's principal functions – that of disseminating Napoleon's personal *gloire* – might appear to be relatively uncomplicated.[14] The role (or roles) of the structure as a reinvention of the Roman arch, nonetheless, was more complex. The regime's relation with the antique was far from straightforward even in the realm of architecture. Napoleon declared that the erection of triumphal arches was a futile exercise, adding that the only reason he considered them worthy of attention was because they encouraged architecture.[15] This point is hardly in accord with his plans in the same year (1806) for the Arc de Triomphe and the Arc du Carrousel, and as noted earlier, with his own announcement that the only honourable route home after battle was by way of a triumphal arch. Temporary Rome inspired arches such as the Pantin arch, built in honour of the Eylau and Friedland victories (1807), were also erected at considerable expense to accommodate Napoleon's triumphal passage into Paris.[16] These inconsistencies should not be looked upon in a negative light: if anything, they reinforce the need to investigate the wider implications of the relationship between the Arc de Triomphe and antique Rome.

The sheer size of the structure already suggests palpable links with the triumphal arch as an emblem of Rome's military force and universal dominion. Unfortunately, the longevity of the monument's construction put paid to its use as a vehicle through which Napoleon and his *Grande Armée* could parade in triumph. His entrance into Paris in 1810 beneath the temporary replica of the unfinished structure with Marie-Louise, however, underlines how the image of this triumphal arch was creatively manipulated as an expression of power (see Figure 4).[17]

Napoleon's vast triumphal monument was erected on Paris' sixth boundary, Claude Nicolas Ledoux's *enceinte des fermiers généraux*. Both this and the important part played by the structure in the Emperor's ceremonial *entrée* into Paris in 1810 (above), introduce its interrelated role as a gateway defining the entrance to the Napoleonic capital. The significance of gateways separating a particularly symbolic space from its surroundings stretches back to antiquity and beyond. The symbolic differentiation of space in Roman times, for example, is highlighted by Lefebvre, who focuses on one of Rome's most popular foundation myths where the city's founder, Romulus, carved out a circle with a plough.[18] The space within the circle was thus given symbolic, religious and political meaning, and legend and reality fused with the realization of Rome's sacred boundary, the *pomerium*. The distinction made between these 'spaces', Lefebvre suggests, should be viewed as both symbolic and practical – as such, this re-emphasizes the differentiation made between the political, judicial and the altogether powerful image of the *Urbs* as opposed to the surrounding *orbis*.[19] The creation of a link between Rome's sacred boundary and Paris is affirmed by a plaque upon which was reference to the *pomerium*. The plaque – which dates to the reign of

Louis XIV – was close to the royal city's new symbolic boundary (the *Cours*), of which more is said in the following chapter.

Bound intricately to Lefebvre's argument is the interrelationship of the Roman road and the city gate. The latter functioned both as a marker defining intra-urban and extra-urban space, and as a symbolic passage through which processions entered and exited a city:

> The Roman road, whether civil or military, links the *urbs* to the countryside over which it exercises dominion. The road allows the city, as people and as Senate, to assert its political centrality at the core of the *orbis terrarium*. The gate, through which the imperial way proceeds from *urbs* to *orbis*, marks the sacrosanct enceinte off from its subject territories, and allows for entrance and exit.[20]

Napoleonic Paris, like ancient Rome, was the kernel of power and a visual lens through which to gauge the politics of its ruler. The interplay between monuments, space and ritual, on both accounts, was employed as a potent tool through which to placate and educate the populace, and simultaneously project the cities' pre-eminence as hubs of culture and universal power. Although a city gate is (or was once) set within the city wall and the Arc de Triomphe has always been a free-standing structure, like Rome's city gates, it would have signalled in a highly visual manner, the symbolic and physical divide between *orbis* and impressive *Urbs*, while also accommodating the passage between these spaces. In this way, Napoleon's arch would mark the spatial limits between the French *orbs* – the rest of France and the empire – and Napoleonic Paris (the *Urbis*). Etlin stipulates that as a capital city, Paris needed a 'physical magnificence worthy of its importance', and that the first requirement in this respect was the entrance as it should encapsulate the image of the city itself.[21] Champagny's reference to the Arc de Triomphe both reaffirms its importance as a spatial marker and as a symbolic gateway to Paris, and underlines how the monument's size and visibility would have increased its efficacy:

> The monument would be seen from afar. . . . It would be visible from the heights of Neuilly and also seen from the Place de la Concorde. It would be admired by visitors entering Paris, for monuments of this kind are more effective when viewed from a distance. By way of its power to penetrate the mind, its incomparable beauty would be engraved on the memories of those separated from the capital.[22]

Champagny was Napoleon's *ministre de l'Intérieur* and heavily involved in the siting and construction of the Arc de Triomphe. His reference to the projected structure, as reported above, has much in common with MacDonald's remarks concerning aspects of the function and spatial location of the Roman arch:

> Placed at nodal armature points, large enough to be seen from a distance and thus impressed in advance upon one's awareness, monumental arches were powerful urban instruments.[23]

The architects of the Arc de Triomphe borrowed additional devices from the Roman world to impress upon the viewer the splendours and power of Napoleonic Paris. Both Kostof and MacDonald underline the importance the Romans attached to the arch as a means of visually framing and regulating a particular view.[24] The authors' combined observations that the view was usually fixed at the end by 'some worthy marker'[25] or 'architectural climax'[26] is also relevant to the view that would have led the eye into Paris when seen through the *fornix* of the Arc de Triomphe. This is explicit in Champagny's conception of the 'majestueuse' and 'superbe' view from the arch of the Palais des Tuileries.[27] Equally significant is his reference to the view an individual would enjoy of the arch *from* the palace, and the emphasis placed on the building's role as the centre of Paris in *its* role as the centre of the Napoleonic Empire.[28]

As Napoleon's imperial palace and seat of power, the Palais des Tuileries acted both as a symbolic climax to the vista *and* as an essential component of his powerful *Urbs*. The view through the arch would thus have allowed the eye to penetrate the spatial limits of the city. This would have accentuated the impact and symbolism of the Champs-Élysées as a triumphal way as it led along the east-west axis towards the Tuileries Palace, behind which was the Palais du Louvre – the Tuileries was set alight by the Communards in 1871 and as a result, the Louvre now forms the perspective's climax.

The use of the Champs-Élysées as a triumphal way re-emphasizes the military character of the Arc de Triomphe. This introduces the monument's links with antique Rome's *porta triumphalis*, as indicated in Champagny's reference to the location of the Arc de Triomphe at the entrance to Paris, and his statement that wherever the visitor stood, entering the city by this route, they would always be opposite the *Triumphator*.[29] Well before Napoleon's 'new Rome' was in the making, the French had been aware that the *porta triumphalis* was located at one of the entrances to Rome and that it marked the symbolic passage of a *triumphator* into the city. It was also understood that although this was an essential element of the Roman triumph, there were still topographical and symbolic links between the *porta triumphalis* and Rome's city gates. For example, Michel de Pure reports that one of Rome's city gates (the Capena gate) was used as a triumphal gate of entry – he also refers to the gathering in the *Campus Martius* prior to a triumphal procession's entrance into Rome.[30] This is not the time to debate the accuracy of Pure's understanding of Rome's illusive *porta triumphalis* – what matters is the importance he attached to the structure's location as a means of entering Rome, and the links created between both the city and the city gate. Here, one is reminded especially of the relationship between extra-urban and symbolic intra-urban space (discussed earlier), and thus the concept of the city gate and the *porta triumphalis* as a mode of passage from the surrounding *orbis* into the *Urbs*. Lefebvre's reference to the relationship between ancient Rome's image and the genesis of various 'spaces of power' also comes into its own.[31] Napoleonic Paris, too, may be seen as a conglomeration of interconnecting spaces of power – each with its images and symbols – representing different, and yet interrelated aspects of the city's make-up. If then we consider the multifunctional and didactic nature of a monument, we see the Arc de Triomphe as a billboard signalling the entrance to various 'spaces of power', which, together, formed Napoleonic Paris. In this way, we may see the structure taking on the interrelated role of the city gate and the *porta triumphalis*, and thus its importance as a marker that signalled the entrance to the civic, political, cultural, religious and military capital of Napoleon's omnipotent empire. The Arc de Triomphe was inspired (in part) by the single-*fornix* Arch of Titus (*c*. 81–2 CE). This structure was not built on Rome's ancient boundaries, but rather, within the city: it stands in the *Forum Romanum* at the point where the road leading to the Colosseum met the *Sacra via* (Figures 5 and 6).[32] We see therefore how the Napoleonic regime mixed, manipulated and reinvented the language of Rome's various arch forms to create a particularly forceful instrument of contemporary propaganda.

Both the *porta triumphalis* and Rome's triumphal arches were essential elements of the Romans' triumphal language and the city's image as *caput mundi*. The Arc de Triomphe, like its antique precedents, was also intended to act as an impressive backcloth for what Kostof would term 'the staging of power'.[33] This was manifest in the re-appropriation of the Roman arch and Triumphal Way, and the ensuing passage through the Arc de Triomphe and along the Champs-Élysées. When reflecting upon the glorious triumphs and eternal monuments of his rule, the ex-emperor Napoleon saw the location of these structures as being at the entrance to the 'Capital of Europe' (alias Napoleonic Paris).[34] The additional relevance of this is clear in the distinction Napoleon then makes between Paris and the 'rest of the universe', and consideration of

Ovid's famous remark that 'the land of other peoples has a fixed boundary; the extent of the city of Rome is the same as that of the world'.[35] The ancient author's inference to the distinction between *orbis* and *Urbs* as Östenberg observes, not only implies Rome's universal hegemony, but could also suggest that the whole world might be seen in Rome.[36] Equally insightful is her subsequent comment that, in 'leading the world into the city, the triumphal procession formed the supreme staging of this notion'.[37] Again, we see what is by now a familiar pattern, for this may be applied as much to the triumphal landscape of Napoleonic Paris and the presentation of the Emperor's capital as *caput mundi* as it could to the triumph and the image(s) of Rome in antiquity.

The physical manifestation of power inherent in the selective adaptation of Rome's image(s), triumphal ritual, route and monuments, of course, was far from unprecedented. This should also be considered when examining the symbolic and topographical relationship between the Arc de Triomphe and the Champs-Élysées.[38] Imperial Berlin's Unter den Linden (1647), for instance, was built as a parade ground and processional way, and it became the symbol of the rise of the Prussian State.[39] Many of the buildings and monuments erected along its axial path had a decidedly military character. The most celebrated structure was the Brandenburg Gate which was built later (1788–91) to celebrate the victories of the Prussian army. Napoleon's own victorious campaigns, moreover, enabled him to manipulate the ideology of Berlin's Unter den Linden and Brandenburg Gate to his advantage. Several days after beating the Prussians at Iéna and Auerstaedt in 1806, he and his *Grande Armée* publicly staged France's military supremacy by their triumphal passage through the Brandenburg Gate and along the city's processional way. Intriguingly, while Napoleon's visions for his own *voie triomphale* were being implemented (in part, at least), the English were also planning a processional route. Had Sir John Soane's project been realized, George IV's London, too, would have boasted a triumphal way interspersed with Rome inspired arches and similarly didactic monuments.[40]

Importantly, Paris itself provided Napoleon and his architects with a wealth of Rome inspired legacies with which to manipulate to the regime's advantage. In an account of a conversation between Napoleon and his *première architecte*, Pierre-François-Léonard Fontaine, the relationship between the Arc de Triomphe and the Roman arch is addressed, whereupon Fontaine emphasizes the salient role of a monument's grandeur and elevation. However, he also suggests that aspects of the Napoleonic arch should resemble those of the Porte Saint-Martin (see Figure 22).[41] This elaborate structure from the reign of Louis XIV was consciously modelled on Rome's triumphal arches. At that time, grandeur and elevation were essential elements of the recreation of Imperial Rome's monumental fabric. Equally, the spatio-symbolic implications of the Arc de Triomphe, the Porte Saint-Martin and the majority of the King's other Parisian arches come into play: while they all drew inspiration from the Roman triumphal arch, they were, for the most part, located on Paris' *enceinte(s)*.[42] These factors illustrate the combined influence of antiquity and Louis XIV, and in turn that of Paris' long-standing *entrée royale* tradition, which itself had found precedent in ancient Rome's passage architecture and the Roman triumph.

By touching upon links between the Arc de Triomphe and former recreations of *Romanitas* in Paris, one is reminded of the tripartite language of Napoleon's didactic monuments. With the cardinal importance of this three-way relationship in mind, one can also appreciate further the potential force of the Napoleonic monument as a political tool. Louis XIV's reign, for instance, was arguably *the* most influential in French history, as were the numerous cultural and urban projects which were such a part of the King's grandiose 'new Rome(s)'. To advertise the dawn of a new era and the all-encompassing power of the Napoleonic regime, the conception of the Arc de Triomphe was related to selectively manipulating the imagery of the Roman world *and* that of Paris' former reinventions of Rome. This fits neatly with the underlying 'horizon of meaning' and 'subcodes' of Lefebvre's 'monument', and thus reinforces the intended role of the Arc de Triomphe as a forceful medium of propaganda.

As outlined previously, the 'subcodes' (or 'pasts') discussed in this chapter are those of Paris' physical and symbolic landscape during the reign of Louis XIV and the revolutionary years. We shall also see how it is these pasts that allow us invaluable insight into Napoleon's exploitation of the city's east-west axis and his recreation of a 'new Rome'. Indeed, here, too, we are able to employ Lefebvre's 'subcodes', as they can be applied to space just as effectively as they can to monuments. The benefits of adopting such an approach are reaffirmed indirectly by Lowrie in his excellent synthesis of a city's layers of space:

> Cities bear a symbolic weight that goes beyond their manifold physical and social structures at any one time because their persistence through history gives layers, sometimes contradictory, to what they stand or fall for.[43]

The author's reference here to a city's sometimes contradictory layers and the accent placed on time, also reflects essential elements of Soja and of course Lefebvre's conception of the often problematic 'interplay between space and time'.[44] The decidedly contradictory nature of Paris' layers (its 'horizon of meaning') in relation to those of the Revolution and the reign of Louis XIV, in particular, underlines further the value of this approach. It also reinforces the potential of employing the basic methodology used by Etlin and Leith: both of whom focus on the Revolution's use of and contribution to Paris' layers of space.[45] The complex interplay between space and time – and 'physical appearance' and 'mental construct'[46] – is also apparent in Lowrie's comment that 'the unconscious only ever comes into consciousness partially', so that we cannot recreate more than a few pasts in our minds at one time.[47] This would have been as applicable to Napoleon and his entourage as it is to the modern investigator, and it underpins the value of exploring the ways in which Paris' past(s) shaped the 'Roman' character of Napoleonic Paris. These considerations also find reference with elements of Marrinan's invigorating portrait of the 'cultural landscape' of Paris between 1800 and 1850. While his study is not orientated towards an investigation of the capital's 'Roman' layers, the manner in which he weaves aspects of Lefebvre's 'multiple levels of meaning' into his narrative of Paris' monuments, spaces and culture, allows us a fuller understanding of the city's multidimensional fabric.[48]

The dominating position of the Arc de Triomphe at the summit of the Champs-Élysées might encourage one initially to associate both projects with Napoleon. Consideration of the multilayered character of this space, however, brings into focus the former appropriation of the area under Louis XIV. The Champs-Élysées was realized by the King's principal landscape designer, André Le Nôtre, and although it had not been employed as a triumphal way, the Vitruvian principals of order, axiality and perspective had governed its creation.[49] Neither was Napoleon the first to envisage the Champs-Élysées as a triumphal way: it had served as just this during the Revolution. There had been various plans to erect triumphal arches along its axial path, typified by an elaborate project, which probably dates to Year II of the Republic, for a single-*fornix* triumphal arch destined to mark the eastern entrance to the avenue.[50] The anonymous plan also illustrates the ways in which the revolutionaries had formerly refashioned antique Rome's triumphal architecture and ritual to express their own forceful rhetoric. This is shown in the procession winding its way around the columns of the arch which, if realized, would have been crowned by the *Horses of Marly*.[51] The replicas of these impressive marble sculptures still frame the eastern entrance to the Champs-Élysées, while the originals – which had been transferred to Paris from the grounds of the Château de Marly under the initiative of David – are now housed in the Louvre. Equally noteworthy are Bernard Poyet's monumental designs in 1799 for the Place de la Révolution (today's Place de la Concorde). His symbolic complex recalling Rome's *campo vaccino* and Capitol was to be integrated into a triumphal route from which, at its most westerly end (the Étoile), it would be possible to view the Tuileries.⁵²

The topographical relationship of the Arc de Triomphe with Ledoux's toll gates (1784–9) serves as a final and a most pertinent example of how space associated with the western limits of Paris was reinstated under Napoleon. The 50 or so classically inspired *barrièrres* were built to collect tax on merchandise entering and leaving the city. Only a handful of them had survived the wrath of the revolutionaries, though two still flanked the Arc de Triomphe while Napoleon ruled (they were destroyed in 1860–1).⁵³ Indeed, as symbols of despotism and oppression, the majority of the toll gates had been attacked and pillaged only two days before the storming of the Bastille.⁵⁴ A contemporary rhyme testifies to their unpopularity: 'This wall enclosing Paris has all of Paris grumbling.⁵⁵ These fiscal barriers had formed part of the *enceinte des fermiers généraux* (noted previously) and, as such, they had redefined both the nature of Paris' gateways and the limits of the city's boundaries. The impact of the Arc de Triomphe – as a monument which both symbolized France's new-found military supremacy and marked the entrance to Napoleon's powerful and improved *Urbs* – would thus have been still more effective given its co-existence with space which had generated such intense hostility.⁵⁶

Napoleon's Arc de Triomphe du Carrousel

The Arc du Carrousel was designed by Fontaine and his co-architect, Charles Percier. The first stone of the structure was laid on 7 July 1806. While both it and the Arc de Triomphe were begun in the same year, the Carrousel arch was completed during Napoleon's rule (1808–9) and employed on a regular basis as a triumphal monument under which he and his soldiers passed.

Legrand and Landon's *Description de Paris et de ses édifices* (1809) was both a guidebook and a blatant piece of contemporary propaganda. In their account of the Arc du Carrousel, emphasis is placed on the monument's location, function and, most significantly, that it was not simply imitating Rome's triumphal arches, but that it was more impressive than its antique precedents.⁵⁷ The authors could not use the size of the Arc du Carrousel as an indication of its superiority, for, unlike the Arc de Triomphe, it was considerably smaller than its Roman counterparts. The guide was charged with political rhetoric, and the allusion to ancient Rome should be interpreted as a further advertisement of the advent of an infinitely powerful and impressive new era.

The construction of the Arc du Carrousel as a celebration of one of the Emperor's most acclaimed military victories underpins the creation of an explicit bond between this triumphal arch and those of the ancient Romans. The Austerlitz victory (1805), moreover, was instrumental in bringing to an end the *Saint Empire Romain Germanique* and as such, this reinforced parallels between the Napoleonic Empire's omnipotence and that of Imperial Rome. This is underlined by Fontaine's reference to the merits of the Arc du Carrousel's antique precedents, especially in relation to the association between these grandiose structures and the conquering Romans' display of power over much of the ancient world.[58] Napoleon was involved personally in the function(s) and siting of the structure, which was also built to unite the palaces of the Tuileries and the Louvre, as well as acting as a free-standing entrance to the former: the Emperor's political headquarters and residence.[59]

The selective manipulation of the Roman world, its symbolism and ideology went further still. The Louvre was a key instrument of Napoleon's propaganda, not least as it displayed the famed Roman booty that he and his republican armies had seized and which later was paraded triumphantly into Paris in 1798. This is especially significant if we recall that the Temple of Jupiter (Rome's sacred Capitol) had symbolized the heart of ancient Rome and its mighty empire, and served as the symbolic terminus for the city's triumphal processions.[60] The Capitol also housed the spoils that Rome's victorious *triumphators* and their armies had captured and paraded through the city.[61] The parallels between the Louvre and Rome's Capitol are therefore unmistakable.[62] This is indicated in Amaury-Duval's praise for the Louvre's 'magnificent' *Musée Napoléon*, in which were exhibited 'the most sublime productions of antique sculpture, immortal trophies of our victories'.[63] The transfer of Rome's power and heritage to Paris demonstrated, in a highly symbolic manner, the capital's role both as a 'new Rome' and as the 'first city' of the Napoleonic Empire. The implications of this relationship are explored further by Mainardi, who also considers the new roles played by ancient Rome *and* the modern city of Rome. She remarks that the booty embodied 'a double authority, both cultural and political; through the agency of these objects both Romes were symbolically relocated in Paris'.[64] The subsequent display of the spoils in the museum was used to underline Napoleon's possession of the 'world's art treasures', both to legitimize the regime and to reinforce the notion of empire and power.[65] This would have been even more meaningful once the Eternal City was under Napoleon's control (1809–14) and Rome proclaimed the 'second city' of the Empire. Such rhetoric was also geared towards justifying the fashion in which the treasures had been acquired – after all, was looting not normal in the grand scheme of empire-building? Had this not been part and parcel of the antique triumph and Rome's display of universal hegemony? Importantly, Quatremère de Quincy's views are illustrative of those who were vehemently opposed to the acquisition and later display of the plunder in the Louvre – indeed, he was so outraged by the imperial government's desire to serve Napoleonic politics, that he accused them of the 'conscription' of culture.[66]

Unsurprisingly, there were additional dimensions at work, not least as the Arc du Carrousel drew inspiration from Rome's Arch of Septimius Severus (Figures 7 and 8). The Severan arch is located in the *Forum Romanum* and stands on the *Sacra via* before its ascent of the Capitoline hill to the Capitol.[67] Although the Louvre was not built on elevated ground, its proximity to the Arc du Carrousel would have found parallels with the spatio-symbolic relationship between the Arch of Septimius Severus and Rome's Capitol. The Napoleonic arch acted as a focal point for the Place du Carrousel ('la cour Napoléon') – an area between the Louvre and the Palais des Tuileries which was synonymous with military activity. We have seen already that the Louvre-Tuileries complex under Napoleon was multifunctional, serving as the sociopolitical and cultural centre of the Emperor's imperial capital. These factors underpin the spatio-symbolic links between the Louvre-Tuileries complex as the nucleus of Napoleon's 'new Rome', and the *Forum Romanum* and Capitol in antiquity.[68]

A grandiose project from 1799 demonstrates how the inventive recreation of Rome's Capitol and *Forum Romanum* had already played a pivotal role in the theatre of legitimation and power. In Bernard Poyet's search for a focal point for a monumental triumphal route, and also a suitable sociopolitical and cultural centre for Republican Paris, he chose to re-appropriate a space already laden with powerful rhetoric. The Place de la Révolution (alias Place de la Concorde) was synonymous with the guillotine; and both the square and its immediate surroundings were to be transformed into a monumental complex reminiscent of the Roman Forum.[69] While disappointed that Paris was unable to boast antique Rome's original monuments, Poyet consoled himself with a plan that would recreate in detail these once magnificent structures.[70] The central feature of this project was to be a group of antique horses, believed to have been captured by the Romans and placed upon the city's triumphal arches.[71] A newspaper article from 1798 underlines the importance the French attached to the provenance of the antique group: it even stipulates (possibly mistakenly) that the horses had crowned one of Nero's triumphal arches.[72] The group was transferred from Rome to Constantinople, and in 1204 it was taken to Venice as booty following the sack of Constantinople. When it was seized by the French Republicans in the late 1700s, it adorned Venice's Basilica di San Marco. As a further demonstration of the French Republic's universal authority, the *Horses of St. Mark's* then played a prominent role in the famed triumphal procession of *spolia* into Paris of 1798 (see Figure 2). Subsequently, Poyet envisaged the bronze horses (pulling a triumphal chariot) on a pedestal surrounded by four Rome inspired temples, each acting as a museum displaying more of the symbolic fruits of the Republic's victories. The Palais Bourbon was to be incorporated into the scheme, as was the 'nouveau Panthéon' (la Madeleine), within which would be placed the *Apollo Belvedere* – another prized spoil of the 1798 *Entrée triomphale*.

Poyet's monumental and highly symbolic design underlines why consideration of former projects is fundamental to a deeper understanding of Napoleon's manipulation of the antique. The Louvre-Tuileries had already acted as a hub of power during both the monarchical periods and the Revolution. One cannot appreciate fully the ideology of Napoleon's 'forum' without reference, in particular, to the respective exploitations of the space under Louis XIV and the Republic. Napoleon was by no means the first (or last) sovereign to envisage a physical link between the palaces of the Tuileries and the Louvre, though interestingly, in their discussion of the topic, the only precedent mentioned by Legrand and Landon is Louis XIV.[73] The Place du Carrousel was also used for celebrations and military tournaments. The space derives its name from the famous equestrian *fête* of 1662, the Grand Carrousel, in which the King as 'Caesar' participated actively in the spectacle. During Bernini's stay in Paris, there was discussion involving the erection of a monument in the area. If construction had gone ahead, an effigy of Louis XIV on horseback between two triumphal structures reminiscent of Trajan's Column would have occupied space that later was associated with Napoleon's Arc du Carrousel.[74] Like so many Parisian projects, these designs were not realized. The plans under the King for the transformation of the Louvre's eastern façade and the creation of the palace's Gallery of Apollo, however, were far more than unrealized visions and as such, they receive specific attention in the following chapters.

As a royal residence and symbol of monarchic authority, the Tuileries had been stormed during the Revolution, renamed the Palais National and re-baptized as a veritable core of revolutionary ideology.[75] The Place du Carrousel served as an arena for military manoeuvres and public display. Plans included a classically inspired gateway to the National Palace which, if built, would have stood close to where the Arc du Carrousel later marked the entrance to Napoleon's legislative centre and residence. Had additional projects been realized, the area would have resembled a new and modified Republican forum with triumphal arches, amphitheatres and arenas. The space in front of the Tuileries also had associations with the guillotine: this might have found parallels with the Roman Forum's original *Rostra*, erected to display the heads of those who opposed the system. The latter analogy is conjecture on my part, but suits the decidedly radical nature of space during the Revolution's more turbulent years. The creation of Napoleon's forum inspired complex, therefore, should also be seen as a deliberate ploy to re-appropriate space associated both with republican fanaticism and monarchical autocracy. In this way, it was possible to legitimize Napoleon's authority and disseminate further his new, improved and exclusive form of power.[76]

If we consider the Arc du Carrousel's intended role as a monumental entrance to the Tuileries, we see again how the past played a fundamental role in Napoleon's psyche. Noteworthy in this respect is the importance in antiquity attached to ceremonial entrances of palaces, temples and other prestigious buildings; and among the elite, to the dwelling as a symbol of status and power.[77] An illustrative adaptation of this phenomenon in France is seen in the modification to Louis XIV's residence at Vincennes by Louis Le Vau, whose plans involved the construction of a Rome inspired triumphal arch at the entrance to the château. John Nash's Marble Arch (1828) reveals the continuation of the tradition in London: prior to it being moved to its present location near Hyde Park, this Constantine inspired arch served as an entrance to Buckingham Palace.

Interestingly, the modest size of the Arc du Carrousel resulted in its limited impact as a monumental entrance to the Tuileries. Napoleon's displeasure, when he inspected the arch once it was free of scaffolding, however, reinforces the pervasive presence both of the Roman world and Paris' former recreations of Rome. He remarked that the structure was more like a 'pavilion' than a triumphal arch, and that Louis XIV's Porte Saint-Denis 'was preferable by its form and grandeur' (see Figure 21).[78] The Emperor's dissatisfaction with the finished product might suggest that he was not actively involved in the detail of the arch. Contemporary sources, nevertheless, emphasize his unrelenting interest in the project.[79]

Although it is important to remain aware of the symbolic and topographical links between the Arc du Carrousel and the Arch of Septimius Severus, the regime's selective exploitation of antiquity resurfaces with the physical likeness between Napoleon's arch, the Severan arch *and* the Arch of Constantine (Figure 9). Percier and Fontaine had a detailed knowledge of the form and iconography of the arches of Septimius Severus and Constantine. In his description of the Arc du Carrousel, Fontaine provides information on the antique structures' respective locations, and he also comments that they combined more perfection than that of any other triumphal monument of the Roman epoch.[80]

The Severan arch, as noted previously, stands at the foot of the Capitoline and is sited on the *Sacra via*. The structure was dedicated in 203 CE to Septimius Severus and his two sons, Caracalla and Geta, and commemorates the Emperor's triumph over the Parthians in 195 and 203 (it also signalled the legitimacy of the new Severan dynasty).[81] The Arch of Constantine (315–16 CE) spanned the Triumphal Way between the Colosseum, the Palatine and the *Forum Romanum*, just before the ascent to the *Summa Sacra via* (leading to the Arch of Titus and the *Sacra via*). It celebrated Constantine's victory over the tyrant Maxentius at the Battle of the Milvian Bridge (312 CE).[82] Both arches were erected by the Senate and the People of Rome to commemorate an emperor's military triumph.

Both the Arc du Carrousel and its antique counterparts boast a principal *fornix* and two smaller subsidiary arches with coffered vaults (see Figures 7–9). They also share eight Corinthian columns with pilasters behind (four to each façade) and an entablature over which is an attic. The rectangular reliefs over the lateral arches of the Arc du Carrousel demonstrate how Napoleon's structure borrowed specific elements from the Arch of Septimius Severus. Nevertheless, similarly pertinent links between the Arc du Carrousel and the Arch of Constantine include the eye-catching use of polychromatic marble; the rectangular friezes of the side panels depicting the feats of the victorious armies and the length of inscription panels on the attics. Perhaps the most ingenious feature is the way in which the variety of intricately sculpted Napoleonic soldiers crowning the Arc du Carrousel's coloured marble columns recall the figures (Dacian prisoners) atop the columns of the Constantinian arch.

Like its Roman counterparts, the Arc du Carrousel reveals the 'Emperor' in all his military glory, a central and dominant figure throughout. One is able to differentiate between the depictions of the respective emperors from those of the other figures simply by the differences in position, attire, gestures and the orientation of those around them. Though generally Napoleon is presented in contemporary dress, the central bas-relief on the structure's interior, for instance, depicts him both as a modern and as a Roman emperor in his imperial robes crowned by the goddess Victory.[83] The translation of Roman imagery into a contemporary context is also manifest in the depictions of Napoleon's victorious campaigns of 1805 where, for example, the battles of Austerlitz and Ulm, and Napoleon's entrances into Munich and Vienna are exhibited in all their majesty.

Although the Arc du Carrousel was not able to translate into a modern idiom the exact form of the missing *quadriga* from the Severan and the Constantinian arches, the Napoleonic structure's crowning piece was none other than the *Horses of St. Mark's*. We might remember that the antique group had already played *the* central role in Poyet's plans for a French Republican forum in Paris. The provenance of the bronze group was again all-important; its significance as a symbol of military dominion, of course, still more meaningful as it had been the focal point of the 1798 entrance into Paris of Bonaparte and the French Republican army's spoils (see Figure 2).[84] Legrand and Landon describe the group's transfer to Paris; how it had originally crowned a triumphal arch in antique Rome, and how these 'objets précieux' after their journeys to Constantinople and Venice, had found their 'destination nouvelle' atop Napoleon's triumphal Arc du Carrousel.[85] That these bronze horses were now a feature of the Napoleonic arch and the Emperor's 'new Rome' says much about the regime's use of triumphal imagery as a forceful political medium. It also illustrates a definite one-upmanship both over the great Roman Empire and Paris' former appropriations of the same antique world.

The Emperor's Director of Museums (1802–15) and artistic director, Dominique-Vivant Denon, oversaw the sculptural decoration of the Arc du Carrousel. He insisted that the empty *quadriga* crowning the arch be accompanied by a statue of Napoleon dressed as a Roman emperor and *triumphator*.[86] This reinforces the monument's unequivocal links with Rome's triumphal imagery and ideology. Equally relevant was Napoleon's negative reaction, and his orders that it be removed immediately. He said that he would never condone the placement of a statue which so obviously glorified his, rather than his army's feats.[87] Such an act is reminiscent of traits attributed to Augustus by influential French figures such as Montesquieu, who had long emphasized Augustus' astuteness and tactical moves to camouflage his autocratic ambitions.[88] It has been argued that an explicit relationship was created between the 'forum Napoléon' and Augustus (as the 'first imperial builder') and that the Arc du Carrousel thus promoted Napoleon as a 'new Augustus'.[89] Whether the building of the arch and the creation of the Emperor's 'forum' were intended to create a specific affiliation with Augustus, however, is open to question. Although the media were known to disseminate more generalized parallels between Napoleonic and Augustan rule,[90] Montesquieu's candid perception of Augustus suggests that Napoleon would not deliberately reinvent himself as an individual who had been recognized popularly as a masked dictator. This is reinforced by the absence of contemporary links created between Napoleon's 'forum' and Augustus' Roman forum, and Napoleon's own reaction to the wording of the inscriptions destined for the Arc du Carrousel:

> Why give the Emperor Napoleon the title of Augustus or of Germanicus? Augustus could boast only of the Battle of Actium . . . There is nothing we can envy in Rome's emperors. What horrible memories for the generations who lived under Tiberius, Nero, Caligula and Domitian.[91]

Napoleon (he often spoke in the third person) continues to assert that Julius Caesar was the only man whose character and actions were truly worthy of note, but that the inscriptions must make no reference to ancient Rome's figures (notably, Augustus and Germanicus), as the title 'Emperor of the French' must stand alone.[92] The Arc du Carrousel and its symbolic surroundings, therefore, were not intended simply to emulate ancient Rome, or to present Napoleon as a 'new' *anybody*. Napoleon's stipulation that the inscriptions be in French and not in Latin – as French was the most cultivated of modern languages and more definable than 'dead languages'[93] – underlines his selective manipulation of the antique to project a decidedly contemporary image of himself as a modern and a singularly distinguished sovereign in his own right.

Paradoxically, the passionate responses the Arc du Carrousel generated after Napoleon's forced abdications in 1814 and 1815 bring into focus a further link between this structure and the Roman world.[94] The alterations it underwent as a result of the heated reactions Napoleon generated recall the practice of *damnatio memoriae*: a common feature of Rome's politically orientated monumental landscape. The destruction and defacement of monuments associated with the assassinated Domitian is to be noted, as is the removal of Geta's name and image on the Severan arch once he had been murdered.[95] The translation of *damnatio memoriae* into a French contemporary context is illustrated most pointedly by the 1789 Revolution's alteration, removal and destruction of monuments identified with the *ancien régime*. These factors both re-emphasize the immense power of monuments as political media and underpin the significance of the post-Napoleonic alterations to the Arc du Carrousel. The monument's fate could have been even worse, for in March 1816, an order was passed saving it from total destruction. This is recounted by Fontaine, who adds that by 1827 the intense animosity directed at the (First) Empire and its symbols had subsided sufficiently for a series of new plans to have been completed.[96] By 1828 the depictions of Napoleon's victories of 1805 were replaced with plaster reliefs illustrating various episodes of the Spanish campaigns of 1823. It was only after 1830 (under Louis-Philippe) that the original reliefs were reinstalled, as were the lead-coated statues discussed earlier.[97] The symbolic *quadriga* had been removed in 1815: the antique horses restored to the Venetians, and the accompanying chariot by François-Frédéric Lemot destroyed (the replacement bronze *quadriga* by François Joseph Bosio now crowns the arch). These politically motivated modifications to the Arc du Carrousel stand as a poignant testament to the power of Napoleon's legacy. Somewhat ironically, they also reinforce the success of this 'pavilion'-like structure as a forceful tool of Napoleonic propaganda.

The western section of Napoleon's *voie triomphale* and the Rue de Rivoli

We have seen already that some years before its destruction, the Palais des Tuileries had served as Napoleon's political headquarters and for a while, also his residence. A reconstruction of the view from the eastern and western sides of the palace provides insight into the ways in which the Emperor selectively restated the notion of ancient Rome's triumphal landscape. A painting of the partially destroyed palace by Meissonnier (1871) hints at the nature of the view from the eastern side of the building. Behind the mountain of rubble, it is possible to decipher the attic and *quadriga* of the Arc du Carrousel. This allows us to conceptualize the impact of the view in Napoleon's day. A painting by Ducis (1824) gives an impression of what the view from the western side of the palace would have offered had the Arc de Triomphe been completed during Napoleon's reign. Though Louis XVIII and his entourage are in the foreground, one is struck by the vista behind, which leads the eye up through the Tuileries gardens and the Champs-Élysées to its architectural and symbolic climax – the Arc de Triomphe. With the aid of these paintings, it is therefore possible to appreciate the symbolic intent of the views from Napoleon's headquarters had his visions been realized in full: on the eastern side a triumphal arch with 'forum' and 'capitol' as backdrops; to the west, a thoroughfare leading to an immense *porta triumphalis cum* city gate signalling the entrance to the Emperor's 'new Rome'.

The arches also formed a fundamental role in Napoleon's ambitious plans for a series of streets which would have completed the bisection of Paris (the various roads which today follow the path of the east-west axis were not interconnected at this stage). Had the projects been completed, there would have been a direct physical link between the Emperor's structures and symbolic spaces, many of which punctuate today's *axe historique* – thus named as it passes through what Lefebvre would envisage as Paris' most poignant 'spaces of power'.[98] While suggesting the potential impact of Napoleon's monumental schemes, and illustrating how urban development was influenced by politics and practicalities such as the facilitation of traffic, in isolation, however, this does not reveal any further links with Napoleon's visions for a *voie triomphale*.

The Palais des Tuileries stood on the axial path between the Arc de Triomphe and the Arc du Carrousel (Figure 10). A road running parallel to the Tuileries garden perspective (above) that also connected the Louvre-Tuileries complex to the Place de la Concorde (and the Champs-Élysées) would therefore ensure a physical link between the two arches. The construction of the Rue de Rivoli achieved this (see Figures 1 and 10).⁹⁹ Although it seems the road's original creation was not governed by this objective as its conception predates that of Napoleon's arches, the spaces these structures would occupy were already charged with symbolic appeal. We might also note Napoleon's instructions that the road be named after the Battle of Rivoli, one of the military victories of his famed 'first Italian campaign'. The regime had planned to open the first section of the Rue de Rivoli in 1802 (from the Place de la Concorde at the junction of Rue Saint Florentin, to the Louvre). However, it was only cut (and named) in 1804, and Napoleon was never to see the project finalized in its totality. The eastern end of the road was extended under Napoleon III, who reunited the Louvre and the Tuileries, and by way of this, completed the city's east-west axis (see Figure 10).¹⁰⁰ This gives an indication of the potential impact of the First Empire's Rue de Rivoli, had the regime's plans reached their fruition. The monumental route would have played a pivotal role in joining the Champs-Élysées (as processional route) and the Louvre -Tuileries (as Napoleon's 'forum') to the existing roads of the eastern section of the axis. As a result, the road would have formed a physical and symbolic link between the Napoleonic city's principal monuments and centres of ritual.

The picture, nevertheless, is still incomplete without reference to the projects of Napoleon's predecessors, not least because those who had shown interest in similar schemes had also attached great importance to ceremonial ritual and Roman symbolism. This reintroduces the relevance of the extension of the western end of the east-west axis during the reign of Louis XIV (Figure 11). At the beginning of the seventeenth century, the Champs-Élysées area was still largely marshland and did little to facilitate communications between the Louvre-Tuileries complex and the King's palace of Saint-Germain. A decree was passed in 1667 stipulating the creation of a promenade: this resulted in the birth of André Le Nôtre's tree-lined avenue, known later as the Champs-Élysées. Although the construction of the Jardin des Tuileries and its palace took place under Catherine de Medici (who assumed power as regent in 1564), the gardens were redesigned in a truly monumental manner under the King. Le Nôtre created impressive pools and terraces, and enlarged the main alley that would run parallel to Napoleon's future Rue de Rivoli. These alterations and the creation of the Champs-Élysées resulted in the magnificent perspective which later formed the symbolic view from, through and to the Arc de Triomphe.

Equally notable are the plans of the *Commission des Artistes* in its quest to 'revolutionise' Paris' urban infrastructure. One of the Republic's priorities was to link the site of the recently destroyed Bastille to the new city's equally symbolic core – the Louvre and its environs. A plan by Jean-Baptiste-Alphonse Lahure involved the building of the National Assembly on a road that would create a physical and an ideological link between the two areas.[101] The road was to be named the Rue National and, if realized, it would have traced the missing section of the east-west axis which later was built (in part, at least) under Napoleon I as the Rue de Rivoli. The Rue National would have also linked the Place de la Révolution (and therefore the Champs-Élysées) to the National Palace (the Tuileries) and the Republic's 'forum'.

Napoleon was clearly aware that the Rue de Rivoli would occupy an area already charged with symbolism. This also suggests how his visions for a Rome-like triumphal way in Paris were influenced by a desire to outclass his Parisian predecessors. Although this discussion has certainly hinted at the triumphal nature of the Rue de Rivoli, it is only with an understanding of the nature and location of the First Empire's Vendôme Column that one is able to appreciate the road's intended role as an intrinsic element of Napoleon's visionary *voie triomphale*.

Napoleon's Vendôme Column

The Colonne de la Grande Armée (1806–10) – a stone shaft covered in bronze helical plates depicting the feats of Napoleon and the *Grande Armée* between 1805 and 1807 – was erected in Place Vendôme and was consciously modelled on Trajan's Column (Figures 12 and 13). The Column of Trajan was dedicated in 113 CE by the Senate and the Roman People. It stands in the largest of Rome's imperial *fora* and celebrates the Emperor's victorious Dacian campaigns (101–2 CE).[102]

The publication of earlier designs for the Napoleonic structure in one of the regime's key media of propaganda, *Le Moniteur Universel*, reveal the column's future role as a celebration of a new era under a modern emperor and hero whose glory was unparalleled.[103] Adjectives such as invincible, immortal, powerful, glorious, brave, heroic and triumphant punctuate the pages of the newspaper – all of which are directed at Napoleon and how his victory at Austerlitz might be immortalized by the construction of a suitable monument. Most recommendations opt for a triumphal structure reminiscent of Trajan's Column: one such proposal envisages an exact copy, with the addition of certain modifications ensuring absolutely that the glorious actions of Napoleon, rather than those of Trajan, be the focus of the monument and its decoration![104]

Although the Colonne de la Grande Armée (or Vendôme Column) differed slightly to the earlier proposal (above), the monument's relationship with

Trajan's Column was certainly no less explicit.[105] The architects of this splendid Napoleonic structure, Jean-Baptiste Lepère and Jacques Gondouin, worked under the direction of Denon. While the Emperor was also directly involved in the project, Denon played a salient role, especially in relation to the finished structure's affinity with Trajan's Column.

Given Paris' long-standing relationship with antiquity, it comes as little surprise that the concept of erecting Rome inspired triumphal columns was far from unprecedented. The sheer number of these structures in existence, both in France and further afield, stands as a testament to this. Of note is the project destined for the Place du Carrousel (noted previously) as it brings into focus, both Louis XIV and his royal predecessors' deep-rooted fascination with Trajan's Column. This is reinforced by the existing drawings, miniature models and casts of the Trajanic structure, well before Percier had himself suspended in a basket to study its reliefs in preparation for his intricately detailed *Envois* of 1788.[106] Examples embrace the sketches by the seventeenth-century French painter Nicholas Poussin and most importantly, the casts undertaken during the reigns of François I and Louis XIV.[107] Due to the replacement of Trajan's crowning statue with St. Peter by Pope Sixtus V, this was about the only part of the column not to have been studied religiously. Louis XIV was even hailed as 'Il Traiano della Francia' in a dedication to the King on Bartoli and Bellori's illustrated edition of the Trajanic casts.[108] Roland Fréart de Chambray's *Parallèle de l'architecture antique avec la moderne* (1650) acts as further testimony to the prestige attached to Trajan and his column prior to Napoleonic rule. According to the author (who had been deeply involved in collecting relevant iconographical data), this celebrated structure was not only one of the most superb (existing) vestiges of Rome's majestic past, but its very presence and nature were also such that it served its role of immortalizing Trajan more efficiently than the hand of antiquity's many historians.[109]

These observations on the long-standing popularity of Trajan's Column call to mind the 'trialectic' nature of Napoleon's exploitation of Rome, and the ever-present one-upmanship, in particular, over Louis XIV's person and reign. This finds reference with the pre-Napoleonic casting campaigns (above) and as Tollfree aptly remarks, with the Emperor's ability to create 'an even greater display of power' by erecting a 'full size version' of Trajan's Column.[110] Neither is it without significance that at an earlier stage, Napoleon is said to have set his sights on transporting the original column from Rome to Paris, though fortunately he was advised that this would destroy the structure. The symbolic nature of the space appropriated by the Napoleonic column is also indicative of this three-way relationship: it was erected exactly where the equestrian statue of a 'Roman' Louis XIV had stood, prior to it being ruthlessly torn down by fervent revolutionaries in 1792 (Figure 14).

Revolutionary projects also reveal a string of proposals for various triumphal columns. A monument by Jean-Nicholas Sobre destined to mark the entrance to Paris' Pont de la Concorde suggests a particularly imaginative recreation of Roman architecture.[111] The plans, which probably date to Year II of the Republic, combine a surprisingly traditional-looking single-*fornix* triumphal arch with two columns reminiscent of the Trajanic structure. Possibly the most Trajan-like of all revolutionary columns, however, was Etienne-Louis-Denis Cathala's proposed centrepiece for the site of the Bastille. The project was conceived during the Revolution's early years. Especially interesting is Cathala's admiration for Trajan's Column as a symbol of force, and the translation of this into a design for a 'republican' column that would be taller than its classical counterpart.[112] The same may be said for the spiral reliefs winding their way around the shaft, as they depict the Revolution's progress, rather than Trajan's victories. The Vendôme Column – like Cathala's visionary structure – was taller than Trajan's Column; it, too, differed from its Roman prototype by glorifying decidedly contemporary triumphs.[113] These observations underpin how Napoleon's victory monument was influenced by such projects, as well as by the display of power inherent in the ideologies of these plans.

The impact of the Revolution's legacy and the royalist associations of the space re-baptized by the Vendôme Column would have influenced Napoleon's insistence that the glorious feats of the *Grande Armée* be the principal focus of the column's iconographic programme. It would seem that these factors may also have had some bearing on his earlier stipulation that the crowning statue be of Charlemagne rather than himself.[114] Due to a number of complex issues, the Emperor, nevertheless, was persuaded eventually that a statue of 'Napoleon' was preferable![115] The Vendôme Column was thus crowned with a colossal effigy of the Emperor (in Roman costume) soaring above the urban metropolis of his mighty imperial capital. Ironically, it would also seem that Pliny the Elder's reference to the placement of statues on columns so that they may be raised above all other mortals, was not lost on the individuals at the helm of the Napoleonic propaganda machine.[116] This fits neatly with Lefebvre's analyses of towering structures and the power of 'vertical space': a 'space', moreover, which has long been associated with masculinity and therefore envisaged as a potent symbol – and display – of fecundity, authority and force.[117]

Linked inextricably to Napoleon's display of power and his preoccupation with France's past was an element of demonstrating the First Empire's pre-eminence over Imperial Rome. Here, Trajan's reputation – as one of history's most highly esteemed rulers, imperial builders and military leaders – would have come into play. By building a structure that was modelled on this famed emperor's magnificent epitaph and by incorporating certain 'improvements', Napoleon and his publicists sought to reaffirm the First Empire's hegemony. Similarities are manifest in the combination of allegory, portraiture and human activity; in the conscious repetition of the respective emperors throughout, and in their eye-catching statues atop the respective columns. The helical reliefs of the Napoleonic column, however, depict a modern Napoleon and his *Grande Armée*, while iconographical tricks simultaneously accentuate the presence of the French nation's champion. Additional observations include the Napoleonic structure's pedestal, for although its resemblance to that of Trajan's Column is patently clear, Rome's triumphal insignia is replaced with contemporary arms, helmets and military costume (Figures 15 and 16). Equally notable is the structure's superior height and also its (part) composition of captured canon: as booty taken from the enemy, this reinforced the First Empire's display of military strength.[118] The Romans were known to have used the spoils of war in a similar way. Pliny asserts that the statue of Jupiter in the Capitol, erected by Spurius Carvilius after his victory over the Samnites (293 CE), was made from captured breastplates, greaves and helmets.[119] Given that Trajan's Column was of marble (as opposed to the symbolic *spolia* that were incorporated into Napoleon's structure), this also suggests a demonstration of the Napoleonic Empire's unrivalled strength.

As a means of displaying the all-pervasive power of the First Empire and its figurehead, it was, of course, essential that the Vendôme Column be erected in a suitably effective location. I am not suggesting that Napoleon and his advisors mistakenly envisaged Trajan's Column as a feature of antique Rome's triumphal route(s). A brief exploration of the Napoleonic column's topographical relationship with the Rue de Rivoli and the Emperor's other monumental landmarks, however, demonstrates a particularly suggestive reinvention of Rome's Triumphal Way.

Given the number and spectacular nature of military parades under Napoleon, it appears logical that a monumental road built in the centre of his imperial capital would prove most advantageous as a triumphal way. It is here that the significance of the Rue de Rivoli's projected extension to the Louvre-Tuileries resurfaces, as many of Napoleon's parades either started or finished at the Place du Carrousel. It is also telling that the conception of the Emperor's Rome inspired victory monuments coincided with his increasingly powerful empire, and that the column and his arches became what Van Zanten would surely class as 'symbolic pressure points' of the city's monumental topography.[120]

Napoleon was actively involved both in the choice of the location and the symbols associated with these monuments.[121] This goes hand in hand with the importance of the Arc du Carrousel and the Vendôme Column's proximity, in particular, to the Rue de Rivoli. The reasoning behind the siting of the Carrousel arch, and the relevance of its topographical relationship with the Rue de Rivoli has already been addressed. What must be asked now, however, is why Napoleon should have opted for the column's location in the Place Vendôme, when other sites had been proposed and rejected (a case in point being the Place de la Révolution as it was here that Louis XVI had lost his head to the guillotine). Firstly, any suggestion that it was built for aesthetic reasons is to be overridden, not least, due to the architectural and spatial incompatibility between column and setting. The square's original monarchical connotations and the Revolution's violation of the site, however, underline how the 'Napoleonisation' of the area had a contextual and a deeply symbolic appeal.[122] This is indicated in the symbolic prelude to the erection of a national column in Place Vendôme after the Marengo victory (14 June 1800), in which Bonaparte (as First Consul) and the other members of the triumvirate (Cambecérès and Lebrun) had processed to the square, the first of the four ceremonial stations they were to visit.[123] The ceremony (14 July 1800) involved the removal of the pedestal which had supported the statue of Louis XIV, prior to its decimation by the revolutionaries. The medals beneath were also removed and, with great ceremony, they were replaced by another medal upon which were depictions of the three consuls (the column got no further than the laying of the first stone and also the construction of a model which was soon dismantled). The location of Place Vendôme in the hub of the Emperor's later imperial capital thus ensured that it was perfectly placed, on both an ideological and a practical level. Further, Napoleon's Rue de Castiglione formed a physical communication between the Place Vendôme and the Rue de Rivoli which, with the construction of the Vendôme Column, created a visual and a symbolic bond between triumphal monument and triumphal route; Napoleonic Paris and Imperial Rome (see Figures 1 and 10).

To appreciate fully the impact of the Vendôme Column and its role as a backdrop to the Rue de Rivoli as a Rome inspired triumphal way, it is necessary to consider the physical and psychological implications of the area's new road network. An individual following the route of the Rue de Rivoli would soon have reached its junction with the Rue de Castiglione (above), a short but grandiose street which offers a spectacular view of the Vendôme Column (Figure 17). Originally, the street (which leads southwards from the Place Vendôme) reached only as far as the Rue St. Honoré. Its extension under Napoleon ensured that the symbolic square was now linked to the Rue de Rivoli and, as a result, also to the Napoleonic capital's imperial core (see Figures 1 and 12). Equally notable is the name Napoleon chose for the street: like the Rue de Rivoli, it evoked one of the victories of his famous first Italian campaign. The street that joined the square at its northern end was also extended under the Emperor and known thereafter as the Rue Napoléon (until its name change during the Restoration to the Rue de la Paix). It would have been difficult for an individual not to have appreciated the didactic imagery at work, inherent in the nature of the Emperor's dominating column and its immediate surroundings.

We have seen that the Rue de Rivoli was not completed during Napoleon's rule. In spite of the road's subsequent limitations as a regular stage set for triumphal spectacle, however, it was used as a processional way, even in its unfinished state, towards the later part of Napoleon's rule. For example, Bausset recounts how Napoleon paraded on horseback across the Louvre and the Carrousel in 1812, and continued his course along the Rue de Rivoli to the Elysée to the cries of 'Vive l'empereur'.[124] Plans also included the paving of the Rue de Rivoli for the imperial couple's entrance into Paris in 1810 (which, as noted earlier, involved the passage of the *cortège* beneath the unfinished Arc de Triomphe). By employing contemporary coverage of the celebrations following Napoleon's victories, it is possible to develop a contextual reconstruction of ceremonial activity on and around the Rue de Rivoli. This will help clarify what surely would have been a common sight had the road and the Arc de Triomphe materialized as planned and, therefore, also how this fitted into Napoleon's grandiose visions to recreate the triumphal landscape of Rome.

Consider for a moment, Napoleon's major political tool, *Le Moniteur Universel*, announcing a victory abroad, and the imperial capital readying itself for the triumphant return of the *Grande Armée*.[125] Visualize the troops' passage through Napoleon's *porta triumphalis* (the Arc de Triomphe) as they enter Paris and parade down the Champs-Élysées to the Place de la Concorde and onto the Rue de Rivoli. Contemplate the visual display of force as the procession proceeds along Napoleon's newly built road; also the tangible fusion of ritual and visual didacticism at work, as it reaches the junction of the Rue de Castiglione from where the Vendôme Column is visible to all (see Figure 17). Imagine the impact of the triumphal column immortalizing the feats of the *Grande Armée*; the crowning statue of a modern Roman emperor that towers above the city's skyline,[126] and the spectators' glimpse of him in person as the procession (with *spolia* in tow) continues its course along the road. Consider the procession's symbolic terminus: the Louvre as Napoleon's 'Capitol', and the location of the Arc du Carrousel in the midst of the Louvre-Tuileries: the Emperor's 'forum'.[127] Sense the spectators' thrill as the *cortège* and the nation's *triumphator* parade under the triumphal Arc du Carrousel as they approach their destination.[128] Finally, imagine the songs sung in the streets, the *fêtes* and the wreaths of laurel decorating the *appartement* façades to celebrate yet another public spectacle glorifying the First Empire's unparalleled military dominion.[129]

The sentiments of a French citizen writing under the Second Empire mirror the relationship created between the Rue de Rivoli, the Vendôme Column and ancient Rome. Having commented upon the impressive nature of the Rue de Rivoli, Léon de Chaumont leads the reader down the road emphasizing the splendour of the immortal column. He then puts into words what the glorious Rue de Rivoli would say to a passing foreigner and in so doing, he ensures that Paris be seen as still greater than both ancient and modern Rome.[130] As always, it is important to contextualize primary material and in this instance, to bear in mind both the extension of the incomplete Rue de Rivoli under Napoleon III and the Emperor's admiration for his uncle, Napoleon I.

An anonymous guide titled *Description de la Colonne de la Place Vendôme* (1818) reinforces the interest the Vendôme Column generated, and its efficacy as a medium through which to perpetuate Napoleon's image once he was no longer master of France. This surprisingly neutral guide – which also supplies visual stimuli – was published while Napoleon was in exile. The way in which it combines a description of the structure's history with details of the opening times, and who to contact to attain permission to enter the column, underlines the monument's additional role at this stage as a tourist attraction.[131] Emphasis is placed on the splendid panorama offered from the column's summit; the author adds that no other view of the Parisian landscape and its wonders was as impressive.[132] Given the column's commanding presence and its proximity to other Napoleonic landmarks, the visitor – willingly or otherwise – would have been left with an indelible impression of Napoleon's urban projects which, of course, were created as lasting epitaphs to the incomparable magnificence of his new imperial capital.

These factors and Léon de Chaumont's allusion (above) to the 'immortal' Vendôme Column bring into play Lefebvre's delineation of a monument's heightened value as a durable entity, and his comment that 'monumentality transcends death' while 'monumental imperishability' also 'bears the stamp of the will to power'.[133] As clarification of Lefebvre's latter reference to 'the monument', we might consider his question just beforehand, asking 'what, after all, is the durable aside from the will to endure?'[134] An understanding of the advantages of a monument as an enduring and a highly visual testament to the feats and all-encompassing power of an individual, of course, stretches back to antiquity and beyond.[135] Given a monument's power and efficacy as such, it could be an equally effective vehicle through which to vilify and/or eradicate the power, memory and ideology of an individual (or regime). Indeed, *damnatio memoriae* had already played a fundamental role in the revolutionaries' desire to cleanse Paris of its 'despotic space' and thus legitimate their new ideology by claiming the city and its landscape.[136] Importantly, if not ironically, the Vendôme Column very nearly received a similar treatment to the equestrian statue of Louis XIV it had replaced. The structure's fate, moreover, was arguably the most spectacular demonstration of *damnatio memoriae* in the city's turbulent and passion-filled history. Chaudet's original statue of Napoleon in Roman attire was torn down by the royalists in 1814, to be replaced eventually by a flag depicting the fleur-de-lys (1815).[137] In 1833, Louis-Philippe had this replaced with a new effigy of Napoleon in contemporary costume, and in 1865 Napoleon III exchanged this for a statue of his uncle as a Roman emperor in classical dress.[138] Then, as a symbolic demonstration of the end of authoritarian rule, in 1871 Gustave Courbet and his Communard associates brought the whole structure, shaft and all, to the ground. The pedestal, shaft and crowning statue of the Emperor were sufficiently unscathed to be restored and re-erected in 1873–5.[139]

This is equally relevant to Lefebvre's allusions to the more negative aspect of 'the monument', explicit in his observation that 'turmoil is inevitable once a monument loses its prestige, or can only retain it by means of admitted oppression and repression'.[140] The convoluted and violent history of the Vendôme Column reinforces the ideological and political impact of the structure as an emblem of Napoleonic authority. It also underlines the extent to which the column as political billboard generated these heated and radically diverse post-Napoleonic reactions during the nineteenth century. The power of monuments and buildings as forceful political tools, in relation both to their projection and reception as such, has been analysed to great effect by Harvey in his paper on the Sacré-Cœur (of which the first foundation stone was laid in 1875).[141] The author examines the basilica's sociopolitical context and subcontexts, and those of the symbolically charged space it appropriated. Likewise, he explores the implications of the building's visually dominant location, and those of the radical and similarly diverse responses it incited. In a fashion, the paths of the Vendôme Column and the projected basilica actually crossed, for both structures were symbols of an ideology which was vehemently opposed by the anti-authoritarian followers of the Commune in 1871.[142] Interestingly, Napoleon had already recognized the benefits of constructing a didactically charged building on the heights of Montmartre.[143] His visionary structure, like the antique temple that once had graced the hill's summit during the city's Roman occupation, was to emanate a divine air, but was to be modelled on Rome's Temple of Janus.[144]

The eastern section of Napoleon's *voie triomphale* and the visionary Rue Impérial

Bonaparte was so impressed by anything large that while looking from the Saint-Germain-l'Auxerrois side of the Louvre one day, he gesticulated in a most significant manner, and exclaimed: 'This is where I will build an imperial road. It will begin here and extend to the Barrière du Trône; the road will be one hundred feet wide and lined with a gallery of trees. The Rue impérial must be the most beautiful road in the universe.'[145]

Napoleon's Rue Impérial remained a grandiose imperial dream. His wish that the immense route extend from the eastern side of the Louvre to the Place (or Barrière) du Trône – today's Place de la Nation – hints at the far-reaching implications of such a scheme. The emphasis Napoleon is reported to have placed on the projected route as 'the most beautiful in the universe' also mirrors his sentiments some years earlier when he had announced that if he were master of France, he would transform Paris into the most beautiful city to have ever existed.[146] Had this visionary route been realized and the Emperor's Rue de Rivoli been finished, he would have succeeded in completing the bisection of Paris along the east-west axis. Accordingly, Percier and Fontaine note the potential impact the projected '*rue triomphale*' would have on the visitor entering Paris by the Place du Trône, and how their subsequent passage along the axis would lead them to the Champs-Élysées and to the Arc de Triomphe.[147] Although Napoleon's Rue Impérial proved to be logistically problematic and too costly to build, these points would suggest that his visions were linked to the creation of a triumphal route which would vie with and even improve upon the idea of ancient Rome's Triumphal Way.

Noteworthy in this respect was a victory column designed by François-Jean Bralle: the structure's erection in today's Place du Châtelet resulted in it punctuating Napoleon's visionary Rue Impérial. The Fontaine de la Victoire was inaugurated in 1808 to commemorate the victories of Arcole, Austerlitz, Dantzig, Eylau, Friedland, Iéna, Lodi, Marengo, Mont-Thabor, the Pyramids, Rivoli and Ulm.[148] The monument is also referred to as the Fontaine du Châtelet and the Fontaine du Palmier – the name 'Palmier' (palm) is illustrative of the monument's Egyptian motifs and its associations with the Battle of the Pyramids.[149] The structure's additional role as a fountain underlines its practical purpose, as well as its importance as an illustration of the Napoleonic regime's technological expertise. This recalls the Romans' use of water as a demonstration both of their power and force over nature. Napoleon and his entourage would have been familiar with Pliny's *Natural History* and, of course, with the Romans' aqueducts, not least Roman Gaul's spectacular Pont du Gard.[150]

Napoleonic Paris was graced with an impressive number of fountains – both monumental and purely functional. Of particular interest were the Emperor's visions for a fountain that would take the form of an enormous elephant. While the structure got no further than a full-sized model in plaster, like the Fontaine de la Victoire, it was unquestionably triumphal in nature and stood on the projected *voie triomphale*. In his *Décision officielle* of 1810, the Emperor stipulated that the fountain was to be erected in the Place de la Bastille; that it be composed of canon captured from the (insurgent) Spaniards and also that its form be inspired by 'les Anciens'.[151]

Reiteration of Napoleon's personal involvement in this project is in order on several accounts. From antiquity, the elephant has been viewed as a symbol of imperial power and military force. Equally, there was a long-standing association between the elephant and acclaimed empire-builders such as Caesar, Alexander the Great and Hannibal who, in their role as such, were perceived by Napoleon as exceptional military commanders of their time.[152] Linked intricately to this was the interrelationship between the display of force, the elephant and the Roman triumph, as shown by Pliny's account of the elephant-drawn chariot of Pompey the Great after his African triumph.[153] A gigantic elephant made from captured canon, in a space associated with the Emperor's visionary triumphal way, would thus have displayed in a most pertinent manner, the unmitigated power of the Napoleonic Empire and its founder.

Napoleon was not the first sovereign – French or otherwise – to exploit the symbolism of antiquity's triumphal elephant. Examples range from a depiction of Marie de Medici on a triumphal chariot drawn by elephants during her *entrée* into Avignon in 1600; the mock elephants pulling a triumphal chariot during Louis XIV's elaborate 'Grand Carrousel' at Versailles in 1664, to an unrealized plan (1758) projected for the Étoile with Louis XV atop a monumental elephant.[154] The elephant was also to prove popular during the revolutionary years. As a symbol of wisdom, it was incorporated into a project (Year II) by Jean-Baptiste-Philibert Moitte. Had this monument materialized, it would have boasted a triumphal arch resting on the backs of eighteen elephants.[155] Again, we see what is by now a familiar pattern emerging, as Napoleon's manipulation of the symbolism inherent in the Roman elephant was also bound inextricably to former recreations of the antique.

This re-emphasizes the importance of considering the symbolic layers of space the elephant fountain occupied. It would appear that the implications of this were far from lost on Napoleon's friend and foe, Chateaubriand:

> What did we erect on the site of the Bastille? First, a Tree of Liberty, which then was severed by the sword of Bonaparte to make way for a clay elephant.[156]

The Place de la Bastille inevitably brings to mind the area's poignant reputation as a synonym for oppression since the storming of the Bastille. Given the Republic's heightened interest in the area's symbolic appeal, it is ironic that none of the Rome inspired projects planned for the space were carried out. It was instead Napoleon's plaster elephant that temporarily filled the space which formerly was occupied by the Bastille and then the revolutionaries' Tree of Liberty.[157] Nevertheless, had this giant and highly didactic elephant fountain ever realized its full potential, its presence within such a space would have furnished the Emperor with an additional tool with which to perpetuate the advent of a new, dynamic and a prosperous era for all.

Prior to the elephant project, Napoleon had envisaged a triumphal arch as both a centrepiece for the Place de la Bastille and as a magnificent marker signalling the force of the First Empire. Interestingly, he was convinced that a monumental triumphal arch was better suited to a different location – hence the birth of the Arc de Triomphe at the western limits of Paris. A major factor persuading him that this location was preferable appears to have been that the area would fulfil the monument's additional role as a highly visual entrance to the imperial city most effectively. Equally, the new site would increase the structure's symbolic impact, both by it being linked visually with the Tuileries Palace and by its location on elevated land at the summit of the Champs-Élysées.[158] Napoleon's original intention to construct an arch at the Place de la Bastille, however, introduces the additional relevance of the area's layers of symbolic space. Henri II's single-*fornix* Porte Saint-Antoine had been transformed under Louis XIV, and until the remaining *portes du Soleil* were built, it was the Sun-King's principal triumphal arch. Importantly, the Porte Saint-Antoine (before its destruction in 1778) had not only occupied space associated with the Bastille, but it had also stood on the path of the east-west axis. The creation of the *portes du Soleil* owes much to a flamboyant exploitation of the antique and to the dissemination of the Sun-King's *gloire*. The interrelated roles of the remodelled Porte Saint-Antoine as a setting for the King's ceremonial ritual and as a grandiose entrance to his Rome-like metropolis, reinforce the heightened symbolic appeal of this space.[159]

Equally telling is Napoleon's wish that the Rue Impérial stretch further east beyond the Place de la Bastille and terminate at the Place du Trône (cited above), for his visions, again, found precedent in Louis XIV and his predecessors' urban and ritualistic legacies. The Cours de Vincennes leading to the Place du Trône from the east, the square itself, and the street continuing the axis to the west (the Rue du Faubourg Saint Antione) had accommodated one of the most spectacular adaptations of the Roman triumph in the city's history. The Place du Trône had served as the principal setting for the magnificent ceremony celebrating the *entrée* into Paris of Louis XIV and his new bride, Marie-Thérèse in 1660. The temporary triumphal arches erected along the path of the couple's passage from the Château de Vincennes to the Place du Trône and onto the Louvre (a less direct route was followed for the latter part, not least as the east-west axis was not complete by this stage) clearly illustrate the exploitation both of the axis and Rome's processional ritual under the King. Further, had the royal capital's most ambitious project been realized, an immense triumphal route would not only have stretched from the Château de Vincennes to the Porte Saint-Antoine (alias Place de la Bastille), but a street from here would have been cut, creating a direct ceremonial link between the city's eastern section and the Louvre-Tuileries.[160] Prior to Louis XIV's rule, the orientation of Paris' traditional kingly processional route had already begun to shift from the Roman city's major axis, the north-south *cardo maximus*, to the less popular east-west *decumanus maximus*.[161] These important developments may also be seen as marking the beginning of a major change in emphasis with regard to the location of the city's processional ritual and a number of its 'symbolic pressure points'.

This is especially noteworthy in relation to Napoleon's ambitious visions for the east-west axis and his re-appropriation of its *western* section as a processional way. Indeed, in building the Arc de Triomphe at the summit of the Champs-Élysées, he set a precedent for the avenue's later role (and continued use) as the capital's major triumphal way.[162] Significantly, the manipulation of the antique and the employment of the east-west axis as a demonstration of authority and change is by no means a phenomenon peculiar to Louis XIV, the revolutionaries, Napoleon *or* even his far-sighted nephew, Napoleon III. This is demonstrated by François Mitterrand's exploitation of the same axis (the path of which is followed by Paris' first and most prestigious metro line). Two of the President's most conspicuous epitaphs have a topographical relationship with the east-west axis and find reference with the antique. Ieoh Ming Pei's 20 m. high glass Pyramid (1989) marks the main entrance to the Musée du Louvre (Figure 18). It stands in the Cour Napoléon within close proximity to the Arc du Carrousel and no less tellingly, also to a 1988 copy of Bernini's equestrian statue of Louis XIV.[163]

The second of the President's structures associated with the axis is the Grande Arche de la Défense (Figure 19). This glass-covered, cube-shaped structure was completed in 1989 and now forms the western limits of Paris' monumental *axe historique*. The monument's design by the Danish architect, Johan Otto von Spreckelsen, was chosen by Mitterrand from 424 projects, and was conceived by its architect with humanist and pacifist symbolism in mind.[164] It perhaps comes as no surprise that Mitterrand's colossal arch is significantly higher than the Arc de Triomphe which, as we have seen, had marked the entrance to Napoleon's magnificent new metropolis.[165]

The monument and the monumental axis in perspective

Driault's veneration of Napoleon's projected *voie triomphale* encapsulates the magnitude of the Emperor's Rome inspired visions for his imperial capital and the pivotal role the city's east-west axis played in these visions. The author begins his discourse by reminding his readers of the path of the Roman triumph to the *Forum Romanum* and Capitol by way of the *Sacra via*. He then describes the entrance(s) into Paris of Napoleon's triumphal processions and also those of the French soldiers during 'la Grande Guerre'. While inferring that a triumphal arch would have been better placed at the eastern limits of Paris for the many soldiers who returned from the east, Driault imagines their ensuing passage as they traverse the city and pass through its historic core. Both this and the emphasis placed on the troops' subsequent ascent of the Champs-Élysées in its role as the 'Voie Sacrée', reaffirm the poignant parallels between the symbolic landscapes of Paris and antique Rome. Equally pertinent is Driault's perception of the Arc de Triomphe as integral to the concept of the Roman triumph and Napoleon's display of power. Finally, we are reminded of the impact the Rue Impérial would have had upon Paris' physical and symbolic character, had the Emperor's monumental *voie triomphale* been more than an imperial dream.[166]

Driault also demonstrates (be it indirectly) how a trialectic way of thinking is as applicable to periods post-dating Napoleon, as it is to the Napoleonic and pre-Napoleonic eras. By way of his praise for the Emperor's visions and (part) recreation of antique Rome's *via triumphalis*, the author is not only advocating the French nation's unity, but also its powerful and influential status within a contemporary wartime context (his work was published when Mussolini had already joined forces with Hitler). The impact of Napoleon's re-appropriation of Rome's triumphal rhetoric was also explicit in Hitler's desire to create a monumental *voie triomphale* and triumphal arch in Berlin. The scheme was inspired both by antiquity, and by the Champs-Élysées and Napoleon's Arc de Triomphe. We therefore see a pattern emerging, for Hitler's monumental axis was to be significantly wider than its Parisian counterpart and his triumphal arch to be over double the size of the Napoleonic structure.[167] Equally suggestive of this pattern, of course, are Mitterrand's time-defying additions and 'improvements' to Napoleon's 'new Rome' and the modern city's *axe historique*: the Pyramid and the Grande Arche de la Défense.

Such a pattern is reminiscent of the symbolic intent manifest in the location, imposing nature, composition and iconography of Napoleon's Vendôme Column. The structure was to rise above and improve upon its Trajanic counterpart and also any subsequent attempts to reinvent antique Rome and its famed column. Although the diminished size of the Arc du Carrousel meant it was unable to compete with the Roman or post-antique world on this particular level, the presence of the *Horses of St. Mark's* ensured it fulfilled its symbolic role admirably. As prized booty, the Napoleonic media hailed as *spolia* the Romans had claimed and placed on their triumphal arches, this demonstrated the First Empire's universal hegemony and its unparalleled authority. This was also expressed in the structure's location in Napoleon's 'forum' and in its proximity to the Louvre (as 'Capitol'), which now displayed more of the Emperor's symbolic spoils.

Here, it is also necessary to return briefly to Napoleon's Arc de Triomphe. Consideration of the multidimensional character of this arch and the nature of the layers of symbolic space it appropriated, reinforce how the structure's 'Roman' language remains unclear without reference to the ways in which its very being was influenced both by former recreations of Rome's triumphal architecture, and by the ideologies of the structures (and plans) associated with the physical space it now occupied. In the context of Lefebvre's definition of a monument's 'horizon of meaning' to Napoleonic Paris, we see now that we cannot appreciate the Arc de Triomphe's complex language (its 'supercoding') without considering its 'subcodes' which, like all Napoleon's projects examined in this discussion, were linked inexorably to antiquity, the *ancien régime* (notably Louis XIV) and the Revolution.

Equally indicative of the above mentioned pattern was Napoleon's exploitation of the Champs-Élysées, his creation of the Rue de Rivoli (also the Rue de Castiglione) and the Vendôme Column, not least as these developments formed part of a vision that took the reinvention of Rome's triumphal route and ritual to exceptional heights. The Emperor's visions, if they had materialized, would have improved upon the monumental plans for Paris' east-west axis under Louis XIV and the Republic. By joining the eastern and western sections of the axis, Napoleon would thus have bisected the capital and created a monumental triumphal way stretching across his new and superior 'Rome'.

The efficacy of the Emperor's monuments as media through which to perpetuate his image and, conversely, the prolific implementation of *damnatio memoriae* once he was no longer sovereign act as final testaments to the impact of Napoleonic Paris' Rome inspired legacies. The far-reaching implications of this are reinforced by the diverse and heated passions these symbolic and politically charged monuments incited. Maxime Vuillaume's first-hand account of Napoleon's statue once the Vendôme Column had been violated for the final time, underlines both this and the continuing influence of Napoleon's affiliation with the antique: he describes in a most poignant manner, a decapitated '*César*' lying on his back, whose laurel-crowned head, like a pumpkin, had rolled to the edge of the pavement.[168]

Reference to the column's force as a didactic medium must inevitably go hand in hand with consideration of the nature of the symbolic space that both it and Napoleon's other Parisian structures appropriated. Lefebvre's synopsis of the power of space comes into its own here, as it embraces the trialectic nature of space and 'the monument', and thus may be used to clarify the essence of this chapter:

> How could one aim for power without reaching for the places where power resides, without planning to occupy that space and to create a new political morphology – something which implies a critique in acts of the old one, and hence too of the status of the political sphere itself (as of specific political orientations)?[169]

The building of the Colosseum (for the 'people') on the site of the Emperor Nero's infamous Golden House underlines how the Romans had been acutely aware of the sociopolitical advantages of re-baptizing symbolically charged space. The translation of this into a contemporary French idiom was manifest in the revolutionaries' destruction of Louis XIV's despised equestrian statue in Place Vendôme, and also in Napoleon's re-appropriation of the space as a means of displaying and legitimating his new and improved form of power. In light of the Emperor's concerted efforts not to be cast as a despot in constant pursuit of self-glorification, the Communards' toppling of the Vendôme Column (and Roman-clad Napoleon) as a symbol of authoritarian rule, acts as a fittingly pertinent, if not ironic, conclusion to this chapter.

Figure 2 Berthault, P.-G. Detail of the *Entrée triomphale des monuments des sciences et arts en France (9–10 Thermidor, An VI)*, 1802. Engraving, BnF, Estampes, inv. Collection Hennin, no. 12452. Photo: BnF, Paris.

Figure 3 David, J.-L. *The Coronation of the Emperor Napoléon I and the Crowning of the Empress Joséphine in Notre-Dame Cathedral on 2 December, 1804*, c.1806–7. Oil on canvas, Musée du Louvre, inv. 3699. Photo: © Bridgeman Art Library.

The Monument and the Monumental Axis 73

Figure 4 Anon. *Entrée of Napoléon I and Marie-Louise of Austria as they near the Avenue des Champs-Élysées (2 April, 1810)*, c.1810. Engraving, BnF, Estampes, inv. Collection de Vinck, no. 8452. Photo: BnF, Paris.

Figure 5 The Arc de Triomphe de l'Étoile. Photo: by author.

Figure 6 The Arch of Titus. Photo: by author.

Figure 7 The Arc du Carrousel. Photo: by author.

Figure 8 The Arch of Septimius Severus. Photo: by author.

Figure 9 The Arch of Constantine. Photo: by author.

Figure 10 Testard, A. A *'bird's-eye view' of Paris*, 1860. Engraving, BnF, Cartes et Plans, inv. GE D-1902. Photo: BnF, Paris.

Figure 11 Anon. Map of Paris (including the city's *fauxbourgs*), c.1720. Engraving, BnF, Cartes et Plans, inv. GE D-5371. Photo: BnF, Paris.

Figure 12 The Vendôme Column (Colonne de la Grande Armée). Photo: by author.

Figure 13 Trajan's Column. Photo: by author.

Figure 14 Friedrich. *The demolition of Louis XIV's equestrian statue in 1792 (Place Vendôme)*, 1793. Engraving, BnF, Estampes, inv. Collection de Vinck, no. 4924. Photo: BnF, Paris.

Figure 15 Detail of the Vendôme Column's pedestal. Photo: by author.

The Monument and the Monumental Axis

Figure 16 Detail of the Trajanic Column's pedestal. Photo: by author.

Figure 17 A view of the Vendôme Column from the Rue de Rivoli. Photo: by author.

Figure 18 The Louvre's glass pyramid by I. M. Pei. Photo: by author.

Figure 19 The Grande Arche de la Défense by J. O. von Spreckelsen. Photo: by author.

The Monument and the Monumental Axis 83

Figure 20 Anon. *Inauguration Ceremony (13 August, 1699) for the erection of Louis XIV's equestrian statue in the (then) Place des Conquêtes, c.*1700. Engraving, BnF, Estampes, inv. Collection Hennin, no. 6440. Photo: BnF, Paris.

Figure 21 The Porte Saint-Denis. Photo: by author.

Figure 22 The Porte Saint-Martin. Photo: by author.

Figure 23 Callet, A. F. *Allegory of the Surrender of Ulm, 20 October, 1805*, first half of nineteenth century. Oil on canvas, Châteaux de Versailles et de Trianon, inv. 3108. Photo: © Bridgeman Art Library.

Figure 24 Werner, J. *Triumph of King Louis XIV of France driving the Chariot of the Sun preceded by Aurora*, c.1662–7. Gouache on paper, Châteaux de Versailles et de Trianon, inv. MV 6927/1. Photo: © Bridgeman Art Library.

Figure 25 Lepautre, J. *Detail of the temporary obelisk-topped triumphal arch erected in the Place Dauphine for the 1660 Entrée triomphale, c.*1662. Engraving, BnF, Estampes, inv. Collection Hennin, no. 3995. Photo: BnF, Paris.

Figure 26 Lepautre, J. *Detail of the temporary triumphal arch erected on the Pont Notre-Dame for the 1660 Entrée triomphale, c.1662.* Engraving, BnF, Estampes, inv. Collection Hennin, no. 3991. Photo: BnF, Paris.

3

The Impact and Implications of the Sun-King's 'New Rome(s)'

The Louvre to continue everywhere. Arch of Triumph for conquests of land. Observatory for the Heavens. Pyramids, difficulty in executing them. Grandeur and Magnificence.[1]

With this famous quote, Louis XIV's most influential advisor, Jean-Baptiste Colbert, illustrates his visions for the transformation of Paris. The King's capital was to signal a new beginning and Imperial Rome was to serve as the precedent. Paris, however, was intended not simply to equal, but to surpass the Eternal City: it was to become a 'new Rome' and instrumental in conveying to the world, the influence of the King and his reign over the past, the present and the future. Paris under Napoleon was a capital city within which a new, a grandiose and an improved Rome could be revealed that would eclipse all other cities in both the present and the past.

Louis XIV and Napoleon hold indisputably commanding positions in French history. They too were masters of publicity and in the manipulation, both of classical Rome and subsequent receptions of Rome. Nevertheless, as Louis Couture argued when he remarked upon the parallels in the sovereigns' unrivalled hold of power in France, there were pointed differences in the implementation of their 'toute-puissance'.[2] The emphasis Couture then placed on the different roles allocated to the French populace under the sovereigns is especially significant, not least given the propagandist overtones of his work and its coexistent publication with Napoleon III's assumption of power (the work was geared towards publicizing favourable links between the newly appointed Emperor and his famous uncle).[3] This already hints at the potential of exploring the similarities *and* the differences in Louis XIV and Napoleon's presentations of *Romanitas*, the mechanics behind the creation of their public images (and with this, their architecture) and also the audiences they and their broadcasters targeted.

In his insightful biography of Napoleon, Forrest comments that the Emperor 'used what he knew of the history of past regimes, from Ancient Rome to the court of Louis XIV, to see how others before him had exploited pomp and symbolism to burnish their image and impose their authority'.[4] Further, the links between aspects of the *Emperor* Napoleon's rule and that of Louis XIV are no secret to those familiar with Napoleonic Paris and its founder. Why therefore has the relationship between the two sovereigns' exploitation of antiquity and their respective recreations of a 'new Rome' not been investigated fully?[5] Reasons for this scholarly gap might stem from the identification of Colbert as the orchestrator of the King's 'new Rome', as well as a tendency to exaggerate Louis' disregard for Paris. While it would be ludicrous to question his obsession with Versailles or to suggest that his interest in Paris did not wane, the capital continued to be a place within which the King's public persona, military force and glorious reign were displayed and reproduced for an influential audience – even after the completion of the Court's transfer to Versailles in 1682.[6] Neither – as Leon reports – should it be assumed that the lifeblood went out of Paris as a political centre after this time.[7]

The less flamboyant manipulation of Roman architecture under Napoleon, combined with a readiness to characterize the architecture of Louis XIV as 'vulgar ostentation',[8] may also have bearing on the lack of analyses exploring the interrelationship of antiquity, the two sovereigns and their respective 'new Romes'. While this helps to explain why advocates of the Napoleonic legacy are reluctant to elaborate upon these parallels, it does not account for the paucity of works among scholars who condemn Napoleon's structures as costly expressions of his inflated ego.[9] It is, of course, essential that we also recall the enormous effect France's turbulent political history had upon the nature of relevant data. The staunch anti-Establishment beliefs of Voltaire (1694–1778) and at times, his criticism of Louis XIV, would have coloured later perceptions of the King's character (as opposed to his glorious *Grand Siècle*). Equally notable is the influence of the duc de Saint-Simon's less subtle allusions to the monarch's flaws in his seventeenth-century *Mémoires* (first published in 1788) and the additional weight of figures such as Rousseau, whose views and Enlightenment ideals had helped fuel revolutionary thinking. A reluctance to draw parallels between France's deposed monarchy and Napoleon – an individual popularly characterized as the people's saviour and child of the French Revolution – could thus be explained.[10] Still more improbable, therefore, would be the elaboration of a perceptible link between Napoleon and Louis: a sovereign who had been cast repeatedly by the revolutionaries as the epitome of absolutism and decadence.

The relevance of this connection in relation to late twentieth-century receptions of Louis XIV – particularly among French scholarship – is explicit in an article on the King by Bluche that is aptly entitled *Arrêtez de démolir Louis XIV!*[11]

We have seen already how the (conflicting) 'Roman' landscapes of Paris under the Revolution and the earlier monarchy were to influence the nature of Napoleon's capital and the visions he harboured for the city's east-west axis. With an understanding of the multidimensional language of the Emperor's 'Roman' monuments and that of the spaces they occupied, it is possible now to examine in greater depth the relationship between the 'new Romes' of Louis XIV and of Napoleon.

The role of antiquity in the Sun-King's new monarchy

Louis XIV's reign (1643–1715) was the longest in French history. The early years were characterized by *la Fronde* (1648–53), a series of rural rebellions which culminated in Paris that were quelled only when Cardinal Mazarin, the chief minister of France, and his protégé, Louis, had returned to the city. With the death in 1661 of Mazarin, Louis made public his intention to rule without a first minister and govern on his own. The King developed a concept of *pouvoir absolu* that did not mean he ruled without reference to an influential group of advisers. In fact, he was very aware of the need to make the most of his authoritative entourage after 1661, not least Colbert, who had worked under Mazarin and remained in the King's service as a member of the *conseil royal des finances* until his death in 1683. Colbert's appointment in 1664 as *surintendant des bâtiments* is particularly noteworthy, as one of his principal concerns was to accentuate the King's glory through the development of an imperial model of kingship and the execution of a series of architectural projects in Paris. These grandiose projects and the King's majestic spectacles formed an integral part of the representation of *pouvoir absolu*.[12] After Colbert's death, the appointment, in particular, of the Marquis de Louvois (1683–91) and Jules Hardouin-Mansart (1699–1708) as *surintendant des bâtiments* ensured Paris' role as an impressive 'new Rome' continued to develop under Louis XIV.

The impact of antiquity on European kingship drew on a plethora of studies made in the Renaissance (and earlier). For example, Vasari remarked that François I's 'hunting lodge' at Fontainebleau could be described as 'almost a new Rome' and later, as seen in the introduction to this book, the Paris of Henri IV was compared to Augustan Rome.[13] However, the revival of the classical past reached new heights under Louis XIV with the *Académie de France à Rome* established in 1666, the *Académie royale d'Architecture* in 1671 and the initiation and reorganization of other influential academies, such as those for the study of epigraphy, sculpture and painting. This resulted in a new phase of the interpretation of antiquity under the patronage of Louis' absolutist monarchy that linked the Roman past with contemporary imagery associated with the King. Detailed images of ancient Rome's architecture were provided by Antoine Desgodetz in his *Les édifices antiques de Rome* (1682).[14] In this work, Desgodetz also critically evaluated the major architectural treatises of his day, including those by Palladio and Serlio.[15] Equally, there was a renewal of interest in Ovid's *Metamorphoses*, stimulated not only by Bensérade's translation of the work into French verse, but also by the King's orders that an illustrated edition be published which recognized Ovid as the individual to have inspired the Crown's decorative programmes.[16] This might also have helped (educated) persons decode the complex allegorical representations of Louis.[17] Claude-Charles Guyonnet de Vertron created an explicit connection between Rome's gods, emperors and heroes and the King that was published in 1685.[18] The Abbé de Villeloin's 1667 translation of the *Historia Augusta* also encouraged the creation of parallels between France's own great age (and monarch) and the antique.[19] Bernard de Montfaucon had spent a number of years in Italy collating data for his *L'Antiquité expliquée*, in which he provided details of the religious, political, military and social life of ancient peoples. His work was first published in 1719 as a five folio-volume collection of visual representations of ancient art and sculpture that was to become the reference work for these subjects until the mid-1800s.[20] Alongside this literary production were the new building projects under the King: the transformation of the palace and gardens of Versailles, Claude Perrault's monumental façade of the Louvre; the Hôtel des Invalides; the Place des Victoires; the Place des Conquêtes (Place Vendôme); the Champs-Élysées; the Cours de Vincennes and Le Nouveau Cours (today's Grands Boulevards). Seen together, Louis XIV and his Court adapted and refined the classical world to create a new definition of civilized behaviour that was soon to be imitated in the royal courts across Europe.

Royal patronage took on a new significance under the King and was defined with reference to antiquity. Burke has identified a reference to Colbert as playing the role of 'Maecenas to Louis' Augustus'.[21] We see within this analogy how Colbert's role was that of Augustus' 'agent' Maecenas – an individual responsible for the dissemination of material which accentuated and glorified his patron's *auctoritas*. As Virgil's epic *Aeneid* drew parallels between Octavian and the mythological hero Aeneas to underline the continuity of Rome's power under Augustus, so Colbert encouraged the circulation of a wide spectrum of literature to reinforce the King's ubiquity and his image as a quasi-mythical hero.[22] The number of active royal image makers speaks volumes about the importance attached to the diffusion of the King's image. Many of France's most acclaimed historians, poets, playwrights, architects, sculptors and artists flourished at this time. This would suggest that figures such as Lebrun, Blondel, Chapelain, Corneille, La Fontaine, Molière, Le Nôtre, Le Vau, Racine, Charles Perrault and his brother, Claude, were playing their own roles as modern equivalents of Horace, Livy, Ovid, Propertius, Virgil or Vitruvius.

The analogies created between the modern world and the antique are typified in Charles Perrault's celebrated *Parallèle des anciens et des modernes* that was published between 1688 and 1697. Perrault acted as Colbert's right-hand man for some 20 years and he provides an insight into the relationship between the contemporary world of the Sun-King's Court and antiquity. The work – an imaginary dialogue between three individuals while walking around the gardens of Versailles – illustrates the superiority of the King and his new Golden Age over the wonders of the Augustan era.[23] It embraces spectacle, literature, sculpture, architecture and art, as well as landscape design and the exploitation of water where, like architecture, technological and aesthetic considerations are borne in mind.

The didactic nature of the *Parallèle* is explicit in the specific roles allocated to each of its three characters. The Abbot (or priest) is cast as a champion of the 'moderns' and as a result, he questions the superiority and originality of the Romans' achievements. Arguing against the Abbot, the President acts as Rome's advocate: he presents a case for Louis' reign as an imitation of antiquity, rather than an innovative age in its own right. Lastly, the Knight plays the vital role of the mediator who ultimately is won over by the Abbot's pertinent arguments. The structure of the *Parallèle* is reminiscent of the dialogues of Cicero. For instance, in the *De re publica* Cicero presents his readers with several players who debate subjects such as the ideal state and the foundation of justice, while arguing for and against the merits of the Romans and the theorizing Greeks.[24] The philosophical dialogue takes place in 129 BCE in the gardens of Scipio Aemilianus, whose role, it appears, is to show through examples that the Roman system was better than the Greek.

The promotional nature of the *Parallèle* is equally clear, for while it praises Augustus and other celebrated figures from Roman antiquity, including Maecenas and Horace, the work also includes the famous poem, *Le Siècle de*

Louis Le Grand, which ensures no reader is left wondering whose Golden Age was the more influential.²⁵

The interrelationship between the cultivation and projection of Louis as an improved Augustus, and consideration of the vital role played by the sovereigns' agents reiterates how the King's exploitation of antique Rome has significant bearing upon Napoleon's reinvention of *Romanitas*. It also brings into focus and underlines the relevance of scholars such as Barker and Burke, whose theories embrace the important question of legitimation, and a leader's cultivation and dissemination of an appropriate identity (or identities). For example, in Burke's excellent analysis of the 'fabrication' of Louis XIV, he explores the mechanics behind the creation of the King's public image. The author places Louis at the top (as he intervened when necessary to either commission or to choose between certain works); then immediately below him, Colbert; followed by Colbert's most influential advisers, notably Jean Chapelain (on literature), Charles Lebrun (on painting and sculpture) and Charles Perrault on architecture.²⁶

Napoleon's broadcasters were also to create analogies between Augustan rule and their own sovereign's unrivalled achievements and success. This is exemplified by an illuminating excerpt from *Le Moniteur Universel* (1810), in which reference is made, both to the merits of Napoleon's rule and the extent of his ever-growing empire, and to the Emperor as a 'nouvel Auguste'.²⁷

We may already envisage links between Vitruvius, whose architectural treatise was addressed to Augustus; Charles and Claude Perrault, both of whom advised Louis XIV on architecture and acted as two of his most prolific broadcasters; and Percier and Fontaine, Napoleon's influential architects and image-diffusers. Equally, there are parallels between Colbert (the King's 'Maecenas') and Vivant-Denon in his influential role as supervisor of imperial patronage (and principal image-diffuser) under Napoleon.²⁸ Although this should not imply that Napoleon sought deliberately to fabricate – or project – such links, these factors suggest already how, like Louis, he created effective systems of representation that were maintained by a central core of advisors, within which there existed an understanding of the interrelationship between architecture, literary works and the Emperor Augustus in antiquity.

Burke's argument (above) that Louis' system of representation was organized from the centre is taken up by Barker, whose *Legitimating Identities* (2001) sets out the wider implications and develops a conception of a leader's (or a government's) legitimation and identification. He argues that legitimation and identification are inextricably linked; that 'the principal way in which people issuing commands are legitimised is by their being identified as special, marked by particular qualities, set apart from other people. When rulers legitimate themselves, they give an account of who they are, in writing, in images, in more or less ceremonial actions and practices. The action both creates and expresses the identity'.[29] Three groups of 'actors' are identified by Barker in the 'drama of legitimation': the 'custodian' as governor (ruler, king, president, etc.); the 'cousins', those who hold a privileged position without actually governing themselves; and lastly, the 'subjects', the ordinary citizens. Within each group, different identities are formed; the 'cousins' play the role of mediating between the 'custodian' and the 'subjects', while simultaneously they influence and draw upon the strengths of the world of the ruler and that of the ruled.[30] This modelling of the relationship demonstrates that leaders, such as Louis XIV, tend to be isolated from their citizens and that their relationship with their citizens is mediated through the action of an inner circle. Importantly, the actions of this inner circle developed a set of imagery for Louis that was designed with the King's tastes in mind, rather more than the ideals or aspirations of the masses. In this endogenous model of government, a 'custodian' can survive a collapse of legitimation among his 'subjects', and his position might be jeopardized if his identity is questioned by the 'cousins', but the regime will only suffer catastrophic consequences if he loses confidence in himself.[31]

Although (as I will soon demonstrate) I have some reservations with regard to the endogenous model of government that minimizes a role for the masses in connection with the government of Napoleon after the Revolution, there are clear benefits of using the model to analyse the construction and consumption of the image of Louis XIV. This can be shown by a reappraisal of Charles Perrault's *Parallèle*, which substantiates further the interrelationship between Augustus and Louis; and Maecenas and Colbert. In the text, the Abbot presents an argument for the originality and superiority of modern architecture:

> I stand by my claim that our architecture be seen neither as imitating that of antiquity, nor that it be considered inferior – our buildings, moreover, have untold advantages over those of the antique world.[32]

The Abbot presents here an argument of one of Barker's 'cousins' and speaks volumes not to the masses, but to the King and the self-identity of the King as a 'custodian', whose place in history is established via the reference point of antiquity. The inclusion of the famous poem to 'Louis le Grand' (above) develops this concept further: with both the achievements of the King and his image in the present being evaluated with reference to antiquity. None of Perrault's characters represent the masses – interestingly, this validates Burke's view that the fabrication of Louis' image was not targeted at the ordinary French citizen, but communicated with the King, his courtiers, persons of similar status from abroad and also posterity.[33] The Abbot and the Knight encapsulate the upper echelons of French society, but in the characterization of the President we see a distinguished foreigner (versed in both Latin and Greek) who we may envisage as the judge of France under Louis XIV. The President (who has not been to France for 22 years), though convinced Roman antiquity still has the upper hand, is dutifully impressed by the wonders and multifaceted achievements of the King's reign.[34] There are also explicit references to posterity in the comparisons made between the durability of Rome's legacies and the unparalleled impact the King's own legacy would have upon the future.[35] Voltaire's famed *Le Siècle de Louis XIV* (1751) serves as a demonstration of the King's (part) success here, for he was portrayed as a *grand homme* whose patronage of the arts and the sciences inspired such outstanding works and men that his century surpassed those of Pericles and Alexander, Julius Caesar and Augustus, and later the Medici.[36] Both this and also the distinction made by Voltaire between the King's person and the greatness of his *siècle* has significant bearing on the later presentation of Napoleon as a new patron of the arts, whose fifth Golden Age of civilization was to eclipse any in history.[37]

This discussion of the creation of the King's image and its legacy therefore has particular relevance for the consideration in this book of Napoleon's tripartite relationship with antiquity. Drawing on the work of Burke, in particular his analysis of the striking parallels (and differences) between Louis and Augustus,[38] it is possible to develop greater insight into the implications of the relationship between the projection of the King *and* of Napoleon as Augustan figures by their respective 'cousins'. In highlighting the cultural differences between the present day and the seventeenth century, Burke argues that the modern concept of propaganda (in the political sense) goes back only as far as the late eighteenth century and developed within the framework of the French Revolution's techniques of persuasion.[39] Hence, when analysing the projection of Louis XIV's image and the audience his 'cousins' addressed, we should not see an appeal to the masses as a primary objective. Instead, it is necessary to understand expressions of the King's power as cultural ideals associated with the Court and as acts of devotion by his most ardent subjects.[40]

Obviously, Napoleon's use of similar imagery, after the Revolution, had a rather different direction to it. The differences in context provide a means for understanding the broad distinctions in the modes of communication and of audience that may have influenced the reception of Roman antiquity in France.

The importance of Louis' place as an absolute monarch with a divine right to kingship resurfaces, for although his broadcasters recognized the benefits of diffusing an image which would add to his *gloire* in the eyes of the appropriate audience, his status as monarch was such that it was unnecessary to resort to mass persuasion to legitimize his position. Napoleon, on the other hand, acts as a perfect counter example, as he did not inherit a throne by divine right but was chosen by the 'people'; he fought tirelessly both to acquire and to maintain his position and, of course, he was the first post-revolutionary ruler. As a result, the projection of Napoleon's image – and the links the media created between his person and figures from antiquity – would have been coloured by the sociopolitical changes wrought by the Revolution. This in turn brings into focus a fundamental difference between the presentation of Louis' image and his manipulation of *Romanitas*, and the persuasive, propagandist and more populist nature of Napoleon's reinvention of Rome.[41]

These observations on the importance of context lead to some reservations, not so much with the endogenous model of government, but with Barker's interpretation of Napoleon. His analysis focuses on David's famous painting, *The Coronation of the Emperor and Empress*, in which Napoleon is shown placing a crown upon Josephine's head (see figure 3). This is seen by Barker to demonstrate how the Emperor sought consent from no other body ('and certainly not the people') and as an expression of his own authority in a 'self-coronation' which, within its setting in Notre-Dame, was seen by a small audience whose most important member for David was the Emperor himself.[42] In some ways Barker's argument is compelling, but we need to consider what Barker and indeed David's painting do *not* say. The Coronation had two façades: one direct and undertaken in front of the painting and the other presented via *Le Moniteur Universel*. This newspaper's leading article demonstrates the appeal to a mass audience: it gives an account of the many and varied entertainments laid on for the people, while simultaneously it describes the whereabouts of an 'immense population' gathered joyously to witness the spectacular *cortèges* as they processed through the Parisian streets.[43]

There are numerous other examples of how media coverage created a role for the citizens of France in the *gloire* of their emperor. For example, newspaper coverage of the forthcoming *entrée* into Paris (1810) specifically identifies the attention paid to the masses' accessibility to an event in which Napoleon and his empress were cast as the principal actors. The *Journal de l'Empire* supplies details of the public celebrations organized for the spectacle, as well as lengthy descriptions of the various public access points to the ceremonial route along which the imperial *cortège* was to pass as part of the '*entrée publique*'.[44] The heightened role of the masses can also be seen from the explanations of the Arc de Triomphe's temporary reliefs (most of which focussed on Napoleon as the principal subject), which sought to interpret the images on the monument for a wider public. All was seen in the context of the monument under which the Emperor and Empress would pass as they marked their entrance into an imperial Paris. Accent is placed on an extract by the author of these bas-reliefs, Monsieur Lafitte, in which he includes reference to a depiction of the imperial couple in a triumphal chariot as they travel through the empire bringing riches and happiness to their people.[45] The importance attached to the public's comprehension of such imagery – and thus the masses' role as an audience – is emphasized with the promotion of a widely available leaflet supplying a fuller explanation of the monument's iconography. The paper even supplies practical information such as the leaflet's price and the outlets from where it might be bought.[46] Although this particular method of persuasion targeted only a percentage of the population who could read and be able to decode the imagery, it reveals the changes and fundamental differences in the nature of the presentation of Louis XIV's image and that of Napoleon. This is reinforced by the difference between the generally succinct coverage of the King and his activities in, for example, the *Gazette de France*,[47] and the more loquacious style newspapers adopted to popularize Napoleon's magnificent feats and actions in general.

The variation in the style of media coverage suggests that Napoleon had to work harder than Louis at projecting an appropriate image to a larger and more diverse audience. This reintroduces the complexities inherent in the differences between their respective use of the Roman past in relation to Louis' divine status and the new context of Napoleon's regime after the Revolution. The Revolution was undertaken in the name of the people and a new ideology of actions undertaken on behalf of the people – a mass audience to be engaged with in the presentation of their leader(s) or 'custodians'. Hence what we see with Napoleon is a shift from an exclusively endogenous form of self-legitimation to one that included an exogenous element – a framework within which Napoleon also sought to legitimize himself in the eyes of the masses. Perhaps, this is seen most clearly in an article in *Le Moniteur Universel* reporting on the distribution and the design of a mass-produced medal struck to commemorate the Coronation of Napoleon:

> In the morning the heralds covered the main areas of the city, and on their passage they distributed a vast quantity of medals of varying grandeur that had

been produced to commemorate the Coronation. Here follows a description of these medals. On one side is the figure of the EMPEROR wearing a 'couronne des Césars' with this caption: *Napoleon, Emperor*. The reverse side reads: *The Senate and the People*.[48]

The Roman past provided the vehicle for the establishment of an emperor, while including reference to the people and a senate. This recalls the restored republic of the Emperor Augustus (while simultaneously it reminds us of the similarities between the emperors' clever disguise of sole power). At the same time, the Emperor Napoleon wore a 'couronne des Césars' rather than a king's crown. This would have created a distance between the monarchical past while also demonstrating that the new present was a 'new Rome' to surpass those created under the monarchy.

Once again, we can identify a trialectic form of reception in this example. Posterity was appealed to as an audience that would view these commemorative medals in the future. Medals were a medium for the creation of a memory of Napoleon's *gloire*, as much as the images found on triumphal arches.[49] Within Barker's model of legitimation, posterity was infinitely more important than the people.[50] If one considers how tradition had compartmentalized Roman emperors as either 'good' or 'bad' depending, in part, on how they were perceived as treating the masses, however, one could justifiably argue that the people and posterity (as audiences) were not mutually exclusive.[51] The use of *Senatus PopulusQue Romanus* (SPQR) in a Napoleonic context legitimized the rule of Napoleon as that of a 'good' emperor who ruled within the limits of the constitution, but also set him apart from the French monarchs who had created an image that was articulated via an equation with the Roman emperors. Napoleon was simply better on all accounts, within both the context of the recent history of France and that of antiquity.

The monarchy – including Louis XIV's band of ardent publicists – had previously recognized the benefits of translating the imagery and ideologies associated with Roman government into a contemporary idiom for the representation of power. This can be seen most clearly in one of the temporary triumphal arches erected for the 1660 *entrée*, upon which were inscribed the initials SPQP (the P for *Parisinis* replaced the R for *Romanus*).[52] The modernization of what might be termed the 'SPQR concept' was then taken to new heights during the Revolution. However, where it had been used as a medium of presenting – and conserving – an image of Louis both as unique (individuals who are marked as special require lesser humans to accentuate their uniqueness) and as a 'good' ruler, it was re-appropriated during the Revolution as a forceful tool of anti-monarchic (and anti-despotic) propaganda to diffuse a new ideology to popularize equality among the citizenry.

The reinvention of this particular aspect of *Romanitas* (as others) under Napoleon was influenced both by a constant drive to be – and to be seen to be – exceptional and to outdo Louis' impressive legacy, as well as an awareness of the dangers of being labelled a despot. To compete with posterity's vision of Louis, Napoleon's *gloire* was expressed within the same language as that of the King and the reinvented imagery that he and his royal broadcasters had drawn from antiquity. This also provided Napoleon with a set of images that could lead to his association with a legitimacy defined during the Revolution with reference to a similar set of images from antiquity. The fusion of both republican and monarchical images expressed via the language of antiquity created a new form of legitimation that focussed at one and the same time on the persuasion of a mass audience, an inner circle and Napoleon himself. The Emperor's 'new Rome' would thus draw into its conception all of history and then surpass it with a view to its consideration by those in the future.

The projection of the Sun-King's capital as a new and a superior 'Rome'

Having explored the dynamics of legitimation under Louis XIV and Napoleon with respect to the reception of imagery from ancient Rome, we need now to consider how these concepts were expressed in Paris – a city under the King that was to become the 'new Rome' of Europe. What we see is that the city itself was interpreted and understood within a prism that was constructed from the ideals present in classical, rather than contemporary authors. For example, Michel de Pure's *Idée des spectacles anciens et nouveaux* (1668) is a valuable piece of contemporary publicity, as well as a testimony to the knowledge of Roman history, spectacle and ritual. Pure compares Paris with ancient Rome and he envisages the King's capital as Rome's successor. He also analyses evidence and the works of ancient authors with a critical eye. The accent placed on antique and modern spectacle illustrates both how the French adapted the rhetoric of ancient ritual to their own time, and how architecture played a vital role in the King's theatre of ritual and display.

Equally revealing is Germain Brice's seventeenth-century *Description de Paris et de tout ce qu'elle contient de plus remarquable*. The painstaking detail and wealth of pictorial material underpin the importance attached to Paris' monumental landscape under Louis. Brice also provides citations to Plutarch, Strabo, Tacitus and Vitruvius, and includes numerous references to antique Rome's monuments and influential individuals. He envisages Paris as the most impressive of cities and throughout, explicit reference is made to the power and grandeur Rome once boasted.[53] Significantly, the grandeur and decadence of ancient Rome is fully represented: a technique used by Brice to underline Rome's ultimate ruin, in contrast to the King's capital, a city for the future. To accentuate the similarities between the two cities and yet the fallibility of Rome, Brice compares the miserable state of the antique city, before its collapse, to its splendour under the great Caesars.[54]

In like fashion, the guidebook wills its audience to draw the all too obvious conclusion that Paris has surpassed ancient Rome through the intervention of the King in the interest of not just the visitor in the present, but also those to come in the future. This is shown in Brice's glowing appraisal of Claude Perrault's arch of Faubourg Saint-Antoine, in which emphasis is placed on the structure's Roman character *and* unparalleled magnificence and also Colbert's desire to immortalize the glory of his master through its conception.[55] Ironically, the monument's excessively elaborate and costly nature resulted in it getting little further than a life-sized model that was erected between 1669 and 1670.[56]

The description by Brice of the equestrian statue of Louis XIV in Louvois and Hardouin-Mansart's Place des Conquêtes (alias Place Vendôme) acts as a further testament to the ways in which the link between the King, Paris and ancient Rome was projected. Having praised the pomp of the inauguration ceremony (1699) and the impressive nature of the square within which François Girardon's statue was set, the author explains how the King was portrayed in antique dress, with neither a saddle nor stirrups 'such as we depict the heroes from the great antique past' (Figure 20). The accent he then places on the colossal size, the beauty, perfection and magnificence of this 'superb monument' reinforces how Louis was presented as an individual whose qualities were such that he rose above even the most celebrated of Rome's military heroes.[57] This, too, is indicated in the King and his image-diffusers' intention that the statue surpass the proportions of its antique prototype: the famed equestrian statue of the Emperor Marcus Aurelius (161–80 CE) on Rome's Capitoline.[58]

The propagation of the King's image in Paris found one of its most ubiquitous forms in the translation of Rome's triumphal arches into a contemporary idiom. Consideration of the Porte Saint-Denis reveals how the reinvention of Rome in the royal capital also involved the use of existing spaces that already had strong symbolic connotations. Nicolas-Francois Blondel's Porte Saint-Denis – like the equestrian statue by Girardon – celebrated the military victories and unparalleled *gloire* of Louis XIV (Figure 21). The difference, however, lay in the structure's location in a space already permeated with a long association with the history of status and power. This brings into focus the importance attached to the Parisian *entrée royale*, as traditionally it involved the passage of the king and his *cortège* into Paris via the Porte Saint-Denis. Given the contemporary projection of Louis as the most superior ruler in history, it is telling that one of his most prestigious structures was built only 56 m. north of the old Porte Saint-Denis.[59] Blondel's grandiose arch would therefore mark one of the principal entrances to the King's magnificent new city and, as a Rome inspired monument considered immediately a *chef-d'œuvre*, the structure was praised accordingly by Brice.[60]

Although Brice does not mention the structure's exact antique prototype(s), a guidebook by Luc-Vincent Thiéry, published in the late eighteenth century, stipulates that it found precedent in the triumphal arches of Constantine and Titus.[61] The importance of the Porte Saint-Denis – like the King's monumental landscape in general – also lay with the juxtaposition of ancient and contemporary imagery. While the allegorical reliefs on the French arch and its ancient model(s) reveal a similar array of triumphal iconography, the symbolism, iconography and the form of the Porte Saint-Denis had a distinctly contemporary flavour. For instance, the absence of a *quadriga* is notable, and while the relief facing the city finds parallels with the heroic image of Caesar, his military exploits and his famous crossing of the Rubicon, Louis is portrayed as a modern *triumphator* crossing the Rhine during his Dutch campaign.[62] Equally relevant are the obelisks and pyramids emblazoned with trophies and fleur-de-lys; also the conspicuous presence of the name of Louis-le-Grand in Latin on the friezes either side of the arch.[63] Louis XIV – like his royal predecessors – drew inspiration from a plethora of individuals from antiquity, not only Caesar and Augustus but also influential figures including Constantine. Given the frequency with which the Emperor's triumphal arch served as a model for those of Louis, we might note the monuments' respective inclusion of *(CONSTANTINO) MAXIMO* and *(LUDOVICO) MAGNO*.[64] With these factors in mind, it comes as little surprise to learn of Charles Perrault's comment that the King's arches were larger than the Arch of Constantine![65]

Brice's guide reveals how the didactic language of the Porte Saint-Denis was equally applicable to its slightly less acclaimed neighbour – the Porte Saint-Martin (Figure 22).[66] This triple-*fornix* triumphal arch (it too, is extant) stands just to the east of the Porte Saint-Denis and in like fashion, it replaced an older gate which had marked the entrance to Paris under King Charles V. Celebratory iconography included the dissolution of the Triple Alliance depicting Louis as a 'French' Hercules crowned by Victory; also the capture of Besançon, in which a personification of the defeated city is shown kneeling at his feet.[67] This is reminiscent of the imagery on Roman coins which portrays the Empire's subjugated cities and provinces: for example, a coin (114–17 CE) from the reign of Trajan depicts Dacia kneeling, with hands bound.[68]

The Porte Saint-Denis and the Porte Saint-Martin were integral to Blondel's ambitious project to replace Paris' medieval gates. Accounts demonstrate how the *portes du Soleil*: the (refurbished) Porte Saint-Antoine (1671–2); Porte Saint-Denis (1672–6); Saint-Bernard (1673–4); Saint-Martin (1674–5) and Saint-Louis (1674) became potent and highly visual vehicles through which to celebrate and diffuse the King's *gloire*.[69] This was also manifest in the structures' laudatory Latin inscriptions. Interestingly, the repetition of symbolism extolling Louis as a deliverer of peace through conquest was translated into the physical destruction of Paris' fortifications. This was combined with their replacement by a boulevard forming a huge arc around the Right Bank which, if fully realized, would have circled Paris. *Le Nouveau Cours* (1668–1705) – punctuated by the *portes du Soleil* – signalled the symbolic (rather than the physical) limits of Paris, and the city was thus hailed as a '*ville ouverte*'.[70] This tree-lined boulevard was interspersed with monumental statues and obelisks reiterating the rhetoric of the *portes du Soleil*. The message was clear: the new city, as a symbol of Louis' monarchical and military supremacy, represented both the transformation of a medieval city into a modern metropolis, and Paris' pre-eminence over Rome – a '*ville ouverte*' that had regressed to a city surrounded by walls under the Emperor Aurelian.[71] Equally, the name of the Sun-King's arches, the *portes du Soleil*, suggests a further link with the antique, explicit in the symbolic association between a ruler's divine authority, the Sun and certain gateways to cities from the Hellenistic and the Roman worlds.[72]

The map by Blondel and his pupil, Pierre Bullet, serves as an additional testimony to the 'Roman' character of the King's capital and the nature of urban renewal. The map, the first of its kind in the history of French cartography (1675), depicted not only existing features, but (in accordance with Louis' wishes) also projects which had not yet been realized.[73] The presence of utilitarian projects such as the improvement of public fountains, quays and streets, reveals how the modernization of Paris involved both aesthetic and practical considerations. The map's eye-catching representations of Louis' triumphal arches say much about the portrayal of Paris as a Rome-like metropolis. The inclusion of humanitarian embellishments reinforces how the advantages inherent in the politics of 'good' emperors such as Augustus, Vespasian and Trajan were not lost on the King and his publicists.

The nature of Blondel and Bullet's map brings into play Paris' expansion and increase in population which, moreover, encouraged the dissemination of further comparisons between the King's capital and Imperial Rome. For instance, while boasting Paris' physical and demographic growth, and its place as the most populous city in Europe, Brice makes explicit reference to Imperial Rome and the equation between the size and the power of a city (accent here is also placed on modern Rome being significantly smaller than Paris).[74] The creation of more subtle parallels is exemplified by the author's mention of a Latin inscription in a garden close to the *Nouveau Cours* and the Porte Saint-Antoine. On both sides of the plaque was the ever-present LUDOVICUS MAGNUS. However, the *faubourg* side of the inscription referred to the *pomerium*, while on the city side, reference was made to Augustus.[75] Following a ritual that was said to stretch back to the days of Romulus, Augustus (and others) had celebrated military victories with a ceremony which enlarged the *pomerium*.[76] The significance of the Parisian inscription is emphasized by the plaque's proximity to the city's new symbolic boundary (the *Cours*) and as noted in the previous chapter, to the importance of the *pomerium* in antiquity as Rome's sacred and ritual boundary. The link here between Augustus and Louis, and the value the King and his broadcasters attached to Paris' growth is also indicative of a convoluted exploitation of *Romanitas* which the average observer would not have readily understood. The inner circle or propagators of the King's image would have had it in mind, as would other members of the Court in their quest to see 'Rome' in their monarch's capital.

The presentation of the King's capital as a 'new Rome' may also be demonstrated by Claude Perrault's *Abrége des dix livres de Vitruve* (1673). This architect's own projects illustrate a palpable awareness of Vitruvian principals and his desire to translate into a modern idiom these principals. Cleary remarks that Perrault 'challenges Louis XIV to surpass Augustus as a patron of architecture'.[77] This is manifest in the frontispiece to Perrault's *Vitruve*, upon which are displayed his designs for the eastern façade of the Louvre, the Observatory and the arch of Faubourg Saint-Antoine. The juxtaposition of modern and antique imagery is typified by the portrayal of a figure whose style of dress is classical but whose presence, explicit in the fleur-de-lys on her robes and on the shield she rests an arm upon, alludes to a distinctly contemporary rhetorical image. The frontispiece also demonstrates how Perrault's projects were to go a step further than the reliable and solid forms of Vitruvian architecture. This is apparent in the depiction of his triumphal arch which, as an elaborate variation on the Roman theme, was undoubtedly the most flamboyant of all Parisian projects at the time. The traditional Roman *quadriga* is replaced with an immense equestrian statue of the King. Equally notable is the elevated position of the statue: had the design been realized in full, this would have resulted in the arch (and 'Louis') standing higher than those of classical Rome.[78] This brings to mind Brice's laudatory description of the structure which, as noted earlier, included reference both to the triumphal arches of Rome and to the unequalled perfection of Perrault's design.[79]

The inclusion in the frontispiece of the Louvre's eastern façade (the 'Colonnade') reintroduces the palace's long-standing role as the supreme symbol of monarchical power in France. As a highly acclaimed adaptation of the classical theme, Claude Perrault's Colonnade thus represented the King's unequivocal power. In short, the frontispiece to his *Vitruve* presents in microcosm the political language of architecture in the Sun-King's new and improved 'Rome'. It is far from coincidental that there are tangible parallels between this valuable piece of pictorial evidence and Colbert's grandiose visions which, as we saw in the opening citation to this chapter, signalled a similarly telling 'Romanisation' of the King's capital city. While these examples and the following discussion prepare the ground for an investigation into the similarities between the grandiose 'new Romes' established under Louis XIV and Napoleon, they also reinforce how the presentation of the King's image appealed largely to a select and a classically trained audience, in contrast to Napoleon's schemes and associated imagery, which targeted a far wider audience.

The Sun-King's 'parallel Romes'

The programme of monumental development in Paris coexisted with a stunning adaptation of Imperial Rome at Versailles, in which the palace and its gardens also served as a visually didactic arena for the dissemination of the Sun-King's image.[80]

> A palace is more than the sum of its parts. It is a symbol of its owner, an extension of his personality, a means of self-presentation.[81]

This is reminiscent of the importance that the more affluent Roman attached to his dwelling as mirror of his status.[82] Louis XIV's palatial residence was a symbol of his power and authority, fused with a sense of good taste that drew on classical conventions to surpass the achievements of the past, including those of antiquity. This is reinforced by our imaginary Abbot in the *Parallèle* who, while seeing Versailles is an image of his century, made pointed references both to the magnificence of the King's palace and gardens, and to imperial residences such as Rome's Palace of Augustus and the Emperor Hadrian's Villa at Tivoli.[83] The palace of Versailles also accommodated the Royal Court – its master's 'vastly extended house and household'[84] – and was open to the public. Although the visual stimuli in the public zones of the palace were profoundly didactic in nature, the ambiguity in the term 'public' inevitably recalls earlier references in this discussion to the select audience Louis and his inner core had in mind. To be eligible, one had to wear a sword: this reveals how only a minority – males with the means either to own or hire a sword at the entrance – actually gained access to the palace.[85] While the King's daily activities in his private space (at least in today's sense of the word) were anything but intimate affairs, the preponderance of didactic stimuli in these private zones reinforces how imagery was fabricated, first and foremost, for the King himself and his inner circle. Again, this finds certain parallels with the Roman world, for ancient accounts suggest that the influential and more reputable Roman should envisage no part of his life or space as wholly private.[86]

The Sun-King's association with Apollo was no less Roman in its origin. It also acts as an illustration of the symbolic parallels at work in Paris and at Versailles. Apollo – the most glorious and beautiful of all Rome's deities, and god of reason, music, poetry and fine arts – was also the Sun God. As Louis was considered a quasi-divine being, his court was seen as a mirror of the cosmos. Consequently, the sun became his emblem: it was translated into a bounty of gold-clad vehicles through which to perpetuate his image as *le roi-soleil*.[87] The prolific use of gold (or gilt) is typified by Paris' golden dome of Les Invalides and, of course, by the decoration at Versailles. The 'sun' also manifested itself as a form of ritual: not least the Sun-King's daily *lever* and *coucher* ceremonies, controlled by the rising and the setting of the sun.

Lebrun's supervision of the building of the palace's State Apartments resulted in numerous allegorical representations of Apollo depicted as the centre of the universe. In light of Augustus' notoriety as a builder and his association with Apollo, a painting of *Augustus Building the Port of Messina* in the Salon of Apollo is revealing. The symbolic link between Louis, Apollo and Augustus is also shown on a medal struck in 1672.[88] It portrays the King on one side, and on its opposite face, Apollo, the Colonnade of the

Louvre and an inscription stating *Apollo Palatinus*.[89] Given the spatial and symbolic relationship between Augustus' Palatine dwelling and the Temple of Apollo, the medal underlines just how adept Louis' image-makers were at translating – and personalizing – Rome's legacies.[90] The medal's depiction of the Louvre is equally telling, for the palace's Gallery of Apollo – like the Salon of Apollo at Versailles – was also designed by Lebrun, acting as a similarly powerful device to disseminate the Sun-King's rhetoric. As Berger comments, the gallery became the Louvre's *'pièce de la résistance*, calculated to bedazzle the visitor'.[91]

Swans are associated with Apollo, and in 1676 Louis had a number of the exotic birds imported and placed on the polluted waters of the River Seine. As graceful and beautiful creatures, they also symbolized the metamorphosis of Paris from a dirty medieval city, to a new and beautiful (Rome-like) modern metropolis. Consideration of the brilliant whiteness of these regal birds and that of white marble brings into focus an additional dimension. This is clear in Henri Sauval's *Histoire et recherches des antiquités de la ville de Paris* (1724), in which we find reference both to Augustus' statement that he found Rome a city of brick and left it a city of marble, and to the Sun-King's capital as the more impressive of the two cities.[92] Even the birds' location on the Seine was charged with meaning, for the island on which they were placed – the Île des Cynes – was visible from the road leading to Versailles and its gardens, within which was a fountain decorated with swans.[93]

Apollo was not the only god to have been exploited with fervour in Paris and at Versailles. Examples include the depictions of the war god Mars both in the Hall of Mirrors (on which construction began in 1678) and on the Porte Saint-Denis. Imagery associated with the demi-god Hercules was also prominent. Similar to the many other mythological characters displayed at Versailles such as Jupiter, Venus and Minerva, Hercules' persona was used in an equally didactic manner in Paris. These mythological characters were linked together via a generic emphasis on the allegorical themes of war and peace. This was also translated into the portrayals of Augustus *and* of Caesar: those of Augustus generally depicted peace in the wake of victory, whereas those of Caesar symbolized war and the art of war, as shown in the depiction of Caesar sending a Roman colony to Carthage in the Salon of Diana. The images at Versailles mirrored the iconographical programme in Paris that alluded to the King's heroic actions and splendid victories leading to the city's prosperity. There was also a fusion of modern with antique imagery in Paris and at Versailles. In Lebrun's painting of the *Second Conquest of Franche-Comté* on the ceiling of the Hall of

Mirrors, Louis is portrayed as a part Roman, part modern warrior, surrounded by mythological figures including Hercules and Minerva.[94] The King's central position in the painting and the personification of the Doubs River at his feet would also have restated the widespread imagery disseminating his military supremacy. Interestingly, in this work, the King's dress is almost identical to the equestrian statue in the Place des Conquêtes that portrayed him as an heroic Roman with his characteristic modern-day periwig (see Figure 20). There are other examples of paintings within the palace that provide direct linkages with monuments in Paris: for instance, the depiction of 'Caesar' inspecting his troops in the Salon of Mars uses the same imagery of Louis as Caesar on the triumphal arch of Saint-Denis.

The association of the image of Caesar with Louis provided a vehicle for the articulation of the King in the role of a Caesar-like general to be seen re-enacting Roman spectacle and reinterpreting ancient events as though they were occurring in the present. Claude-François Ménestrier's *Traité des tournois, joustes, carrousels et autres spectacles publics* (1669) places emphasis on antique spectacle and the Roman nature of the King's *spectacles publics*. While highlighting Louis' portrayal as Caesar in Paris' famous 1662 *carrousel*, Ménestrier refers to the device on the King's shield that depicted a sun and the inscription UT VIDI VICI (as I saw I conquered).[95] He provides an equally vibrant account of Versailles' 1664 *carrousel*, in which the King is again shown playing a central and a similarly heroic role in an event described as no less Roman or spectacular than its Parisian counterpart.[96]

The areas that accommodated these magnificent spectacles served as stage sets upon which the King was able to display his authority. Equally significant in this respect was the didactic statuary that graced the public spaces of Paris and the gardens at Versailles. Although Louis possessed an impressive number of original statues from antiquity such as the *Germanicus* and the *Cincinnatus* (these were housed in the palace's State Apartments), his sculpture collections were for the most part copies of classical Rome's most celebrated pieces. There was a belief that the copies should be 'more perfect than the antique'[97] – this would have created a repertoire of modern images that symbolized the superior nature of the King over all of history. This can be seen in Lebrun's interior designs at Versailles and in Paris. These set out an identical message to the monumental creations of Le Nôtre who incorporated sculpture and an elaborate manipulation of both water and light into his grandiose schemes. The fountains, pools and groves, combined with the extensive use of hydraulics in the gardens at Versailles, increased the drama of the aquatic displays. They also demonstrated the King's ability to outclass the Romans' display of power through their ability to control nature.[98] This is typified by Le Nôtre's ingenious triumphal arch water feature. It was completed in 1684 and is no longer extant, but a painting by Jean Cotelle (1708) reveals its gilded three-bayed arch; its obelisks, and its numerous jets of water which apparently created a crystal-like effect.[99] We should recall that the palace's gardens were used as the setting for Perrault's didactic dialogues in the *Parallèle*, in which the Abbot had argued convincingly for the superiority of Louis XIV and his splendid era over the achievements of the ancient Romans. Equally, the impressive water features may have illustrated the King's ability to surpass *modern* Rome and, for example, the unfulfilled design by Bernini (1629) for the present Fontana di Trevi. Although I have focussed on the gardens of Versailles, the far-reaching impact of Le Nôtre's handiwork in Paris (and throughout Europe) must not be underestimated. Further, reference to the King's capital brings to notice the general image of the city's monumental landscape which, like Le Nôtre's projects at Versailles, improved upon the *horti* and gardens of the Roman world by taking the concept of grandeur, order, axiality and perspective to new heights.[100]

The reception of the Sun-King and his 'new Rome(s)'

One of Louis' principal audiences (discussed earlier) shared fundamental traits with Perrault's imaginary President: an influential foreigner whose status and knowledge of ancient Rome were so great that he needed to be reminded of the current *Grand Siècle* and its splendours. Classically educated foreigners visited Paris and gazed on its monuments. John Locke's account of his travels in France (1675–9) demonstrates a deep interest in the classical world and also a tangible appreciation of the country and city he was visiting. In his *A Journey to Paris in the Year 1698*, Lister goes a considerable step further when describing the King's capital as a 'new' city that is 'so much altered for the better, as to be quite another place'.[101] He also praises the discipline with which the King kept 'this great city' and even the ways in which his orders were 'cheerfully obeyed'.[102] When he addresses Louis' classically inspired monuments (rather than the city in general), however, his tone becomes less adulatory. This is explicit in his reference to the statue by Martin Desjardins that was unveiled in 1686 as a centrepiece for Hardouin-Mansart's Place des Victoires. He begins by presenting his reader with the image of a 'vast' winged Victory who, while resting a foot on a globe, held a laurel crown over the King's head. We learn, too, that the structure was gilded in gold with an inscription that announced to all: *Viro Immortali* (to the Immortal Man).[103] He then comments:

> But that which I chiefly dislike in this performance, is the great woman perpetually at the King's back; which, instead of expressing victory, seems to act as an encumbrance, and to fatigue him with her company. The Roman Victory was of a very different description: it was a small puppet carried in the hand of the emperor, and which he could dispose of at pleasure. This woman is enough to give a man a surfeit![104]

Lister's account serves as a vivid illustration of the city's poignant adaptation of Roman symbolism. It also acts as a valuable piece of contemporary evidence that favours authentic reproductions of the antique over the reinterpretation of antiquity that was prevalent in Paris and at Versailles. His rather amusing disapproval here also demonstrates how a foreigner with a keen interest in the workings of the Roman world reacted to the ubiquitous diffusion of the King's image.

The description by Lister of the equestrian statue in the Place des Conquêtes allows us further insight into the reception of the King's 'new Rome' – while describing this colossal structure, he adds:

> In this statue the King is arrayed in the habit of a Roman Emperor, and sits the horse without either stirrups or a saddle. But to confuse the whole, the head is covered with a large French periwig a-la-mode. I am quite at a loss to conjecture, upon what principals or precedent this confusion of costume is to be justified.[105]

Having commented upon the prudence of following the 'ancient manner of simplicity' and in consequence, the statue's misappropriation of Roman costume, Lister states that it would certainly be thought 'strangely ludicrous' if Louis were actually to appear as such at the head of an army.[106] What Lister expected was not the fusion of modern with the antique, but the reproduction of one or the other. What he sees as of little merit is the modern reinterpretation of classical imagery under Louis XIV to present the King as a monarch who surpassed all others in history. This is in contrast to Brice's reference (noted previously) to the statue as an image of the King as an heroic figure of his own age, whose brilliant victories were such that he surpassed antiquity's great heroes.

Unlike Perrault's imaginary knight in the *Parallèle*, Lister was not won over. He continued to maintain that antiquity remained unrivalled – a position that was reinforced by his critique of the imagery associated with the King's 'new

Rome'. Lister's sentiments may be seen as indicative of other foreign perceptions of such imagery, though inevitably there were still those whose views regarding the King's projects (*and* person) were decidedly more derogatory.[107] These views contrast with the French guidebooks for foreigners that set out the merits of these monuments and building projects. Lister's reflections also reveal the deliberate modernization of Imperial Rome in Paris, made explicit in the triumphal imagery of the statues and in their roles as symbolic centrepieces for the city's monumental squares.[108] It was no coincidence that as media used to diffuse Louis' *gloire* the statues were related topographically: initially an ambitious project had been planned connecting the Place des Victoires and the Place des Conquêtes with a monumental triumphal avenue.[109] If the avenue had been realized, both statues would have faced each other; thus creating a most symbolic physical and visual link that would have been accentuated with the military connotations of the original names given to these squares. Lister's perception of the statues would also suggest that if an educated individual did not appreciate fully the complexities of such imagery, then the illiterate French masses with infinitely less knowledge of the Roman world stood little chance of decoding the complex language of Paris' cityscape.

The imagery of the 'new Rome' established during the Sun-King's reign continued to be discussed after his death. While emphasizing the Roman character of the capital, French pre-revolutionary accounts appear generally to treat the King's legacies with respect. For instance, in his description of Blondel's Porte Saint-Denis, Henri Sauval underlines the monument's impressive nature and that it was intended not simply to imitate, but also to surpass antiquity.[110] A similarly adulatory account by Luc-Vincent Thiéry in his *Guide des amateurs et des étrangers voyageurs à Paris* (1786) describes how this 'superb' monument was to better the triumphal arches of Constantine and of Titus.[111] Additional references to the King's legacies follow a similar vein: examples range from the 'vast and magnificent' project for the Place Louis-le-Grand (Place des Conquêtes) and Perrault's magnificent 'new Louvre', to the presence in Le Nôtre's '*chef-d'œuvre*' (the Tuileries gardens) of impressive statuary – some of which, notably *Aphrodite*, are described as being finer than the originals.[112] Jean-Aymar Piganiol de la Force's *Description historique de la ville de Paris et de ses environs* (1765), on the other hand, at times is more critical. In his account of the King's Porte Saint-Antoine, for example, he infers that the structure had neither the grandeur nor the magnificence to embody the image of a city which, despite its defects, remained the most celebrated metropolis of the universe.[113]

If, however, Piganiol de la Force paints a slightly less complimentary picture of certain embellishments under Louis XIV, material associated with the revolutionary era takes the slurring of the King's legacies to unparalleled heights. The final volumes of Mercier's *Tableau de Paris* (1781–8) were published only a year before the official outbreak of the 1789 Revolution. The republican overtones and the abusive manner in which the King's projects are addressed underline the blatant politics at work here. Mercier comments that Paris would be a far richer and finer place if, instead of building Versailles for himself, Louis had 'built' Paris for the people.[114] He also laments the decadence of the Roman Empire, and when commenting upon the arch of Faubourg Saint-Antoine, he rejoices that this costly and futile project that was intended both to flatter the King's pride and surpass the triumphal arches of ancient Rome, never reached fruition.[115] Accordingly, Mercier's criticisms had a distinctly cautionary tone, explicit in his remark that a government's worst enemy is the architect and that Louis' Rome-obsessed architects had killed their monarch's *gloire*.[116]

We see here how posterity, an important element of the audience to which Louis XIV and his inner circle had appealed when fabricating the King's positive self-image, had now become part of a critique of the monarchy. The significance of Mercier's cautionary overtones in relation to Napoleon's exploitation of antiquity is underlined by his own stipulation that Louis' architects had ruined the great King as he had been unable to count.[117] This reinforces how consideration of the reception of Louis' legacies is crucial when assessing the projection both of Napoleon's image and the character of his 'new Rome'. Negative perceptions of the King's appropriation of *Romanitas* – as Mercier's views demonstrate – acted as poignant reminders of the dangers inherent in the conception of Napoleon's capital as a mirror of Louis' decadent and grandiose 'Rome'. The political intent of negative links created between the King's architecture and antiquity is reinforced by earlier material such as the anonymous pamphlet, *Nero Gallicanus* (1690), in which comparisons had been made between Louis' extravagant building projects and those of Nero's Rome. The circulation of these parallels, no doubt, would have been fuelled further by the knowledge of Nero's appropriation of Apollo and the omnipresence of immense 'golden' media through which to display the Emperor's affiliation with the Sun God.[118] Napoleon's comprehension of the dangers of being tarnished with the same brush as Louis were surely heightened by his awareness of the Revolution's defacement and destruction of the King's most potent symbols. In 1807 an article in *Le Mercure* actually drew comparisons between Napoleon and Nero – this resulted in Chateaubriand being relieved of his position as editor and in the newspaper's suppression.¹¹⁹ The diverse receptions of the King's architecture would also have reminded Napoleon continually of the power of the classically inspired monument as a vehicle through which to either make or break an individual's self-image. These factors reinforce the importance of the distinction made earlier in this chapter between the narrower audience Louis and his 'cousins' had targeted, and the recognition by Napoleon and his inner core of the people as both participants and as an essential recipient of the Emperor's imagery.

Positive receptions of the 'new Rome' established under Louis XIV would have had an equally profound impact upon the nature of Napoleon's image and the creation of his new imperial capital. His own reflections regarding the influential nature of the King's reign and legacies are undoubtedly significant in this respect:

> Louis XIV was a great king: it was he who made France the most prominent nation in Europe.... Ah! Does not *even* the sun itself have its imperfections?¹²⁰

One might, however, observe Napoleon's delicate allusion to the King's flaws here, the subtlety of which contrasts with his more reproachful comments on Louis' ruinous architecture and excessive expenditure (noted earlier). Such a contrast in tone exemplifies the ambiguity inherent in Napoleon's treatment of the King. Nevertheless, we see in the above citation that the more favourable references by Napoleon to Louis XIV come from the time of Napoleon's exile. This would suggest that while he was actively in the public eye, he strove to deter the creation of explicit analogies between himself and Louis, but that once he was no longer master of France, he had considerably less to lose by expressing his personal and deep-rooted admiration for the King and his impressive achievements. Napoleon's preoccupation with Louis' influential legacy is underlined further by his recognition of the short time he had been in charge of Paris, compared to the longevity and the many accomplishments of the King's reign.¹²¹ The Emperor's own blunders and his discreet allusions in his memoirs to those of the 'grand roi' suggest that he was contemplating the role he, too, would play on posterity's stage. Such observations reinforce the impact the King and his impressive legacy had upon the fabrication of Napoleon's own image(s) and the nature of his imperial capital when he was emperor of France. Although this analysis has led inevitably to a discussion of how interpretations of Louis XIV and his legacy influenced Napoleon, before delving into the links between the sovereigns' 'new Romes', it is important to consider briefly how the Napoleonic media were to project the King's imperial capital.

Napoleon's publicists and the Sun-King's Paris

Legrand and Landon's *Description de Paris et de ses édifices* (1806) serves as a lens through which to gauge the projection of the Sun-King's capital when Napoleon was in power. The guidebook's introductory section reinforces the pivotal importance attached to the King's *Grand Siècle* for the Napoleonic era:

> Paris under the Bourbons – besieged, nourished, conquered, embellished and made prosperous by Henri IV; torn apart again by the civil wars under Louis XIII; brilliant under Louis XIV; agreeable though corrupt, under Louis XV; restless and troubled under Louis XVI; devastated and almost annihilated during the storms of the Revolution; and triumphant and glorious under the empire of Napoleon I.[122]

The accent placed on the brilliance of Louis XIV's reign, the devastation wrought upon Paris during the revolutionary years, and the glorious and triumphant nature of the Napoleonic capital, underlines how the Emperor's publicists used the city's past as a forceful medium through which to project the unprecedented magnificence of the present. The above citation also demonstrates that even at this early stage of the Emperor's rule (1806), his propagandists were already distancing Napoleonic Paris from the Revolution. It is important here to distinguish between memories associated with the social turmoil of the revolutionary era that these publicists sought to create a distance between, and the Revolution's egalitarian ideology which, as its *raison d'être*, inevitably influenced Napoleon's rule and the nature of his imagery. These factors fit with the model of legitimation outlined earlier in this chapter, as we see how Napoleon's broadcasters used Paris' diverse past(s) to project an image of a new capital which, while finding parallels with the greatness of Paris under Louis XIV, was now governed by a sovereign whose very different ideals within a post-revolutionary context rendered his rule and capital city superior to any in France's history.

In Legrand and Landon's laudatory account of Blondel's Porte Saint-Denis, favourable comparisons are made between the iconographic depictions of Louis XIV and Rome's celebrated Trajanic column.[123] The authors' delineation of the structure and the Sun-King's other *portes du Soleil* is equally revealing: they are described as 'veritable' triumphal arches which, although serving no longer as gateways to Paris, were sumptuous monuments built to celebrate – and perpetuate – the glory and military victories of a great king.[124] The authors bestow similar praise upon additional structures that had celebrated Louis' *gloire*: reference even is made to the 'superb' statue of Louis XIV in the Place des Victoires.[125] This is of particular interest, for the four personifications of enchained slaves at the King's feet, especially, had attracted untold criticism. Mercier's condemnation of these slaves as symbols of tyrannical and self-aggrandizing rule certainly found no parallels with Legrand and Landon's allusion to the same figures as representations of the King's military force.[126] Such differences in the reception of the statue are indicative of the changing perceptions of Louis' image and capital from the revolutionary era through to the Napoleonic epoch. Although direct comparisons drawn between the sovereigns would still have been potentially catastrophic (the edition in question was published in 1809), it appears that the guide was preparing the public ground for a new grandiose capital which was to reinvent Imperial Rome, and also personalize and improve upon the 'new Rome' of Louis XIV.

From the Sun-King's Paris to Napoleon's 'new Rome'

There are a number of similarities in the overall character of the projects for the development of Paris that were established under both Louis XIV and Napoleon: grandeur, order, axiality, the use of perspective and a reinvention of the antique. This is shown in Le Nôtre's creation of the Champs-Élysées (and its environs) and in Napoleon's re-appropriation of the area in the guise of a monumental perspective stretching from the Arc de Triomphe to the Tuileries Palace. The city of Paris became the vehicle both for the expression of power in the present, and for a sense of the place of that present within history, as seen in the opening quotation to this chapter, in which Colbert declared his visions for his king's Rome-like metropolis. His statement might be equally relevant for the explanation of the development of Paris under Napoleon. The Louvre formed an integral part of the publicity campaigns under the two sovereigns, as did the construction of monumental triumphal arches which, on both accounts, served to immortalize their personal identities and military achievements. The reference by Colbert to the Observatory and the heavens reiterated Louis' place as both a mortal and a god, and here again we find parallels between the Roman world and Napoleon. Colbert's mention of pyramids brings to mind the sovereigns' selective exploitation of additional ancient civilizations. His reference to pyramids also reveals a certain awareness of the practical limitations confronting the King's architects of power; this, too, is reminiscent of the unrealized and equally grandiose visions of Napoleon. Further, the nature of the two sovereigns' highly symbolic monumental landscapes encapsulated the very notion of 'Grandeur' and 'Magnificence'.

Similarities between the imperial capitals of Louis XIV and Napoleon also include the translation of Roman imagery into a contemporary idiom, and its importance as an expression of the sovereigns' modernity and an ability both to compete with and to better ancient Rome. This is indicated in Blondel's depiction on his triumphal arches of modern weapons, and in the inclusion of contemporary military equipment on the pedestal of Napoleon's Vendôme Column (see Figure 15). Equally notable are the visual representations of both individuals as thoroughly modern, and yet Roman-like heroes, whose military prowess and omnipotent empires also rendered them still greater than even Caesar himself. Indeed, the didactic juxtaposition of modern and Roman imagery (and architectural form) in the King and Napoleon's respective capitals was a pivotal element in both the projection of their images, and in the newness and superior nature of their rule. However, as Legrand and Landon's appraisal of Paris suggests (above), there was an additional dimension at work in Napoleon's 'new Rome', and this was bound intricately to the Emperor's concerted efforts to outshine the Sun-King.[127]

Napoleon's obsession with acquiring an unprecedented quantity of Rome's treasures demonstrates this competitive one-upmanship over the acquisition of antiquities. One of his primary concerns was to better his predecessors. François I had made concerted efforts to transfer the prestige of Rome to France.[128] Louis XIV surpassed all other French kings in his acquisition of antiquities and in their reproduction in a still greater number. The intention was clear and made explicit by Colbert: 'we must ensure that France has everything that is beautiful in Italy'.[129] The acquisition and imitation of ancient Rome's most potent images were integral to the recreation of Rome in Paris and at Versailles.[130] The seizure by Napoleon of numerous antique treasures during the Italian campaigns and later, the exhibition of these (and other) acquisitions in the Emperor's *nouveau Capitole* (the Louvre), brought to a conclusion a process initiated by Colbert and his predecessors. Where Louis had made do with imitations – a bronze copy of the *Apollo Belvedere* and the failed attempts to cast a full-sized *Laocoön* – Napoleon (and the influential Vivant-Denon) transferred the originals to Paris. This does not mean that we should make a direct linkage or continuity between Napoleon's projects and those of Louis XIV and see the Emperor merely completing the King's projects. The continuity and reference back to Louis was made to project an image of Napoleon as better and engaged in a critique of the King. For example, the duc de Saint-Simon's criticism of the abandonment of the Aquéduc de Maintenon project under Louis XIV could lead later to Napoleon's claim that if he had undertaken the scheme, it would have been completed.[131]

Seen in the context of Napoleon's construction of the Canal de l'Ourcq (noted in my introduction), this would undermine the King's fantastical water features and set the Emperor up as having a humanitarian intention that would surpass all his predecessors, including the Romans, via the application of modern technological expertise to 'control' nature.

There is a sense in which Napoleon took over Louis XIV's 'new Rome' and grafted on to his monuments a new post-revolutionary significance that reinvented Paris as a new city. This can be seen clearly in the project to redevelop the Place des Victoires. In 1803 – thus before Bonaparte's transformation into the Emperor Napoleon – the space that had formerly housed a modern *Louis à la romain* was to be re-baptized with a statue of the general, Desaix. The structure would have underlined publicly, not the First Consul's own heroic actions (as the earlier statue celebrating Louis' personal *gloire*), but rather those of a hero who had died while fighting for the nation's common cause at the battle of Marengo in 1800.[132] This was a truly republican re-appropriation of space, by which a monument to the Sun-King's personal *gloire* was replaced by that of a martyr who had saved the nation and its citizens from oppression. This is different from Napoleon's later reinvention of the King's remaining Parisian *place royale*, in which the Emperor, while sharing his *gloire* with his triumphant *Grande Armée*, was represented as a modern hero *à l'antique* crowning the colossal Vendôme Column.

The relationship with the monuments of Louis XIV is also clear in a communication addressed to Napoleon by Vivant-Denon in February 1806. He suggests how the people of France might celebrate the Emperor's magnificent reign by constructing a suitable building (or buildings). Denon includes a résumé of Paris' embellishments; the longest section concerns those of the King. The discussion is tinged with both an air of reproach and of grudging admiration. Denon then suggests how Paris might be improved and in so doing, he stipulates that the capital had never been graced with a forum.[133] No reference, however, is made to an elaborate project under Louis XIV (1685–91) to construct multipurpose buildings and an associated triumphal arch (in the very space that would become synonymous with Napoleon's towering Vendôme Column). One is struck by the project's conception at a time when Louis' force was at its zenith: even the original name of the square – the Place des Conquêtes – had decidedly triumphal connotations. The prestigious complex would have beautified the capital and flattered the King's image. As Cleary notes, it was also to create explicit parallels with the function and appearance of Rome's imperial *fora*.[134] Equally, the sociopolitical connotations of the imperial *fora* and the advantages of translating their language into Paris' *place royales* were not lost on either the King or his successor, Louis XV.[135] Napoleon and his entourage would doubtless have been aware of the grandiose scheme under Louis XIV when work began to transform the Louvre-Tuileries into a forum-like arena of power and the first stone of the Arc du Carrousel was laid in July 1806. It would appear, too, that while Napoleon's visions for his own monumental complex were linked symbolically to reinventing Rome's *Forum Romanum*, they were also fuelled by his desire to go a step further than the abortive project for the King's magnificent Rome inspired forum. We may recall that Denon supervised imperial patronage under Napoleon and was arguably the most influential member of the Emperor's inner core. Denon's comment (above) that Paris lacked a forum, combined with his explicit reference to the role of the people, also suggest that the masses were to be perceived as playing an active part both in the 'construction' and in the subsequent use of these schemes. Additional embellishments envisaged by Denon included public baths, a public space for festivals, a theatre and even a covered promenade for the populace (as it rained in Paris for eight months of the year!).[136] These observations fit with the model of legitimation set out earlier in this chapter, as we see again how Napoleon's inner circle also appealed to a popular audience – this would have created a certain distance between Napoleon's grandiose projects and those under Louis XIV, while simultaneously reinforcing the Emperor's ability to better the 'new Rome' of this king.

In Chapter 1, discussion included the importance of Napoleon's occupation of Rome and the regime's archaeological activity which, above all, focussed on rediscovering the ancient city's *Forum Romanum*. We also saw how the 'excavation' of the Forum was a hugely symbolic undertaking that would signal Napoleon's ultimate superiority over antique and modern Rome. By the same token, the Emperor's recreation of this sacred space would eclipse the unsuccessful attempts under Louis XIV to reinvent a forum in Paris. Napoleon's 'resurrection' of the antique city's symbolic heart would thus have reinforced, in a most poignant manner, his ability to surpass the King in his quest to better Rome and to conquer the universe.

The creation of the *Prix de Rome* (1663) and Colbert's establishment of the prestigious *Académie de France à Rome* (1666) were also to play a major role in Napoleon's efforts to surpass his omnipresent 'predecessor'. The King's Roman Academy had provided an unparalleled and a highly organized system of architectural education for successful *pensionnaires* who were in a position to experience, first-hand, the classical landscape of Rome. Similarly, established 'artists' residing at the Academy had returned to France armed with a wealth of information with which to lecture their pupils and recreate a distinctly Roman landscape in Paris and at Versailles.[137] We should recall the casts and imitations of antique sculpture, the perfection and quantity of which had also generated immense interest in Rome itself. Many of Louis' influential image-makers, not only Colbert and Lebrun but others, too, including Blondel, the Perrault brothers and Girardon, had links with the Academy, thus reinforcing its paramount importance as a medium of transmission between Rome and Paris. Equally relevant in this respect are the intricate drawings of structures such as the arches of Septimius Severus, Constantine and Titus by Desgodetz and the popularity of his *Les édifices antiques de Rome* as a major source until well after Napoleon's death.

Napoleon's hand in rejuvenating the King's Parisian academies, the *Académie de France à Rome* and the *Prix de Rome* after the disruptive revolutionary era was such that students once again were able to receive an uninterrupted professional training.[138] The Emperor's influential image-makers also benefited from Rome's French Academy and its new location now in the majestic and visually dominating Villa Medici (the Academy was transferred from the Palazzo Mancini to its present location in 1803). Importantly, the detailed information gathered was instrumental both in the creation and the projection of Napoleon's new and improved 'Rome' in Paris. Now a 'superior' patron of the arts, the Emperor had his own band of publicists: figures including the omnipresent Denon; Vaudoyer, Percier and Fontaine, and also Jean-Nicolas-Louis Durand whose *Précis des leçons d'architecture* . . . (1802–5) would be seen to improve upon architectural works under Louis, such as those by Desgodetz, Blondel, De Chambray and Claude Perrault.[139] The extent to which Napoleon's re-appropriation of the Academy was instrumental in superseding its founder is also illustrated by the major role it played in the Emperor's 'excavation' of ancient Rome. We must remember that Louis had possessed two magnificent 'Romes': Paris and the palace (and gardens) of Versailles. The Emperor, however, went a significant step further, for while Paris (his 'first city') became a grandiose 'new Rome' and the new cultural capital of Europe, he could even boast possession of the Eternal City itself and label it the 'second city' of his empire.

Newspapers also played a major role in the projection of these links between Rome and Paris, for Napoleon, as for Louis XIV. For instance, while a 1682 edition of the *Mercure Galant* stated 'we may say that Italy is in France and that Paris is a new Rome',[140] a 1662 edition of the *Gazette* had already detailed the magnificent festivities held in Rome to celebrate the birth of the King's son. The *Gazette* gives a vivid impression of the extensive nature of these celebrations.

We learn of a vast temporary theatre on the heights of the Pincio (so placed as to be seen from the whole city); an enormous effigy of the Dauphin outside SS.Trinita dei Monti; the revamping of Piazza Navona; the decoration of Rome's streets with French imagery; also fireworks and additional celebrations at the Vatican and on the Capitoline, Aventine, Esquiline and Quirinal hills. The paper's description of these festivities (which lasted three days) includes a *Te Deum* held at S. Giovanni in Laterano, as well as reference to the immense crowds gathered in still more areas of the city.[141] Newspapers were also employed to disseminate Napoleon's influence in Rome. *Le Moniteur Universel* had both *Intérieur* and *Extérieur* sections, and once Rome had succumbed to Napoleonic rule, the city was placed under the former. Examples range from details of the Napoleonic troops' activities in Rome, and the city's exhibitions and theatrical performances, to its splendid festivals such as those held over a period of days to celebrate the Emperor's marriage to Marie-Louise (1810), which, the newspaper informed its readership, were accompanied by cries of '*VIVE L'EMPEUREUR*'.[142] Press reports thus ensured that the French were reminded continually both of Napoleon's achievements in the Eternal City, and also his unprecedented authority as universal conqueror and patron of the arts. Although his son, 'the Eaglet', died prematurely in 1832, the nature and magnitude of the Emperor's visions may be seen in the title he chose for his heir, *le roi de Rome*.[143] In this way, Napoleon could demonstrate further his universal hegemony and it would appear, also his ability to better Louis XIV in his quest to supersede Rome and all that this great city stood for.

Napoleon's numerous and ambiguous comments, both flattering and reproachful, help clarify this relationship, and underline further the influence of the King's Rome inspired legacies. For example, with one stroke, he stated that the Crown's architects had ruined Louis XIV, and yet we might also remember that he informed his own architects that the Arc du Carrousel resembled a *pavillon* and that he preferred the grandeur of the King's Porte Saint-Denis. When Cellerier restored the Porte Saint-Denis (1807–9), he even re-established the huge *LUDOVICO MAGNUS* inscription.[144] The Porte Saint-Martin was restored by Cellerier (1809–10) and both triumphal arches were worked on again (by Delannoy) towards the end of Napoleonic rule. Flattering accounts by Napoleon's publicists provided descriptions of the structures' sculptural detail and inscriptions.[145] We might also reconsider Fontaine's stipulation when initially contemplating the design of the Arc de Triomphe that it should be based both on a Roman form and on the King's Porte Saint-Martin.[146] Louis XIV's *Mémoires pour l'instruction du Dauphin (1661–68)* were even published under Napoleon: the two editions in question (1806), moreover, were the most complete versions to have been published at that time.[147]

The former importance attached to Versailles as an expression of the King's person, authority and his superiority over antique and modern Rome underlines why consideration of Napoleon's contradictory treatment of the palace and its gardens is of immense relevance. Some of the palace was restored (Napoleon even stayed there on occasion), though simultaneously other royal legacies were eradicated. The King's triumphal arch water feature (discussed earlier), for example, was demolished rather than it being left as a testament to the ingenuity and beauty of the *Grand Siècle*. Amaury-Duval's negative appraisal of Versailles in Baltard's *Paris et ses monumens* (1805) demonstrates how, for some, the intense antipathy that the palace had generated as a symbol of decadence and luxury during the Revolution, remained a political issue of considerable importance:

> After more than a century, must we still respect the sad fantasies of Louis XIV, who claimed to have built the most sumptuous of palaces in the midst of barren sands and foul marshlands?[148]

This is particularly ironic given Napoleon's desire to erect an imperial palace for his son, *le roi de Rome*, on the heights of Chaillot which, as Percier and Fontaine note, would have dominated Paris and rivalled Versailles.[149] Elsewhere, Fontaine recounts a discussion he and Napoleon had held on the project, in which the Emperor enquired about Imperial Rome's extant palatial structures. We learn of Fontaine's reply and his reference to the remains of splendid residences including Rome's 'palace of emperors on the Palatine', Hadrian's Villa at Tivoli and Diocletian's palace.[150] Napoleon's vast scheme – envisaged by Horne as a 'display of true *folie de grandeur*' – would have involved the destruction of existing structures in the area, while space occupied by the palace's immense park would have compromised the lives of still more Parisians.[151] Here, one is reminded of the references by Pliny and Suetonius to Nero's excessively lavish *Domus Aurea* taking over much of Rome.[152] Indeed, the extravagances of Nero and his Golden House were a subject that French historians too, were more than willing to recount. For instance, Royou cites Pliny and attacks 'the barbarous Nero' for his grandiose 'Palace of Gold' and the 'gigantesque monuments' of his 'new city'.[153] Although Napoleon's palace got little further than a small pavilion (work began in 1811), his wish to complete the project – which would have covered about half of today's sixteenth *arrondissement* – never waned.[154] Its conception in 1806 and later, its birth at a time when Napoleon's power-hungry ambitions were at their height, might explain why his generally more astute behaviour was now cast aside. While it would be a mistake to compare the Sun-King's 'golden' palace and the gardens of Versailles with the Emperor's unrealistic palatial visions in Paris there are, nevertheless, tangible similarities in the grandiosity of these projects and also in the circulation of material associating their respective persons with Nero.[155] The magnitude of Napoleon's vision underscores the increasingly autocratic nature of his rule, while simultaneously this serves as a further demonstration of the sovereigns' similarly elaborate and poignant exploitations of the Roman world. Napoleon's surprisingly honest ruminations on St. Helena, moreover, stand as a most pertinent example of how his ambitious visions for his imperial capital were bound intricately to the King's monumental legacies. This is seen in the ex-emperor's reference to Versailles: while conceding that he had once condemned its creation, he then admits that the palace had played an important role in his dreams and 'sometimes gigantesque' plans for Paris.[156] Versailles and Paris, after all, had been recreated when it was possible both to display *and* to celebrate its monarch's absolute power – a point which also goes a significant way towards explaining the ambiguity inherent in Napoleon's relentless manipulation both of classical Rome and the 'new Romes' of Louis XIV.

Interestingly, when work began on the Emperor's Chaillot Palace in 1811, the architect Scipione Perosini was concocting a ludicrously ambitious and costly plan for a vast imperial palace on the summit of Rome's Capitoline. Unlike the partially realized Napoleonic project to personalize the papal Palazzo del Quirinale, Perosini's palatial complex – that would extend into the forum (and beyond) and involve the demolition of certain ancient structures – was never to see the light of day.[157] However, had the plans for this immense palace that would dominate Rome not been rejected, Napoleon's critics would doubtless have found still more ammunition with which to create links between his self-aggrandizing embellishments and those of both Nero and Louis XIV.

This brings into play the relevance of Napoleon and Louis' respective admiration for colossal structures, and the equation between size and beauty.[158] It would seem that the King's admiration for immense and highly visible structures was not linked only to his own epitaph and to bettering Rome, but that it also stemmed from a desire to demonstrate his supremacy over the present *and* his predecessors: notably, Henri IV.[159] An effective way was by his being seen as more powerful than Imperial Rome, and in possession of structures larger than those of Rome *and* those inspired by Rome. The same may be said for Napoleon, except in this instance his manipulation of the antique was linked intricately to improving upon Louis XIV and his impressive legacies.

The Emperor, of course, also had the legacy of the Revolution to contend with. Though the majority of his classically inspired projects were as large and as grandiose as those of Louis (and some, still larger), the iconography and the nature of the accompanying inscriptions were seen to combine Napoleon's military *gloire* with that of his victorious armies. The elaborate language and imagery propagating the Sun-King's self-glorification found no obvious parallels with Napoleon's 'new Rome' (especially during the earlier years of his rule). The Emperor's perspicacity, nevertheless, resulted in a symbolic cityscape which, beneath the façade, promoted only a single man's power.

4

The 'Roman' Triumph and the Language of Power

> ... men in general are more affected by what a thing appears to be than by what is, and are frequently influenced more by appearances than by reality.[1]

The pages of the *Gazette de France* describing the *Entrée triomphale* of Louis XIV and his queen in 1660 contain numerous references to the ceremony as a magnificent theatre.[2] Likewise, the city of Paris – as the stage upon which this imaginative recreation of the Roman triumph was performed – is envisaged as the 'Theatre of the Universe' and 'the Capital of this Triumphant Monarchy'.[3] The newspaper describes at length the flamboyant temporary triumphal arches through which the immense *cortège* passed, and its pages are interspersed with references to the splendour of the King's capital and his kingdom.[4]

As noted in the introduction to this book, the Roman triumph encapsulated the notion of conquest and domination, and in essence it was a ritualistic ceremony of entrance. The ceremonial passage of the 1660 *cortège* into Paris via an arch, and the title attributed to the ceremony, found precedent with the symbolic entrance of a *triumphator* into ancient Rome. Equally, the nature of the procession and the allusions by the media to the royal capital as the centre of the universe established explicit links with the rhetoric of Rome's triumphs. The 1660 *Entrée triomphale*, however, was celebrated before Louis XIV and his influential entourage had transformed Paris into a capital that could justly claim its place as Europe's most powerful and impressive metropolis. These factors, combined with the theatricality of the event (and its projection as such by the Crown's publicists), exemplify the need to bear in mind the contextual background both of the 1660 *entrée* and any triumph inspired spectacle thereafter. The ceremonies, moreover, were bound to a long tradition of processional activity in France (and Europe), in which the language of Rome's triumphs had been dramatized to create a visionary exhibition of a ruler's reign and power. The Roman triumph, too, had served as a vehicle through which to dramatize and project the heroic (and godly) image of the post-antique *triumphator*, and also the unprecedented force and influence of a ruler and his capital once he was crowned.

In this book, we have seen the importance of considering Napoleon's relationship with antiquity and the changing face of his capital within a tripartite framework that embraces both the revolutionary *and* the pre-revolutionary eras. Given that the language of the Roman triumph and its post-antique counterparts was integral to the physical, symbolic and ritualistic make-up of Napoleonic Paris, I donate this final Chapter to a more detailed investigation of how the diverse legacies of the triumph were to influence the nature (and projection) of Napoleon's image(s) and his 'new Rome'.

The Roman Triumph: Evidence and conceptions

Material from the Napoleonic era and earlier suggests that the French placed little interest in the Roman triumph's complex origins. Likewise, there was scant analysis of the differences between the early triumph under the Etruscan kings, republican triumphs and those reserved only for the emperor and his family during the imperial period. These points are relevant not only to certain limitations of knowledge which, in the light of more recent scholarship on the triumph, has developed a greater understanding of the ceremony over time, but also to the selection of material from antiquity on which France's many re-enactments of the triumph were based.

The French, nevertheless, were able to draw on a wealth of primary evidence from antiquity upon which to base their perceptions of the triumph. The fragments of the consular *Fasti* (a register of triumphant generals) were discovered in the Roman Forum in 1546–7.[5] The marble plaque, also known as the *Fasti Triumphalis*, would have furnished the French with the dates of a given general's triumph(s) and the peoples over whom he had triumphed. Numismatic material was equally accessible: examples embrace a silver *denarius* commemorating Marius' triumph (101 BCE), upon which is depicted the general in his four-horse chariot.[6] The popularity (and accessibility) of such stimuli in France is explicit in Michel de Pure's comment (1668) that he would not supply details of Rome's triumphal monuments as the reader could consult an infinite number of antique coins (as well as more recent architectural works and engravings).[7] Works both during and prior to Napoleonic rule suggest that a wide range of ancient authors were utilized, including Appian, Dionysius, Livy, Pliny the Elder,

Polybius, Plutarch, Suetonius, Valerius Maximus and Varro. Although we must proceed with care as it is all too easy to fall into the anachronistic trap of using evidence unavailable to Napoleon and his forebears,[8] the very presence and the topographical relationship of Rome's existing triumphal arches would have helped to clarify and even interpret the references from ancient literature.

The iconography and inscriptions on triumphal monuments would have also served as a source for those who had visited Rome. The depiction on the Arch of Constantine of a triumph under Marcus Aurelius and a further relief revealing Constantine's triumphal entry into Rome are notable. Triumphal insignia and symbolism in general were equally visible, as was an inscription dedicating the arch as a mark of triumph (*ARCUM TRIUMPHIS INSIGNEM DICAVIT*).[9] The same may be said for the Arch of Septimius Severus, not least as it boasts a frieze above the lateral arches, upon which captives and booty are displayed. The Arch of Titus had been incorporated into the Frangipani Fortress, was in a terrible state of repair and still burdened with buildings prior to the early nineteenth-century clearances. Desgodetz's description of the two bas-reliefs representing the triumph that Titus (and his father Vespasian) had celebrated in 71 CE, however, demonstrates how the French had long been aware of the monument's triumph-related iconography.[10] The reliefs – positioned on the inner walls of the archway – include a depiction of the triumphal procession as it is about to pass beneath 'an' arch, Titus driving a four-horse chariot, the soldiers, the senators, the lictors and also the spoils that the victorious army had seized from Jerusalem.[11]

Although one should not underestimate the symbolic implications of the 'resurrection' of ancient Rome during Napoleon's occupation, the clearing of the arches (above) revealed no additional information regarding the Roman triumph. Montfaucon's *L'Antiquité expliquée* (1719), for example, described the triumph-related iconography of these arches.[12] Equally, in Desgodetz's *Les édifices antique de Rome*, we find intricately detailed accounts and visual representations, not only of the Arch of Titus but also of the arches of Constantine and Septimius Severus.[13] The *Sacra via* was unearthed in 1811 during the Napoleonic interlude. As symbolic as this find was, the Sacred Way's depth beneath ground level resulted in only parts being cleared. An understanding of the Arch of Titus' location on the *Sacra via* and of its passage (and that of Rome's *triumphators*) through the Arch of Septimius Severus before the procession ascended the Capitoline, demonstrates how the French had long considered a link between the Sacred Way and the Roman triumph.[14]

The discovery in the late 1800s of the silver Boscoreale cup, with its intricate details of the Tiberian triumph, was too late to have provided a source of inspiration. The iconography of the columns of Trajan and Marcus Aurelius, however, would have served as visual stimuli with which to gauge aspects of Rome's military activity and imperial might. The presence of triumphal imagery on monuments gracing soil once subject to Roman domination, such as the honorary arch at Orange, would have provided the French with additional visual stimuli, as would the decoration of the Arch of Trajan at Benevento (114–18 CE) in southern Italy. The relief panels and the small frieze running around the arch narrate the ceremony from its beginning to its end. Among an array of triumphal imagery, it is possible to make out Trajan in his chariot; the spoils; the prisoners; the musicians; the lictors; the senators; the priests and also the axe lifted in readiness for the sacrificial ox in the Temple of Jupiter. The three Capitoline deities are represented on the attic: Jupiter is flanked by Juno and Minerva, and the lesser gods Hercules, Bacchus, Ceres and Mercury are present too. The arch presents the triumph in microcosm: we see the symbolism inherent both in the *triumphator*'s entrance into Rome and the moment at the ceremony's climax when he receives the thunderbolt from Jupiter, and is thus attributed with the power and divine qualities of the 'Greatest and Best' of Rome's deities.[15]

Equally relevant to this discussion is a grasp both of how the French perceived the Roman triumph, and the implications of earlier interpretations of the triumph upon Napoleon's imagery as *triumphator*. The French works discussed here are not analysed within any particular temporal framework, but instead, are used to demonstrate a general conception of the triumph, its characteristics and topography from the beginning of the ceremony to its climax on the Capitoline.

Michel de Pure's comment that 'The triumph was without doubt the most superb Roman spectacle' is illustrative of the importance the French attached to the antique triumph.[16] Although his *Idée des spectacles* was published under Louis XIV, no other later French work provides a similar depth of detail prior to the fall of Napoleon. When examining aspects of the ceremony (albeit within no particular temporal framework), Pure draws from Rome's tradition of *triumphators* and includes a wide range of figures such as Romulus, Tarquinius Priscus, Aemilius Paullus, Marcellus, Pompey, Scipio Africanus, Caesar, Augustus and Trajan. Consideration is given to the meeting of the *triumphator* with the Senate outside the city and the procession's passage into Rome through the *porta triumphalis*.[17] The role of the people of Rome is apparent, in relation both to their participation and their reaction to the triumph.[18] While exploring the ways in which the victories and image of the *triumphator* were immortalized, he places emphasis on the erection of triumphal arches.[19] Equal attention is paid to the procession's display of 'extra-ordinary' *spolia* and its importance as an 'immortal monument to the victory and the magnificence of the *triumphator*'.[20] Pure also analyses the differences between the *ovatio* (*minor triumphus*) and a full triumph, and explains how the latter was a far more significant celebration of an individual's achievements.[21] This is elaborated with reference to the triumph's additional 'pomp' and 'magnificence', and the *triumphator*'s right to ride in a richly decorated four-horse chariot rather than entering Rome on foot or on horseback.[22] The author cites, among other sources, Plutarch, whose description of a 'major' triumph includes reference to the *triumphator*'s crown of laurel (*corona laurea*) and the trumpeters heralding his passage in the procession[23] (a general celebrating an *ovatio* did not have the right to be crowned in laurel, but instead wore a crown of myrtle). The laurel – symbol of victory and peace – appears repeatedly in ancient literature and as Pure explains, the *triumphator* carried a laurel branch in one hand, while in the other he held an ivory sceptre topped with an eagle.[24] In Pliny we learn that the eagle was one of nature's fiercest creatures, that it became the Roman legions' principal standard and was believed to be Jupiter's 'armour-bearer'.[25]

The significance of these observations in relation to Napoleon's re-appropriation of antiquity is explicit in his adoption of the eagle as his principal symbol, and also in the ubiquitous imagery depicting him as a laurel-crowned *triumphator*. These important observations were touched upon in Chapter 1, and may be illustrated further in Antoine François Callet's allegory of a 'Roman' Napoleon after his Ulm victory in 1805. One sees the eagle hovering near the Emperor's laurel-crowned head, as well as a standard-bearer and trumpeters parading alongside the two-wheeled chariot (Figure 23). The two-horse chariot, rather than the traditional four-horse *currus triumphalis*, exemplifies the selectivity inherent in depictions of Napoleon as *triumphator*.[26] Although his attire is clearly Roman, the purple robe of the antique *triumphator* is replaced by red – a colour synonymous with Napoleon's ceremonial activity.[27] Further alterations include the replacement of the *triumphator*'s sceptre and branch of laurel with Napoleon's sword and shield. The Emperor has golden rays radiating from his head: this increases one's perception of him as the central figure and *triomphateur par excellence*, while reinforcing his place as a quasi-divine hero. His role as such is underlined by the presence of the winged white horses. Here, one is reminded of the interrelationship between the triumph, white horses and a *triumphator*'s claim to superhuman status.[28] Napoleon's divine qualities and the links created between his person and Jupiter are manifest in the depiction of the thunderbolt-clasping eagle.[29]

It has been suggested that Callet's portrayal of a triumphant Napoleon is illustrative of the links forged between the Emperor and the famed Macedonian empire-builder, Alexander the Great: in his analysis of the painting, Briant, for example, describes Napoleon as a 'nouvel Alexandre'.[30] Examination of the similarities and differences between the painting and an allegory of Louis XIV as Apollo, however, allows us additional insight into the development of a new iconography for Napoleon as *'triumphator'*. While Louis is attributed with similar triumphal regalia such as a crown of laurels, Roman garments and a chariot drawn by magnificent steeds, there are differences explicit in the four horses of varying colours, the glowing whiteness of the King's godly person and the Apollonian harp in his left hand (Figure 24). This provides us with a point of reference from which we may begin to understand the relationship of Napoleon not just with the triumphal imagery of antiquity, but also with that of Louis XIV. Napoleon was not the first modern *triumphator*, but at the same time, his use of the imagery did not simply reproduce the triumphal iconography of his predecessors in France. Both sovereigns' quasi-divine status is represented by the rays radiating from their heads. While we cannot determine the number of the rays in the portrayal of Louis, Napoleon's rays appear to be twelve: in the *Aeneid*, we read of Latinus driving a chariot wearing 'twice six gilded rays around his glittering brows in token of his ancestor the sun'.[31] Indeed, it is possible that the symbolism here was also linked to aspects of the Sun-King's 'Augustan' legacy, and Napoleon's convoluted quest to outshine his rival in *la gloire* and the same king's influential Golden Age.[32]

The quasi-divine nature of the imagery associated with the depictions of Napoleon and Louis XIV underlines the need to evaluate how the French perceived the antique ceremony once the *triumphator* had reached the Capitol: centre of the State cult and home to Jupiter (*Iuppiter optime maxime*) – father and ruler of gods. Pure provides a vivid description of the triumphal procession's passage along the *Sacra via* to its symbolic terminus, from where (he adds) 'a thousand sacrifices, songs and joyous ceremonies' were performed to pay homage to Jupiter for the success he had granted the *triumphator*.[33] Pure's reference here to the sacrificial nature of the ceremony, combined with his later condemnation of the massacre of Rome's captives on the Capitoline,[34] underscore the selectivity involved in post-antique appropriations of the Roman triumph. In Joseph-Jérôme Lefrançois de Lalande's *Voyage d'un françois en Italie* (1769) too, emphasis is placed on the procession's terminus.[35] Elsewhere in his guide, we learn how the once magnificent Temple of Jupiter was filled with trophies acquired by victorious kings, consuls, generals and emperors.[36] The importance Napoleonic publicists attached to this is typified by Royou in his *Histoire Romaine* ... (1809), in which we find an account of how the 'dépouilles *opimes*' were brought to and deposited in the temple.[37] Edwards notes that the Capitol was perceived by the Romans as the heart of their empire, the symbol of Rome's invincibility and the locus of the Roman state religion.[38] While exploring further the religious nature of the ceremony and its importance as 'the moment when man came closest to god', she comments that it was little wonder the Roman imperial family 'monopolised' the triumph for themselves.[39] These observations underpin why the ceremony was reinvented repeatedly as a forceful power-diffusing device. Equally, they may be used to contextualize further the quasi-divine depictions of Napoleon and of Louis XIV (above), and also as a prelude to a more detailed investigation in this chapter into the re-appropriation of the triumph in France. The French conception of the Capitol, both as the centre of the Roman Empire's undying power and as a symbolic mediator between man and god, is reinforced by the wording of an anonymous guidebook:

> From childhood, accustomed to equating the centre of Roman power with the Capitol – an elevated site upon which the world's conquerors decided the fate of other mortals – foreigners imagine that here they still may find the Earth's most esteemed monument. It was from here that the Scipios, Pompey and Caesar left to subjugate the universe.... This power had been so immense that we have seen the Capitol as accessible only to the Romans and their gods, who together and with equal force, appear to have claimed the sceptre of the universe.[40]

The eighteenth-century guide's allusion to Rome's great *triumphators* and their subjugation of the universe, combined with the reference by Gibbon (in a French edition of his famed work) to the Capitol as this 'antique dwelling of heroes and demi-gods',[41] emphasize the area's heightened symbolic appeal. Accordingly, the Napoleonic decree (1808) formally annexing the Papal States to the French Empire was read on the Capitoline. These considerations reinforce the allure of the Roman triumph and its powerful rhetoric, and explain further why the symbolism of ancient Rome's Capitol was central to the projection of Napoleonic Paris as *caput mundi*.[42]

The Triumph of the Caesars and the *entrée royale* of the kings

From the fourteenth through the seventeenth centuries the French *entrée royale* was one of the principal ceremonial ways used to dramatise political concepts.[43]

The Parisian *entrée royale* recreated and dramatized only what was necessary, exactly as Napoleon (and others) were to manipulate Rome's triumphs to furnish their respective images and politics.[44] Traditionally, the Parisian *entrée royale* symbolized a new monarch's first public entrance into and possession of the city. After his coronation in Reims, the newly appointed king travelled to the abbey of Saint Denis, in which he deposited the *regalia*. He then made his way to the Porte Saint-Denis where the officials greeted him and handed over the keys to Paris. Having passed beneath the symbolic gate and through the city to Notre-Dame, the procession (and the monarch astride a horse) then proceeded to the Palais de la Cité. The Porte Saint-Denis was decorated accordingly, and the Rue Saint-Denis – which often acted as the procession's principal route – was punctuated with decorations celebrating the king's entrance and the dawn of a glorious new era.

The *entrées* of Renaissance France were especially influential: it was at this stage that they flourished, became less judicial and more military in nature, and began to resemble more the triumphs of Imperial Rome. One of the principal characteristics shared by the Roman triumph and these royal entries was the display of power and its physical manifestation in the ceremonial passage into the *Urbs*. The importance attached to Paris' entrance gate, both as a symbolic marker and as an expression of the city and its ruler's authority, recalls a further (though interrelated) analogy. Since early primitive culture, the city gate had symbolized power and was used to mark the sacred boundary between intra- and extra-mural space. Under the Romans this appears to have been translated into Rome's *porta triumphalis*, and later, the arches built to celebrate an emperor's *adventus* (ceremonial arrival).[45] The ceremonial meeting of a king with his officials at Paris' entrance gate found parallels with the Roman Senate's meeting with the *triumphator* outside the *porta triumphalis* and also, in a broader sense, with aspects of the ancient imperial *adventus*.[46]

Certain Renaissance *entrées* appear to have been more 'Roman' than others. Architectural licence was rife with the variety of architectural forms: these ranged from entrance gates and portals dressed as triumphal arches, to the erection of temporary free-standing arches on bridges and roads. Linked to the evolution of kingly status; the pomp and the heightened *Romanitas* of the ceremony was the projection of a king as a singularly glorious Rome-like hero.[47] Strong remarks upon the evolution of the *entrée* as a reflection of the changing political climate in France (and elsewhere), and how the characteristic dialogue between ruler and ruled of the earlier entries, gradually ceased and developed instead into 'an absolutist triumph in emulation of those of Imperial Rome'.[48] Schneider explores the links between the Parisian *entrée* and the antique triumph by highlighting the principal route's place as Rome's *Sacra via*.[49] The author then compares the Cathedral or *la maison de la ville* with Rome's Capitol, and subsequently likens the mass given at the procession's terminus with the sacrifices offered on the Capitoline.[50] The relevance of this is reinforced by the fusion between man and god on Rome's Capitoline and the politico-religious nature of these later *entrées*. As the ceremony evolved into a veritable Renaissance spectacle, the sacro-religious language of the triumph was translated both into Christian and 'humanistic' idiom, thus providing a king with an ideal stage upon which to amplify his power and quasi-divine status.[51]

A king's ceremonial entrance was not *always* marked by his passage under the Porte Saint-Denis, neither were French *entrées* in a wider sense of the word, peculiar to Paris alone. A new monarch's first stately visit to his kingdom's cities was lavishly celebrated: pictorial evidence reveals magnificent Renaissance *entrées* into cities such as Avignon, Aix-en-Provence, Lyon and Rouen. Neither was it always the principal sovereign whose entrance found parallels with triumphal ritual, as Marie de Medici's *entrée* into Avignon (1600) indicates. A depiction of François I's *entrée* into Lyon (1515) suggests that royalty sometimes approached a town by boat. The engraving also illustrates the juxtaposition of Roman and contemporary imagery: the *currus triumphalis* (in this instance, a boat) is not drawn by four white horses but by a half unicorn, half stag-like creature, upon which stands the modern *triumphator* holding a laurel-like branch.

Additional pictorial evidence underlines the tangible parallels between the Renaissance *entrée* and the triumph. An engraving of Henri IV's entry into Lyon (1595) depicts an array of triumphal architecture *à l'antique* along the ceremonial route. Interestingly, the basic subject matter, the theatricality and artistic style of the engraving – also those depicting other European *entrées* – are reminiscent of the many portrayals of Rome's papal processions. A work by Alessandro Specchi, for instance, depicts Pope Innocenzo XII's procession (1692) from St. Peter's to S. Giovanni in Laterano as it winds its way along a route interspersed with triumphal arches and other ritualistic stations.[52] The use of ornate triumphal arches for this and other papal processions reiterates the palpable presence of *imitatio imperialis*.[53] Ironically, the structures, regalia and ritual that the Catholic Church re-appropriated sprang from Rome's 'pagan' and 'decadent' past.[54]

The impact of the papal processions' selective *imitatio imperialis* upon French recreations of Roman ritual, calls attention to the many spectacular Italian entrances during the *quattrocento* (and earlier). These entries – examples include the Duke Borso d'Este's entrance into Reggio (1453) – were influenced by primary sources and also by secondary material: notably, Petrarch's epic account of Scipio Africanus' triumph (*Africa*) and poem *I Trionfi*. *I Trionfi* (c.1338–74) was presented as a series of illustrated editions revealing imaginative triumphal chariots bearing personifications of virtues such as Fame and Eternity, and later they were to play a significant role in France's re-enactments of the triumph.[55] This introduces the relevance of additional spectacle such as Alfonso d'Este's marriage ceremony in Rome (1501), during which the triumphs of Caesar, Aemilius Paullus and Scipio Africanus were staged.

No example of triumphal (and imperial) *renovatio*, however, was more influential than the spectacular entries enacted over a period of almost 40 years by the Holy Roman Emperor Charles V.[56] The ceremonial route for Charles V's imperial coronation (1530) was punctuated with triumphal arches on which were a variety of Roman themes symbolizing aspects of his forthcoming rule as emperor. Although Charles V wore modern armour, he held a sceptre in his hand, and was accompanied by standard-bearers, one of whom carried an outspread imperial eagle. The entrance gate into Bologna was decorated with imagery associated with figures including Caesar, Augustus, Vespasian, Trajan and Scipio Africanus, and also with inscriptions assuring still greater glory under an emperor whose rule would juxtapose the qualities of these pagan heroes with his role as a mediator between god and man. Strong emphasizes the 'universal impact of Charles V's Idea of Monarchy' and the influence his 'absolutist' triumphs had upon Renaissance entries as vehicles through which to display a monarch's imperial power and divine right to kingship.[57] Significantly, we see how the rhetorical language of the 1530 entry finds certain parallels with that of the allegorical works depicting Louis XIV and Napoleon as omnipotent and glorious god-like *triumphators* that were discussed earlier in this chapter.

The most poignant of Charles V's spectacles *all'antica* was his entrance into Rome in 1536. This involved his ceremonial passage under antique triumphal arches (once he had entered Rome via the Porta S. Sebastiano) and the construction of a new Sacred Way between the arches of Titus and Septimius Severus. Although the procession terminated at St. Peter's, both the nature of the ceremony and the famous 'clearing' of the Forum demonstrate an elaborate manipulation of Imperial Rome.[58] While I have found no evidence to suggest that Napoleon was intentionally emulating Charles V, there are similarities not only with the sovereigns' re-appropriations of the triumph as an expression of unprecedented imperial might, but also with the symbolic clearing of the Forum under Charles V and Napoleon's grandiose plans to create a *passaggiata pubblica* in Rome's antique core.

The magnificent entries of Charles V – and earlier Renaissance spectacles – fuelled the widespread circulation of works including Vitruvius' *De architectura*, Franceso Colonna's novel, *Le songe de Poliphile* (1499) and Sebastiano Serlio's sixteenth-century *Tutte l'opere d'architettura e prospettiva*. Colonna's *songe* reveals imaginative obelisks, temples, pyramids and triumphal arches, as well as gods and goddesses astride elaborate triumphal chariots drawn by exotic animals.[59] The translation of the work into French by Jean Martin – literary organizer of Henri II's Parisian *entrée* (1549) – underlines its popularity in France. The ceremony's heightened accent on the Roman triumph is widely acknowledged. The impact the 1549 *entrée* had upon later versions of French triumphalism was still more pronounced given the exceptionally rich documentation of the event.[60] The ceremonial route was adorned with ornate temporary structures including fantastical (*songe*-like) obelisks and columns, as well as triumphal arches at important nodal points such as the Pont Notre-Dame and the Palais de la Cité.[61] Giesey notes that the features of the Gallic Hercules on the Porte Saint-Denis resembled those of Henri II's predecessor, François I, and he uses this as an example of the ceremony's novel blending of contemporary and classical themes.[62] Hercules (who in his quintessentially Roman form was son of Jupiter and had played a salient role in Renaissance Italy's entries) was later manipulated both as a kingly and a revolutionary prototype. Henri II's *entrée* also left as a legacy Paris' first permanent triumphal monument: Pierre Lescot and Jean Goudin's elaborate Fontaine des Innocents (the structure exists still, although it has been remodelled and moved from its original site). The mixture of triumphal symbolism and the use of water find parallels with the construction of Napoleon's Fontaine de la Victoire on his visionary *voie triomphale*. This should not suggest that Napoleon sought deliberately to emulate Henri II, but rather that this structure and also the Emperor's plans for a triumphal elephant fountain (Chapter 2) underpin the interrelationship between antiquity, the Renaissance and later versions of *Romanitas*. For centuries, the elephant had been very much a part of Europe's ritualistic landscape(s); it was depicted frequently in idealized representations of Henri II's *entrées* and those of other French sovereigns.[63]

The impact of imperial *renovatio* upon French *entrées* and their combined influence upon later ceremonial display in France, calls attention to the manipulation of *la gloire césarienne*. We have seen the frequency with which Caesarian imagery appeared in Renaissance Italy's spectacles *all'antica*. Ancient accounts of Caesar's achievements – notably, the reference by Suetonius to Caesar's Pontic triumph and the famous words '*veni, vidi, vici*' – were employed.[64] A secondary, but equally influential source of inspiration lay with Andrea Mantegna's nine life-size paintings of *The Triumphs of Caesar* (c.1485–92). These elaborate canvas panels have been housed in the Orangery at Hampton Court Palace since the seventeenth century, but were commissioned originally to decorate the public areas of the Gonzaga family's palace in Mantua. They were to become one of the most famed and copied artworks of the sixteenth and early seventeenth centuries; their importance is reinforced as they stood to be the first attempt at an accurate visual representation of the Roman triumph.[65] *The Triumphs of Caesar* played a decisive role in Henri II's *entrées*, and during the earlier reign of François I they were re-enacted in towns such as Caen (1513), in which the King was projected as a veritable *triumphator*.[66] If we consider Henri II's affinity with François I and in turn, the fractious relations between François I and Charles V (the most powerful 'Caesar' of his time), we are reminded that the exploitation of the Caesarian legacy was hugely complex. Later, monarchs such as Henri IV cultivated images of Caesarian glory and as we saw in Chapter 3, Louis XIV famously exploited the *veni, vidi, vici* motto during his grand Carrousel in 1662. We therefore see in these examples a convoluted pattern taking form that underlines the value of adopting a tripartite approach to the reception of antiquity.

These observations affirm how the contemporary analogies created between Caesar and Bonaparte, explicit in Thibaudeau's assessement of the Marengo victory (1800) and his choice of the words *veni, vidi, vici* can only be understood fully if placed in within a sufficiently wide historical context.[67] This is apparent in Saunier's similarly adulatory account of the Marengo triumph and in his perception of Bonaparte as 'the greatest of the Caesars'.[68] Of particular interest is his insistence that this did not relate only to world conquest but more importantly, to the liberty of man in the wake of despotism.[69] Saunier was suggesting not so much that Bonaparte had surpassed the *Césars* of antiquity but more specifically, France's own reinvented 'Caesars' – the most conspicuous of whom (given the reference to despotism) being Louis XIV. This is indicative of the evolution of Napoleon's changing persona, for at this earlier stage (c.1800), his image was still associated with the ideals of Republican France and Rome.

The Renaissance 'triumph' is equally valuable for the establishment of a fuller picture of the links created between Napoleon and Augustus. I have argued in this book that an understanding of these links is incomplete without reference both to the image of Louis XIV as a modern Augustus and the nature of the King's imperial capital. This relationship, as we have seen, was part of a still wider pattern that embraced Henri IV's achievements and 'transformation' of Paris. Augustan ideology had already infiltrated France and Europe, and was bound to Charles V's influential exploitation of *Romanitas*. It was central to Charles V's entry into Bologna (noted above) where the imagery juxtaposed his place as *dominus mundi* with that of Augustus' imperial might. A further example is seen in the entry into Florence (1539), at which an arch dedicated to Charles V bore the inscription: *AUGUSTUS CAESAR DIVUM GENS AUREA CONDIT SAECULA* (Augustus Caesar, the offspring of gods, founds a Golden Age): this quotes the famous prophecy of imperial greatness in the *Aeneid*.[70] Here, we should consider Virgil's reference to symbolic gateways, the significance of the Augustan *adventus* and also the popularity of Ovid's *Metamorphoses* which, like the *Aeneid*, advocated a peaceful and golden future under Augustan rule.[71] These factors, in turn, had bearing on the symbolism inherent both in the French kings' semi-divine passage into and through the *Urbs*, and in the entries as manifestations of a monarch's future rule. The symbolic language of these 'absolute' *entrées* subsequently found parallels with the rhetoric of triumphal display in post-Renaissance France. It then rematerialized in a post-revolutionary form under Napoleon – once, of course, he had evolved from a republican hero into an imperial *triumphator* whose own empire and Golden Age were to rival those of Rome *and* the most influential of its post-antique counterparts. An awareness of this pattern, moreover, underlines further the significance of the allegorical representations both of the Sun-King and Napoleon as radiate-crowned *triumphators* in their triumphal chariots.

The 'Triumphs' of the Republic

Revolutionary triumphalism was part of a wider pattern that would affect Napoleonic rhetoric, but itself was linked inextricably to monarchical spectacle *à l'antique*. The Revolution's exploitation of Republican Rome (and its ideology) drew simultaneously from a history of triumphal *renovatio* that embodied the very notion of imperial Roman grandeur and autocracy. The paradoxical nature of this relationship may be clarified through an illustration of the 'triumph' as an effective means both of distancing revolutionary ideology from that of its despotic predecessors, and also a vehicle through which to transmit (and legitimize) the dawn and power of a new era. By viewing these 'Roman' spectacles as mirrors through which to gauge the politics and diverse phases of the Revolution, it is also possible to gain insight into the nature of the Napoleonic 'triumph'. For reasons of clarity, I have divided this section into four subsections which, broadly speaking, begin with the Revolution's earlier years and end with the period that witnessed Republican Paris' famed 1798 *Entrée triomphale*.

The 'Triumph' of the Citizen King

The Festival of the Federation (14 July 1790) encapsulated in a highly visual manner the politics of the Revolution's earlier and less radical years. It was staged in a vast amphitheatre in Paris' Champs-de-Mars (1765–7). As its name suggests, the space evoked Rome's *Campus Martius* and it, too, was synonymous with the war god Mars and used initially as a military training ground. The Champs-de-Mars was re-baptized to serve the rhetoric of the 1790 *fête*: a military festival celebrating the official beginning of the Revolution a year previously and the newfound unity of the nation and King. Etlin's comment that the spectators (citizens) were portrayed as soldiers for the cause and that the parading soldiers envisaged also as citizens,[72] suggests how the spectacle manipulated the Roman triumph and the 'absolute triumphs' of an autocratic past to reinforce the new egalitarian ethos of the present. This is shown in Frederick George Byron's watercolour (1790), in which the participation of the spectators and the soldiers are shown to be of equal importance.[73] Particularly notable is the absence of Louis XVI as *triumphator* and his relegation to peripheral space as 'Citizen King' (the *pavillon* in which he sits is seen in the distant background).[74] Likewise, a painting of the festival by a French artist, Charles Thévenin (1764–1838), portrays the revolutionaries' Citizen King as a mere spectator.

The regime's politics were also manifest in the iconography and the setting of a visually dominating triumphal arch: this again played on the triumph and the French monarchy's 'Roman' *entrées*. For instance, a relief on the structure depicted a chariot of the Law that symbolized the Revolution's triumph over oppression and a newly acquired unity, peace and liberty.[75] The King (on the same relief) was no longer portrayed as a glorious semi-divine hero – imagery akin with the *triumphators* of Imperial Rome and France's past – but instead, as a most human figure among his family and fellow citizens. Equally telling is the monument's location at the entrance to the Champs-de-Mars, for while this found parallels with Rome's *porta triumphalis* and France's kingly *entrées*, the ideologically charged bridge that led to the arch, joining the Left and Right banks of the Seine, reinforced the event's rhetoric as a celebration of an improved and a united nation.[76] These factors also help clarify aspects of Napoleon's re-appropriation of *Romanitas*: not least as they reveal how the festival's egalitarian language and aspects of Louis XVI's image as a citizen-sovereign would have influenced the populist tones of Napoleonic spectacle *à l'antique*.

The 'Triumph' of the radical revolutionaries

The Festival of Unity and Indivisibility (August 1793) post-dated the abolition of the constitutional monarchy (August 1792) and took place only a short while after the execution of Louis XVI in January 1793. The festival was staged to consolidate the achievements of the recently proclaimed Republic. Classically inspired props advocating a united future under the nation's Citizen King, were replaced by structures championing a still brighter future under a regime that had annihilated the tyrannical despots of the past. As a way of reinforcing this message, the festival and procession through the Parisian streets, reinvented (and juxtaposed) aspects of the Roman triumph and the monarchy's 'Roman' *entrées*. The six stations punctuating the ceremonial route served both as didactic billboards and as ceremonial centres. As such, they found parallels with *entrées* including those of Henri II (1549), Louis XIV (1660) and Renaissance Italy, as well as those of Papal Rome – ironic as this may seem, given the absolutist rhetoric of the former examples and the Christian idiom of the latter example were abhorrent to revolutionary ideology. The resemblance between the triumphal arch (the second station) and the Arch of Titus suggests how the festival also manipulated Imperial Rome to fuel its rhetoric. When searching for reasons to explain these paradoxes and, of course, the exploitation of Imperial Rome – which now embodied decadency and unadulterated luxury – we might consider the nature of the 'chariot' crowning the arch. It was not a traditional *quadriga*, but instead a group of women pulling a canon, whose presence symbolized the heroism of the *sans-culottes* in their fight to overthrow tyranny.[77] While this emphasizes the employment of such props as a means of disassociation, a contemporary reporter's claim that the triumphal arch surpassed those of antiquity,[78] suggests how the structure was also used to demonstrate the regime's superiority both over Imperial Rome *and* the French tyrants associated with this offensive past.[79]

The fourth station – a figure of Hercules representing the French People on an immense mountain – reinforces how the symbolism of antiquity and the royal *entrées* was vital to revolutionary propaganda. It seems that the symbolic intent here was emphasized with a link between the French citizens as 'Hercules' and the apotheosis of his Greek namesake (Heracles) on Mount Olympus. Where Hercules had served as a potent symbol of the monarchy's 'Roman' *entrées* as an *Hercule Gaulois*, now he was reincarnated as a powerful emblem of the new order's force, unity and longevity.[80] The pre-event coverage by the media allows one invaluable insight into the dissemination of the festival's rhetoric. The reference in the *Journal de Paris National* to the symbolic *spolia*, the parading infantry; also the triumphal chariot to be pulled by white horses, found precedent in the symbolism of the Roman triumph. Equally significant, however, were the differences, explicit both in the newspaper's reference to the eight horses (as opposed to the traditional four) and that of a chariot accommodating the ashes of the Fatherland's great heroes (rather than a glorious *triumphator*). The impassioned tone of the paper when describing the spoils as egotistical playthings of an 'ignorant' and a 'vile aristocracy' re-emphasizes the poignant ways in which Rome's triumphal language was manipulated to debase France's past and propagate the ideology of a new symbolic order.[81]

The Festival of the Supreme Being (June 1794), like the 1793 *fête*, culminated with a final ceremonial station in the Champs-de-Mars. Where the earlier festival had marked its final station with a Doric column and an Altar to the Fatherland, the terminus of the 1794 procession incorporated a column of the same order crowned with a figure of the People and a colossal mound topped by a Tree of Liberty. The symbolism of the structures – they evoked Nature, Reason, Liberty, Equality, Loyalty and the suppression of Tyranny – mirrored the language of this infamous revolutionary spectacle which served as a forceful tool through which to transmit Robespierre's most sinister version of Republican *virtus*.[82] Such observations underline how the ancient world and post-antique triumphal ritual were manipulated to magnify and legitimize a new symbolic beginning, and abuse further the tyrannical *triumphators* of the monarchical past. The fervent overtones and the egalitarian language of these spectacles and their press coverage would doubtless have influenced the populist nature of Napoleonic triumphalism. Equally, this would have reminded Napoleon of the dangers involved in his being labelled a despotic and an 'absolute' *triumphator*.

The 'Triumph' of French Republican Rome

Once the Revolution had settled back into a less radical, though a far from stable phase, the projection of France's united force was also channelled into popularizing her power and military prowess abroad. It was here that the dynamic general fighting for the revolutionary cause, 'Bonaparte', entered the scene. His string of military feats came to dazzle the French nation; and the Italian campaigns resulted in the Republic's possession of the Papal States and later, of course, also the occupation of Rome itself.

Bonaparte declared that the Roman people, as descendants of Brutus and the Scipios, were the French Republic's friends; that the new Republic would set up statues to honour antique Rome's great heroes; free the people from their long slavery *and* restore the once omnipotent Capitol.[83] The symbolic role-reversal of the French Republic and ancient Rome was still more insulting to the Romans as the Capitoline Museum and other hubs of culture were systematically stripped of their antique (and post-antique) treasures. The invasion of the Papal States had resulted in an armistice stipulating that one hundred works of art were to be ceded to the French. Eventually, in accordance with the infamous Treaty of Tolentino (February 1797) and also after further pressure from Bonaparte, the first of the four convoys of booty was on its way to Paris.[84] The importance the French attached to the treasures is reinforced by Mainardi who notes that as soon as the first convoy had left Rome (April 1797), plans were already underway for their triumphal entrance into Paris.[85] Further, while these treasures – and others seized by Bonaparte and his armies during the Italian campaigns – were making their laborious journey to Paris, Rome was being transformed into a veritable tool of propaganda and a stage set for the French Republic's triumphal ceremony. Potent symbols of Republican Rome's ordered authority such as the lictors' *fasces* were now reinvented to display the force of the French, and they became common features of the city's new Roman landscape.[86] A vast triple-bay triumphal arch, consciously modelled on the Arch of Constantine, was erected at the entrance to the Pont de la République (Ponte S. Angelo) for the Festival of the Federation in March 1798. The arch was awash with imagery celebrating the power of the French Republic and the glorious Italian victories of Bonaparte, such as those of Arcole and Castiglione. It was crowned by figures representing 'la Francia che unisce alla Libertà' and, to add insult to injury, the inscription lauded the French as founders of the new Roman Republic.[87] In true triumph-like style, the parading troops passed under their visually didactic triumphal arch. Then, having crossed the (aforementioned) bridge, the procession continued to the Piazza San Pietro, in which an Altar to the Fatherland provided further stimuli attesting to the new Republic's force and its role as *liberatori*.[88]

The similarities between the triumphal arch (above) and the Arch of Constantine underline how the regime also exploited Imperial Rome's language of power to disseminate their own republican rhetoric and force. This, too, was translated into the re-baptism of symbolically charged space associated both with republican *and* Imperial Rome. While the Capitoline itself was not used as a terminus for the 1798 procession (above), the presence of a Tree of Liberty here was laden with symbolic meaning (it was planted on the 15 February, 1798: the day the French Republic was proclaimed).[89] Equally significant was the re-appropriation of the space in 1799 for the staging of Voltaire's republican play *Le mort de César* (and even the use of the bronze she-wolf as a stage prop).[90]

A further Tree of Liberty was planted in the *Forum Romanum*. The symbolism involved was undoubtedly heightened with knowledge of the sacred fig tree that once had graced the antique Forum, having served as a reminder of the tree under which the Roman Empire's 'founders' Romulus and Remus had been suckled as infants by the she-wolf.[91] The Forum was also used as a stage set for the Festival of the Perpetuity of the Republic (15 February 1799), which marked the proclamation of the Republic a year previously. Artistic depictions of the event reveal a Doric column crowned by a figure of Liberty (under which is a vast podium adorned with four eagles) amidst parading soldiers and a crowd of spectators. Equally notable, however, are the rather sorry-looking remains of the Basilica of Maxentius and the Temple of Antoninus and Faustina in the background and, a little further away, the Colosseum. The nature and visibility of the backdrops in these illustrations underscore the spatial and ideological relationship forged between the new regime's reinvention of the area and the existing antique structures, both in and around the Forum.[92] Further, by staging its festival in the very space that had accommodated the passage of ancient Rome's great *triumphators* as they neared the Capitol, the regime was able to project its force in a most pertinent manner.[93] The presence of parading soldiers within such a hugely symbolic space would have reaffirmed the new Republic's subjugation of modern (and ancient) Rome, and with this its universal dominion.

The 'Triumph' in print: 'Rome' in Paris

The powerful language of the Forum-staged Republican festival (above) would have been still more meaningful for the role-reversal of the two great empires had already been cemented with the 1798 *Entrée triomphale*. Given the Roman triumph's reputation as a ceremony of entrance that encapsulated the notion of universal domination, the symbolism of the procession of Roman (and Italian) treasures into Paris was all the more poignant. It is important to recall that Bonaparte had been involved both in the acquisition of the *spolia* and later, in their ceremonial entrance into Paris. These observations also underpin why readers of this book are already familiar with aspects of the 1798 *entrée*, especially in relation to the impact it was to have upon the role(s) of Napoleonic Paris as a 'new Rome'. The implications of this hugely symbolic festival, however, are such that they require a deeper investigation, not least as the manner in which the event was relayed by the media reveals the intensity with which Rome's triumphal rhetoric was exploited (and reinvented) to serve political ends.

The *entrée* (27–28 July) had been planned to coincide with the 14 July celebrations. Due to the late arrival of the last convoy of booty from Rome, the event was incorporated into the *Fête de la Liberté* (an annual festival celebrating the downfall of Robespierre 3 years previously). Subsequently, the French Republic's symbolic spoils became the focus of the *fête*. This is reflected in newspapers such as *Le Patriote Français*, in which glowing accounts of the procession and the many chariots charged with the Republic's 'trophies of glory' are combined with reference to the spectacular triumphs of ancient Rome.[94] A particularly revealing excerpt from another newspaper, *Le Moniteur*, reveals the important role played by the Aemilian triumph:

> The whole world has been drawn upon to enrich the most beautiful of our *fêtes* so that it might be as magnificent as those of the Romans and the triumph of Aemilius Paullus.[95]

The links created between the 1798 *fête* and the 'republican' triumph of Aemilius Paullus after his victory over the Macedonians (167 BCE) are significant on several accounts, and may be clarified by citing Plutarch:

> Three days were assigned for the triumphal procession. The first barely sufficed for the exhibition of the captured statues, paintings, and colossal figures, which were carried on two hundred and fifty chariots.[96]

Plutarch's allusions to the might of Rome and reference to the impressive display of booty-laden chariots demonstrate why the Aemilian triumph was particularly fitting as an antique precedent. Additional parallels were explicit in the nature of the spoils for, in a similar fashion to those paraded in triumph in 167 BCE, the French Republic's many chariots were weighed down with 'statues, paintings, and colossal figures' (among an array of additional booty). Importantly, the 1798 *entrée* was vital to Bonaparte both as a tool of self-propaganda and as a vehicle through which to fuel his future recreations of the triumph and display of power.[97] We must also consider the absence of Aemilius from the two first days of his triumph, and its relevance in relation to the absentee *triumphator*, Bonaparte. His absence, moreover, was not without its advantages: it would have placed increased accent on the *fête* as a symbolic representation of the citizens' 'triumph', while also augmenting their general's national (and international) image as a glorious republican hero fighting (in Egypt) for the good of the French nation.

Unsurprisingly, the *Fête de la Liberté* (Festival of Liberty) has generated a considerable amount of scholarly interest.[98] There are those, moreover, who have explored the 'Roman' character of the ceremony in some depth. For instance, Mainardi examines its political and cultural ramifications to great effect: she addresses the implications of the procession's display of *spolia* and in turn, she highlights its importance in relation to the 'symbolic displacement of the capital of Western civilisation from Rome to Paris'.[99]

Earlier in this chapter we saw how the *porta triumphalis* and Rome's triumphal arches played an intrinsic role in post-antique re-enactments of the triumph. It is not only surprising, but surely relevant that newspapers covering the 1798 procession pay little attention to these architectural features. By placing emphasis on newspaper coverage of the event and the widely acclaimed song composed for the occasion, it is shown how we may gain further insight into the Roman nature of the 1798 *entrée*.[100]

Songs had accompanied many a French procession, as they had during the triumph of Aemilius Paullus and other *triumphators* as they entered Rome and made their way to the Capitol.[101] The refrain of this particular song, however, demonstrates how aspects of the ceremony were intended to take the exploitation of Rome's triumphal ritual to new and to unprecedented heights. The wording of the chorus reiterates the intrinsically meaningful message of the spectacle: that Rome was no longer in Rome, for now it was all in Paris. The *Journal de Paris* underpins the song's importance by citing it in its entirety on the first day of the celebrations. The paper's readership would have been hard pushed not to miss the song's meaning, as the first chorus illustrates:

> All heroes, all great men
> Have changed countries
> *Rome is no longer in Rome*
> *It is all in Paris.*[102]

The French already had paraded spoils around their capital in triumphal fashion, but the press made sure that no procession should be considered more suggestive – or momentous – than this symbolic display of Roman *spolia* (see Figure 2). The emphasis on 'Rome' being in Paris, also implies that the orchestrators of the *fête* (and the media) saw little point in following their predecessors by placing accent on imitations of Rome's *porta triumphalis* and triumphal arches – for Rome, after all, was now *toute à Paris*.

Key words of the chorus were changed to reinforce the powerful rhetoric of the festival. The first chorus (above) begins with 'all heroes'; the reader is reminded that the principal hero was the absentee *triumphator*, Bonaparte.

The song thus reveals how the media were already promoting parallels between the glorious triumphs of antiquity's heroes and those of the young general Bonaparte, well before he became First Consul and later, Emperor. This is seen in the pointed references to the Aemilian triumph (above) and also in the prolific diffusion of Bonaparte's 'republican' image as an heroic *triumphator*:

> O Bonaparte, why were you not here in your crown of laurels! But foreign climes were calling you. Glory to you, young conqueror of Italy! Glory to your illustrious brothers in arms![103]

Here, we also find a resemblance between Bonaparte's heroic image and the ways in which the French kings had been portrayed as *triumphators*. For instance, a piece in *La Gazette de France* (1660) had hailed a triumphant Louis XIV as France's 'chef de lauriers'.[104] The references in Republican papers both to despotic France and to the advent of a new era underline how the song's projection of Bonaparte as a glorious hero, referred not only to antique Rome but also to a deliberate disassociation with France's past. The song's inclusion of 'all heroes' therefore had a most contemporary significance. Like the press, it also alluded to the pivotal role played by Bonaparte and his army as saviours of the Republic in the wake both of the Robesperrian Terror and the French monarchy's former reigns of despotism. In *Le Patriote Français*, for example, the French kings are labelled as despots, and in another newspaper the words tyranny and despotism are used in conjunction with the Triumvirate of Robespierre, Couthon and St. Just.[105] Neither could the despotic emperors of Imperial Rome and their plundering antics escape the wrath of the media, as is abundantly clear in an edition of *Le Patriote Français* published two days after the *fête*.[106] Ironically, Bonaparte and his republican compatriots had acted in a similar manner by their seizure of Rome's treasures. We have seen, too, that there were objections on this very account, notably by Quatremère de Quincy, though clearly this was something the media kept under wraps.[107]

The second chorus of the song replaces 'all heroes' with 'all gods'; the third chorus becomes 'all art'.[108] The refrain, therefore, made clear that the procession of spoils represented a symbolic role-reversal of Republican Paris and Rome's once omnipotent empire – in the political, cultural, spiritual *and* the physical sense of the word. The message was reiterated with a conspicuous banner in the procession, reading: 'Greece surrendered them, Rome lost them; their camp has changed twice and it will never change again.'[109]

The song's publication in the papers also gave the crowds gathered to watch the ceremony, the opportunity to participate personally by singing along with the official members of the procession. Similarly, the literate person's understanding would have been cemented with detailed descriptions available prior to the event, in which the nature and order of the booty's place in the procession were made known. The *Journal de Paris* provides details of the antique treasures to be paraded triumphantly through Republican Paris.[110] Examples include the *Apollo Belvedere*; the bronze bust of Lucius Junius Brutus; the marble head of Marcus Brutus; the *Laocoön* and the bronze *Horses of St. Mark's*. Such publicity was necessary, for although inscriptions and banners advertised the booty's nature, most of the *spolia* were stacked in sealed packing cases.[111]

Certain pieces such as *Apollo*, however, were given visually prominent locations. The bust of Junius Brutus – one of the French Republic's major figureheads and symbol of Republican liberty – was placed in a conspicuous position on a pedestal opposite a figure of Liberty.[112] As Caesar's assassin, Marcus Brutus was also perceived by the revolutionaries as an enemy of tyranny, though during the *fête* he was assigned a very secondary 'role'. For example, in the *Journal de Paris* his bust was merely listed along with the other booty, while the paper informed its readership that the bust of Junius Brutus was carried ceremoniously at the end of the *cortège*.[113] Scholarly accounts of the festival tend generally to gloss over the implications of this relationship and as a result, a fundamental aspect of the ceremony at the procession's terminus is de-emphasized.[114] Roman tradition had labelled Junius Brutus a courageous fighter of tyranny who successfully dethroned the Tarquins and contributed personally to overthrowing the monarchy. According to Livy, Junius Brutus was the first to have had the 'rods' (*fasces*), the significance of which is reinforced as this potent symbol of the Roman Republic's force and unity was integral to French revolutionary ideology.[115] The Romans had erected a bronze statue of their 'Liberator' on the Capitoline, and as a further symbolic gesture, they placed it in the midst of their kings.[116] The French Republicans' placement of the Junius Brutus bust on the pedestal (above) and their perception of the bust as the original, reinforce the complex ways in which antiquity was exploited. This was reiterated on the pedestal's inscription which stated that Rome was first governed by kings and that under the Republic, Junius Brutus had given Rome its liberty. We saw earlier that before its re-appropriation by former revolutionary regimes, the area in which the ceremony took place, the Champ-de-Mars, had been synonymous with kingly force and military activity. As a space highly charged symbolically, it served as a most fitting stage upon which to diffuse the new regime's unrivalled power and its triumph over the tyrants of France's past. Newspapers reveal that for the duration of the *fête*, the space evoked Rome's Capitol and, as the ceremonial terminus for the procession of Roman spoils, that it was transformed temporarily into the capital of 'Capitols'.[117] The relationship becomes more poignant still if we consider how the regime translated into a modern idiom the Roman tradition of placing a branch of laurel in the lap of Jupiter Optimus Maximus in the Temple of Jupiter. Junius Brutus, rather than Jupiter, became the focus of the ceremony, as members of the Directory ceremoniously placed a laurel branch, not in the lap of a statue of Jupiter, but on the pedestal of the bronze bust of Brutus in the centre of the new Republic's 'temple magique'.[118]

Visual links between the Roman triumph and the procession were also manifest with the eye-catching *Horses of St. Mark's* heading the third – and final – division of booty (it represented fine arts). The bronze horses were not stacked in cases: an understanding of their relationship with Rome's horse-drawn *currus triumphalis* and their placement upon the antique city's triumphal arches was provided both by the accompanying inscription and newspapers.[119] It was shown earlier in this chapter how the monarchy had formerly reinvented Rome's traditional four-horse chariot as a demonstration of contemporary power. The *Horses of St. Mark's* (as ancient Rome's own booty) were thus to represent the most striking display of French Republican force. Further, *Le Patriote Français* boasts that they were to be attached to a triumphal chariot and placed in the Place de la Révolution: a space associated formerly with monarchical and Robespierrean despotism.[120] Although these visions – and those of Poyet for his Republican forum – never materialized, we may remember that the bronze group was to serve later as an illustration of Napoleon's supreme power by gracing the summit of the Arc du Carrousel. Given the Emperor's constant struggle to disassociate himself with France's despotic past, the group's reputation both as a symbol of antique Rome's universal dominion *and* French Republican liberty would prove most advantageous.[121]

Media coverage of the 1798 *entrée* demonstrates how the people were also considered a vital element of the ceremony's spectacular reinvention of the Roman triumph. The *Journal de Paris*, for example, stresses that citizens were invited to accompany the *cortège*; it informs the chosen representatives exactly where and at what time they were to assemble, as well as providing details of how each division of booty would be accompanied by students whose studies related to the various themes.[122] To an extent, the egalitarian language and the political overtones of the *entrée* and former revolutionary spectacle *à l'antique* would always influence Napoleon's recreations of the triumph. However, given the advantages of the 1798 *entrée* as a vehicle of self-propaganda for the absentee *triumphator*, Bonaparte, this also acts as a suitable point from which to examine the implications of the changing face of the 'triumph' and crowd participation once he had evolved into the Emperor Napoleon. This is demonstrated by an article in *Le Moniteur Universel* printed after the Austerlitz victory in 1805:

> O the glory of the Romans shines once more: it is engraved upon the dust of the remaining vestiges of their magnificence. The Senate and the people erected statues, triumphal arches, columns and temples for their emperors. The emperors gave the people circuses, spectacles and public baths.[123]

By this stage, *Le Moniteur Universel* had become the regime's official newspaper and Napoleon's principal tool of propaganda. The reference here to the erection of triumphal monuments by the Senate and the People of Rome is especially telling as the paper is publicizing a recent proposal (from a member of the *French* Senate) for a triumphal column to immortalize Napoleon's Austerlitz victory. The desire for elaborate Rome inspired monuments through which to magnify Napoleon's feats reiterates just how marked his evolution now was from republican general to grandiose emperor. This also underscores how aspects of Napoleonic rhetoric had become increasingly distanced from the republican 'triumph' of 1798, when the citizens (and Roman spoils) had served as the principal focus. This, as the above excerpt also illustrates, is not to say that the people were insignificant under Napoleon but more that their role was becoming secondary to the quasi-mythical *triumphator* 'Napoléon-le-Grand'. Accordingly, *Le Moniteur Universel* venerates Napoleon's Austerlitz triumph and describes the joyous and respectful spectators pressed together as they waited eagerly to view the Emperor leading his heroic *Grande Armée* through the Parisian streets.[124] The paper recounts in dramatic detail, the display of the symbolic eagle, the glorious trophies of war and even the presence of laurel-clad busts of Napoleon in many of the dwellings the *cortège* passed by.[125] These observations also underline similarities between the fashion in which both Louis XIV and Napoleon were to reinvent the Roman triumph. The value of exploring further this relationship is now demonstrated in the final section of this book.

The staging of power: A tale of two 'Triumphs'

> The staging of power is a matter of managing appearances. The managers have a choice audience in mind, an impression they wish to create for it, and a visual language that can bespeak, in a proper measure, regimentation, pomp, and delight.[126]

Kostof and other scholars exploring the spatial, ritualistic and theatrical role of a city as a microcosm of an individual's image and rule, base their studies on a diverse mixture of ages and political regimes from antiquity to the present day.[127] The following pages continue with this theme by revealing the links between the Roman triumph and the 'staging of power' in Napoleonic Paris and the Paris of Louis XIV. This is developed through an evaluation of the ways in which the imperial triumph was selectively reinstated during the entry that celebrated Napoleon's marriage to Marie-Louise (1810) and the *Entrée triomphale* following the wedding of Louis and Marie-Thérèse in 1660. By way of this, it is also shown how we may gain a deeper insight into Napoleon's exploitation of antiquity and the nature of his imperial capital. A final point before I begin: while we should not forget that the 1660 *entrée* took place before the influential Mazarin died and Louis assumed *pouvoir absolu*, neither should we neglect the implications of Bryant's appraisal of this event and his comment that 'the focus was never for a moment taken off the person of the king who was made to will all things'.[128]

Napoleon's *Entrée solennelle* into Paris was not engineered as a re-enactment of the 1660 entry – the principal reason being that no post-revolutionary sovereign would deliberately project parallels between himself and the French Republic's archetypal despot. Nonetheless, by 1810, the shadow of the Revolution was becoming increasingly distant and there were signs that the Emperor's thirst for personal glory resembled more closely the absolutism of Louis' personal rule.[129] Significantly, a piece in the *Journal de l'Empire* (5 April 1810) illustrates how it would have been all too easy to draw parallels between the two sovereigns *and* their *entrées*. Moreover, in an attempt to disguise any discernible relationship, the references in the newspaper to the King inadvertently substantiate the similarities:

> When in 1660 Louis XIV married Marie-Thérèse of Spain, all the poets of the age hastened forth to compete with one another in their quest to celebrate this happy union which brought peace to France.... The century of Louis XIV, cited as the century of taste, has since been considered a century of poor taste.

A little later the paper states:

> When today an Emperor who has achieved by his glory what the ill-fated Louis XIV could only dream of, marries Marie-Louise of Austria, our poets burst forth with the same speed, the same zeal.[130]

This paper's combined use of the words 'glory' and 'peace' also introduces how the respective entrances were broadcast as modern adaptations of the triumphal theme. In both cases, the media referred to the peace and prosperity that imperial activity had brought to the nation and how the marriages would cement this further by unifying Europe. In consequence, Louis' Franco-Spanish marriage united France and Spain, and was projected as a 'triumph' of peace, while press coverage of the 1810 entrance stressed how Napoleon's union with Marie-Louise would seal relations between France and Austria.[131] For the entrances, the sovereigns' *gloire* was tinged with domestic and Augustan connotations, rather than Caesar-like qualities. The anonymous *Entrée triomphante* (1662) – a luxury folio edition that drew from contemporary pamphlets covering the event – makes explicit the links between Louis XIV and Augustus, both of whom, as fathers of their respective countries, had brought peace and joy to their people.[132] A few days prior to the 1810 *entrée* Napoleon was hailed as 'un nouvel Auguste'.[133] Another newspaper covering the *entrée* includes an ode to 'Napoleon-le-Grand', in which the Parisian streets were seen to reverberate both with chants of victory *and* with hymns of love in celebration of the return of the nation's glorious hero.[134]

The accent placed on the ceremonies as contemporary adaptations of the triumph is reinforced by the projection of the respective couples as modern *triumphators*. Although the imagery adorning the architectural stage sets depicted each couple in Rome-like chariots, in reality, only Marie-Thérèse rode in a 'Caléche' resembling the *currus triumphalis*.[135] Louis maintained the *entrée royale* tradition of a king on horseback, and rode in procession a distance before his queen. Napoleon and Marie-Louise, on the other hand, sat in a richly decorated modern-day carriage drawn by eight white horses.[136] While both ceremonies maintained the Roman tradition of the *triumphator* (though here, *triumphators*) 'riding' in mid-procession, all four figures were dressed in contemporary costume.

This exemplifies how ideological depictions of Napoleon and Louis were distanced from their physical reinstatements of the triumph and the average onlooker's perception of the spectacles. We might recall the allegory of Napoleon by Callet in 1805 (see Figure 23) and consider how the laurel-crowned Emperor in Roman military dress and his triumphal chariot differed to his physical presence (and image) as *triumphator*. Although this is explained, in part, by a tradition in France by which the *currus triumphalis* and the attire of the *triumphator* were translated into a modern idiom, and idealized depictions generally painted the sovereign in a more Roman light, it does not disclose the reasoning behind these differences in presentation. Strong highlights the importance of this within a generalized context by noting that imagery and the written word underlined the contemporary language of spectacle.[137] We see, therefore, how the physical manifestation of Napoleon as 'himself' promoted his individuality (and the modernity of his regime), while the written word, visual stimuli and the language of classically inspired stage sets, worked together to reinforce such rhetoric and diffuse further his image as a powerful and an exceptional being. This also fits neatly with Wisch's comment that 'the protagonist of power, who usually participated in person, became, in effect, a representation of himself'.[138] If we apply these observations to Napoleon's 1810 entrance, we return inevitably to the pivotal role of the media. The accent the Napoleonic press placed both on ancient Rome *and* the differences between the *entrées* of 1660 and 1810 would have reinforced the visual language of Napoleon's spectacle. This, in turn, would have underlined the Emperor's powerful self-image and his place as a modern *triumphator* whose politics and persona, moreover, were not to be likened to the absolutism of Louis XIV and his personal rule.

This brings into play the value of examining the respective ceremony's visual representations of the people. We might, for instance, note the triumphal arch topped with an obelisk in the Place Dauphine: the final station of the 1660 *entrée* (Figure 25). The anonymous *Entrée triomphante* stipulates that the Rome inspired arch represented the people, while the obelisk symbolized the King.[139] Scholars observe that the 'people' represented the foundations upon which the monarchy was based.[140] This recalls my discussion in Chapter 3, in which the chasm between the French populace and Louis XIV (as a singularly unique and divine being) was addressed: for we see here how the imaginative structure (above) was built not as a forceful vehicle of propaganda, but rather as an expression of Louis' greatness and legitimate role as king of his people. The impact of this structure and that of the other classically inspired stations would have been accentuated as they were positioned to be seen and admired from afar.[141]

The location and size of the imagery-laden arches present for Napoleon's entrance, suggest they too were eye-catching symbols of authority that were equally convincing as didactic media when viewed from a distance (see Figure 4). Additional similarities include the respective depictions of both Louis and his queen; and Napoleon and his empress in triumphal chariots bringing peace to their people.[142] The allegories of the people on the Emperor's temporarily decorated Arc de Triomphe also served as a vehicle through which to recognize publicly the role of the populace. As always, however, it is vital we consider the populist nature of Napoleon's post-revolutionary propaganda and as a result, how the symbolic representations of the people here inevitably contrasted to those of the 1660 *entrée*.

We have seen already that an effective way of demonstrating authority is either by means of exploitation and disassociation, or/and by improving upon legacies associated with the antique and a more recent past. This is indicated (in part) in the diffusion of the 1810 entrance as the most spectacular to date, in terms both of its magnificence and benevolence.[143] Moreover, the derogatory portrayal of Louis in the *Journal de l'Empire* (above) suggests that while attempts were made to disassociate Napoleon's reign with that of the King's absolute rule, Napoleonic publicists also sought to demonstrate how the event would eclipse the 1660 *entrée*. A brief study of the topographical layout and the spatial language of the structures erected (or transformed) for the respective *entrées* allows us a fuller understanding of this relationship.

The principal archway of a triumphal arch has the potential of framing and therefore attracting the eye to a particular scene (noted in Chapter 2). This was explicit in the temporary triumphal arch at the Pont Notre-Dame through which could be viewed a bridge transformed into a gallery of kingly portraits and a further triumphal arch (Figure 26).[144] The bridge (the fourth station of the 1660 *entrée*) also boasted medallions and inscriptions relating to past monarchs, as well as an image of Louis XIV: under which was a caption: *Consilis armisque potens* (Mighty in council and in arms).[145] Equally, the location of the temporary arch in the Place Dauphine (above) was such that it was possible to gain a perspective view of the equestrian statue of Henri IV through its archway (see Figure 25).[146] Louis was ever keen to surpass this highly-esteemed king, whose popularity and many achievements ensured his *légende dorée* was still very much alive at this time. We may also remember that Henri IV was seen to modernize Paris as Augustus had transformed Rome. The didactic nature of the view through the arch is underscored by the inclusion in the *Entrée triomphante* of an inscription which lauded Louis for the peace he had bestowed upon the whole universe, as opposed to that which Henri had brought only to certain peoples.[147] Further, an inscription at the same station, read '. . . . And if these sumptuous arches of our beloved King rose above the colossus of Henri'.[148] The projection of Louis' superiority over Henri IV would have been accentuated with the diminished proportions of the equestrian statue when viewed through this immense arch. The visual didacticism at work here would have been reinforced with the (temporary) metamorphosis of the space within which the arch was erected – the Place Dauphine, though relatively small, was a celebrated and an innovative urban feature created under Henri IV.

The transformation of the Pont de la Concorde for Napoleon's 1810 entrance exploited the 'view through' concept in a somewhat different, but no less didactic manner. It also finds reference with the 'triumphal bridge' (above), which, itself, had borrowed from the language of Henri II's *entrée* (1549) and former adaptations of the Roman triumph. Napoleon's bridge was decorated with obelisks and star-crowned columns and, as the procession crossed its axial path, the eye would have been drawn to the Palais du Corps Législatif (the Palais Bourbon) which, for the occasion, was transformed into a Temple of Hymen. The 1660 entrance (and previous *entrées*) had already reinvented the symbolism of the obelisk and the star. According to Pliny, the star was most powerful, and an omen of 'great significance'; it shone around men's heads in the evening and was associated with Augustus.[149] This recalls the allegorical representations of Louis and of Napoleon as radiate-crowned *triumphators* and my suggestion that the symbolic intent of the latter was linked to Napoleon's complex quest to outshine the Sun-King's impressive Golden Age. The façade of Napoleon's Temple of Hymen was adorned with statues, including those of Colbert (Louis' 'Maecenas'), Sully (Henri IV's principal minister) and Minerva.[150] Moreover, these statues – associated with antiquity *and* France's monarchical and Republican past(s) – were positioned below the conspicuous figures of the Emperor and Empress.

The Arc de Triomphe was also able to exploit the 'view through' concept to its full potential. The scene viewed through the structure (facing Paris) would have framed the Champs-Élysées as it led majestically to another triumphal arch (at the main gate to the Tuileries gardens). The viewer might also have caught a glimpse of the thirteen smaller temporary arches framing the latter part of the route leading to the procession's terminus – the Louvre-Tuileries complex. Although the procession began at the Palais de Saint-Cloud, it only entered a more symbolic phase once it reached the Arc de Triomphe. Both the elevation of the arch and the axiality of the principal route would have lengthened the perspective which, in turn, would have enabled bystanders to view the procession's 'beginning' and possibly the environs of its symbolic terminus.

In the anonymous *Entrée triomphante*, emphasis is placed on the antique triumph and its associated architecture as an enduring expression of the esteem and impressive achievements of Rome's *triumphators*.[151] This brings into focus the value of exploring further the interrelationship between the 1660 and 1810 *entrées*; and ancient Rome's triumphal architecture and route(s). Both *entrées* had their own *porta triumphalis* under which the processions passed – the symbolic entrance of the *triumphator* into Rome was thus reinvented in both cases to mark a ritual of marital transition or passage and with this, the sovereigns' success in bringing peace and prosperity to their nations.[152] The structures' respective topographical relationship with the boundary separating Paris (as *Urbs*) from the surrounding *orbis* underlines their links with Rome's *porta triumphalis*. In the case of the 1660 *entrée* and the temporarily decorated Porte Saint-Antoine, this is reinforced by the reference in the *Entrée triomphante* to the welcome Louis XIV and his queen received at the arch as 'Triomphateurs'.[153] This has bearing on the 1810 entry, for once the procession had arrived at the Arc de Triomphe – envisaged now as *the* symbolic (though unfinished) entrance into Napoleon's expanding imperial capital – the public and officials were given the opportunity to welcome publicly the Emperor and Empress. While these factors highlight the Napoleonic ceremony's links with Rome's (imperial) triumphs, they also suggest how the 'Roman' language of Paris' Renaissance *entrées* and that of the 1660 *entrée* was manipulated in an equally pertinent manner by the Emperor and his entourage. The importance of this goes further, for at the time, Napoleonic imperialism was nearing its zenith and Rome had only recently (February 1810) been proclaimed 'the second city of the Empire'. Napoleon's *porta triumphalis* therefore signalled the entrance into a magnificent metropolis now labelled 'the first city of the Empire'. This would have underlined his superiority over Rome *and* any French sovereign who had striven to surpass Rome and its heroic *triumphators* – and here, one is reminded especially of Louis XIV and the King's influential 'Roman' legacy.

It was shown earlier in this chapter how the majority of Paris' *entrée royales* had passed beneath the Porte Saint-Denis and followed the city's north-south axis on their ceremonial passage to Notre-Dame and the Palais de la Cité. As a further indication of the similarities between the imperial entrances of Louis XIV and of Napoleon, we see that neither sovereign followed Paris' traditional kingly 'triumphal route'.[154] In both cases, the processions terminated at the Louvre and adopted a route (albeit less than direct) that traced the basic line of the city's east-west axis. The only notable difference in this respect was that while the King's *cortège* set off from the Chateau de Vincennes and entered Paris from the east, Napoleon and his empress began their ceremonial route at the Palais de Saint-Cloud and entered the city from the west. Although triumphal arches and the symbolism of the *Sacra via* had long been features of Paris' 'Roman' landscape(s), the link between the respective triumphal routes followed by Louis and Napoleon suggests why this particular relationship should be explored further. The nature of the route the royal couple followed to the Louvre bore a resemblance symbolically to ancient Rome's *Sacra via* and Capitol. The imperial couple's passage to the Louvre along a route also punctuated with triumphal arches was equally reminiscent of Rome's Sacred Way and Capitol.

The implications of this relationship become clearer with consideration of the Louvre's evolution. In 1660, the palace's principal importance lay with its long-standing role as the monarchy's stately residence and seat of power. Although it served admirably as a terminus for the 1660 *entrée*, the palace had not yet been transformed into a visual exhibition of Louis' rule. It was only later, with the creation of Claude Perrault's eastern Colonnade and Lebrun's Gallery of Apollo that the Louvre became a powerful tool through which to disseminate the King's image and omnipotence. This, as we saw in Chapter 3, went hand in hand with the execution of the Sun-King's omnipresent *portes du Soleil*. If the 1660 *entrée* had taken place some years later, the refashioned Porte Saint-Antoine and possibly more of these elaborate testaments to the King's personal *gloire* would have decorated the triumphal route leading to the Louvre.

Napoleon's imperial capital was no more impressive than the 'new Rome' of Louis XIV and it was certainly unable to boast the creation of as many buildings and triumphal arches. The timing of the 1810 entrance, nevertheless, ensured that Napoleon already had at his disposal, permanent triumphal structures of his own that he could use as poignant didactic stage sets if he wished. The Louvre, moreover, once synonymous with the grandiose 'new Rome' of Louis XIV, was now the Emperor's most forceful power (and image) diffusing medium. This was apparent in the 'replacement' of the King's Gallery of Apollo with Napoleon's Apollonian gallery. Even the façade of Perrault's celebrated Colonnade was reinvented as a veritable display of Napoleonic propaganda: the bas-reliefs of the building's pediment were to represent Minerva and the Muses paying homage to the great Emperor (whose bust was speedily removed once he had fallen from power and 'Louis XIV' had reclaimed his rightful place as the composition's centrepiece). As the terminus of the 1810 *entrée* and ceremonial procession, the Louvre's *Salon Carré* became a similarly potent device through which to display the Emperor's rhetoric. The salon was transformed into an elaborate chapel for a ceremony which would bind Napoleon and his empress in holy wedlock – even the masterpieces that had adorned its walls were dismantled for the wedding. The splendour of the event is captured in contemporary etchings, one of which reveals the imperial couple and the accompanying *cortège* as it makes its ceremonial passage along the palace's vast *Galerie du Musée* to the *Salon Carré*.[155] This, too, finds reference with the language of the Roman triumph, not least if we recall Lalande's account of the Capitoline, and the once magnificent Temple of Jupiter being home to the trophies of Rome's great conquerors.[156] Since the *Musée central des arts* had been renamed the *Musée Napoléon* in 1803, the exhibition in the Louvre of Rome's antique and post-antique treasures would undoubtedly have accentuated Napoleon's omnipresence. The display of these famous (or infamous) spoils of war which, of course, had been integral to the

1798 *Entrée triomphale*, was still more meaningful once the Eternal City itself had fallen to Napoleonic imperialism in 1809. This is seen in the decoration of an exquisite 'Etruscan' style vase in porcelain by Antoine Béranger (1813), upon which is an idealized version of the 1798 procession and its booty-laden chariots passing under an arch labelled 'MUSÉE'.[157] The scrolled handles of the vase are adorned with medallions which represent Napoleon, Augustus, Pericles and Lorenzo de Medici – all of whom would stand alone in history in their combined roles as exceptional rulers and makers of the greatest of Golden Ages. A representation of Louis XIV in his equally influential role as a patron of the arts, however, is notable by its absence. Both this and the nature of the imagery on the vase allude to Napoleon as Patron of the Arts *par excellence*: a figure whose authority was such that he was able to acquire *and* to display the world's art treasures in his *nouveau Capitole*. Like the Capitol in antiquity, the Louvre served as the heart of its emperor's impressive empire and symbol of his magnificent capital's invincibility. The heightened symbolic role of the Louvre demonstrated further Napoleon's superiority both over antique and modern Rome. On such a level, this also left the 1660 *entrée* and even the Sun-King's 'new Rome' inferior in comparison. This, in turn, would have reinforced Napoleon's unequivocal power and his new imperial city's unchallenged place as cultural capital and *caput mundi*.

Conclusion

He who takes it upon himself to look after his fellow-citizens and the city, the empire and Italy and the temples of the gods, compels all the world to take an interest.[1]

Paris under Napoleon became the venue for the visual exhibition of the Emperor's pre-eminence over the past, the present and the future. Like Rome in antiquity, Napoleonic Paris was to serve as the sociopolitical, cultural, religious and monumental locus of its ruler's expanding empire. By promoting Paris as the 'first city' of his empire, and possessing Rome, his 'second city', Napoleon sought to display his superiority, not only over ancient and modern Rome, but also over any post-antique sovereign who had attempted to surpass the Eternal City. Paris as Napoleon's imperial capital, with its new triumphal architecture, became a stage set for the recreation and reinvention of the Roman triumph. These events amplified Napoleon, in both his power and his image as a modern hero and an empire-builder. Although the Napoleonic city was never able to compete physically or culturally with the 'new Rome' established under Louis XIV, the display of Napoleon's magnificent Roman treasures in the Louvre, the 'new Capitol', provided the opportunity to outshine the Golden Ages of antiquity, the Renaissance and even the Sun-King. It also needs to be remembered that Napoleon's humanitarian projects and his influential reforms (namely, the *Code Napoléon*) would have demonstrated, in a most pertinent manner, how this modern emperor, like Rome's 'good emperors', looked after his fellow-citizens. This, too, was crucial to Napoleon's image as a successful post-revolutionary sovereign, who, while striving to create an imperial capital and a legacy that would better those of Louis XIV, was acutely aware of maintaining the semblance of the Revolution's egalitarian ethos. In these ways, Napoleon was able both to relocate a singularly exemplary 'Rome' in the present day and, as Horace asserted, when speaking of Augustus, 'to compel all the world to take an interest'.

In this book I have examined the multifaceted language of Napoleon's imperial capital and with this, his image and exploitation of antiquity. In 1828, Victor Hugo wrote an ode to Napoleon, titled *Lui*, in which he said of the recently deceased ex-emperor: 'You dominate our age; angel or demon, it matters not?'² Although these contentious facets to Napoleon's character have incited heated and conflicting responses, and will continue to do so, we should perhaps take heed of Hugo's allusion to the futility of dwelling on whether he was an angel or a demon (or even a 'good' or a 'bad' emperor). Less difficult to dispute, as Hugo infers, was Napoleon's influential legacy which, to this day, holds a commanding position in both French and European history and in its wide-ranging historiography. Hugo's synopsis of Napoleon also reminds us, be it indirectly, of Thiers' distinction (1845–62) between the republican and monarchical phases of Napoleon's rule, and the emphasis in this book on the opposing ideologies inherent in his evolution from hero of the Revolution to a sovereign whose personal rule, in some ways, may be seen to resemble that of Louis XIV. Napoleon's rise to and use of power was complex, as was his relationship with antiquity; it was at once clear-cut and ambiguous, static and changeable and at times, simply paradoxical and unfathomable. This is indicated in Napoleon's unyielding fascination with antiquity, and yet the distinct contrast between the grandiose imperial emperor he became and the dynamic young Republican characterized by Pascal Paoli as a figure cut from the cloth of antiquity – 'un homme de Plutarque'.³ Napoleon's desire to surpass and over time, to recreate Rome and antiquity's great exemplars in Paris, was linked inextricably not only to the universal influence and the lure of antiquity, but also to its diverse re-appropriations during both the Revolution and the *ancien régime*.

While these factors underpin the hurdles that the scholar faces when examining primary sources and later interpretations of Napoleon, they are also indicative of the potential of investigating the wider implications of Napoleon's relationship with *Romanitas*. The unique historical situation of Napoleon, as France's first post-revolutionary sovereign, has some importance for defining the methodology of reception studies. Fundamental to the interpretation set out here is a recognition of not just the relationship between Napoleon and the Revolution with antiquity, but also the influence upon Napoleon of earlier receptions of Rome, in particular that of Louis XIV. This may be described as a tripartite relationship (or trialectic) between antiquity, Napoleon and earlier appropriations of Rome. By way of this approach, I have sought to establish how we may increase our understanding of Napoleon's display of power and the reinvention of Napoleonic Paris as a 'new Rome'.

The influence of the French Revolution upon Napoleon and his 'new Rome' has generated considerable scholarly interest. Napoleon's visions when he was a youth to become his own Plutarchian hero, after all, were bound intricately to the *oeuvres* of the 'father' of the revolutionaries, Jean-Jacques Rousseau. However, we cannot gain a comprehensive picture of Napoleon's exploitation of antiquity unless we have an understanding of how pre-1789 receptions of Rome shaped his – and the French Republic's – relationships with *Romanitas*. By means of disassociation, the revolutionaries promoted a new and an improved era which drew from Republican Rome, but which rejected the decadence, luxury and despotism associated both with Imperial Rome and the *ancien régime*. The ideological chasm between the French Republic and, in particular, Louis XIV, whose absolute rule and manipulation of Imperial Rome were seen to be the antithesis of the revolutionaries' *raison d'être*, clearly had an immense impact upon their re-appropriations of *Romanitas*. This relationship inevitably influenced the ways in which Napoleon was to reinvent antiquity and as a result, it is central to interpreting the nature of the Emperor's imagery and his 'new Rome'. These factors also beg the question: why should Napoleon's rule as emperor and his 'new Rome' have found parallels with Louis XIV when, as France's first post-revolutionary sovereign, he realized the dangers inherent in a link drawn between his person and the King?

I do not profess to have answered this question in its entirety (and would suggest that it is a near impossible task). It does, however, underpin an underlying argument of this book: that there is a tangible link between Napoleonic, revolutionary and pre-1789 receptions of antiquity. This is reaffirmed (indirectly) by Napoleon's ruminations on St. Helena and his perception of himself as 'the natural mediator between the old and the new order'.[4] These factors cause us to question historical periodization and underscore why we might rethink the views of Hobsbawm and others who envisage a pre- and a post-1789 divide in France. As stated in my introduction, my aim was to bridge this divide, and the gap between scholarly compartmentalizations, which tend to concentrate either on the exploitation of antiquity under Louis XIV and the *ancien régime* or on the association between antiquity, the Revolution and Napoleon. This has been demonstrated through an investigation of the multidimensional language of Napoleon's triumphal monuments and that of the symbolic spaces they re-appropriated. From antiquity, monuments have been used as powerful emblems of authority through which to make or indeed break an individual's image. Like Rome, Paris is a city of conflicting pasts within which its rulers recognized the ideological and the political power of monuments and the spaces they occupied. We have seen how a city's pasts and its layers of space have an 'horizon of meaning' which exists on both a physical and on a cognitive level. This also recalls

Lefebvre's synthesis of the contradictory nature of 'the monument' (quoted in my introduction) and to its many 'subcodes'.⁵ By adapting the theories of Lefebvre and other spatially-oriented works to Napoleonic Paris, this book has explored how the nature of Napoleon's 'new Rome' was shaped not only by antiquity, but also by the physical and symbolic landscapes of the Revolution *and* the French monarchy. Central to this relationship was the contradictory language of the imperial capital of Louis XIV and the (visionary) 'Roman' landscape(s) of Republican Paris. The Napoleonic regime manipulated these diverse recreations of Rome to reinvent Paris and simultaneously project a new, prosperous and an unrivalled era. Although the Emperor was to imprint his ubiquitous image upon Paris in the mode of Louis XIV, he was acutely aware of the radical responses the King's symbols of authority had aroused, and he also used to his advantage the egalitarian and utopian language of the French Republic to disguise his despotic visions of grandeur. The imagery of antiquity enabled Napoleon and his architects to articulate their messages: the Roman world was used as the unifying language of 'the monument' and as a means of reinforcing the Emperor's authority and the dawn of a new superior age.

This is indicated in the Arc du Carrousel's crowning feature, the *Horses of St. Mark's*. As Roman booty that once graced Imperial Rome's triumphal arches, the bronze horses (drawing a *quadriga*) conveyed Napoleon's unparalleled authority as emperor, imperial empire-builder and reinvented monarch. Napoleon was also able to exploit the egalitarian connotations of the antique group, as shown both in the pivotal role it played in the *Entrée triomphale* into Republican Paris of 1798 and the plans by Poyet to incorporate it into his visionary forum. Further, while 'negative' aspects of Lefebvre's 'monument' are explicit in Napoleon's desire that the size of the Arc du Carrousel resemble that of the dominating architecture under Louis XIV, the reverse is true of the Emperor's insistence that the crowning statue of himself be removed from the arch. This contrasts with Napoleon's acceptance of a grandiose effigy of himself (in Roman dress) atop the Vendôme Column. The space within which the column was erected had strong ideological links with Louis XIV and the Revolution, and while its colossal size and crowning statue were reminiscent of the King's self-aggrandizing architecture, the monument's inscriptions and imagery celebrated the military glory both of Napoleon *and* his *Grande Armée*. The later fate of the column and the radically diverse reactions it incited, serve as a potent reminder of the power of Napoleonic monuments as political tools – though somewhat ironically, this also finds reference with the link between the Emperor Napoleon's monuments, those of Rome's vilified emperors *and* those of Louis XIV during the Revolution.

An understanding of the interrelationship between antiquity, Napoleon and the contradictory symbolism of Louis XIV and the Revolution is central to interpreting the Emperor's ambitious plans to complete Paris' east-west axis and transform it into a monumental *voie triomphale*. The use of Paris as a theatre upon which to display contemporary power by the restaging of Rome's triumphal ritual, of course, was not peculiar to the Emperor, the revolutionaries or Louis XIV, and must be considered when evaluating their diverse interpretations of the Roman triumph. The symbolic passage into Paris beneath a modern *porta triumphalis* found precedent with Renaissance France's absolute *entrée royale*, whereupon the monarch processed along a triumphal-arch studded route (normally via the city's *cardo*) to the procession's terminus. It was really only under Louis XIV and during the Revolution, however, that the potential of transforming the city's east-west axis (its *decumanus*) into a triumphal way was fully recognized. While Napoleon's projected *voie triomphale* was linked to outdoing Rome's triumphal landscape, it was also governed by a desire to implement and personalize these earlier plans (above). Further considerations embraced the re-appropriation of symbolic space already associated with the axis which, in the main, had associations with the Sun-King's 'new Rome' and with the revolutionaries' obsession with cleansing Paris of its despotic past. Although the Emperor's visions were not fully realized during his rule, the notion of power inherent in Rome's *porta triumphalis*, its triumphal arches and route(s), was a crucial component of his designs to create a new city which would surpass all others in history. This was explicit in the (partial) building of the Arc de Triomphe at the entrance to Napoleon's *Urbs*, and in the structure's intended roles both as a backdrop for triumphal display and as an eye-catching expression of the city's multifaceted wonders and image as *caput mundi*. Equally important is the spatio-symbolic relationship between the Arc de Triomphe as a *porta triumphalis*, the Champs-Élysées and the Rue de Rivoli as triumphal routes, the Arc du Carrousel as a triumphal arch set within the Napoleonic 'forum', and finally, the Louvre as 'Capitol'. The creation of the Rue de Rivoli and the Rue de Castiglione linked the Vendôme Column to the Champs-Élysées (and therefore to the Arc de Triomphe). Further, Napoleon's two roads joined his triumphal column to the Napoleonic city's symbolic heart, the Louvre-Tuileries. If these grandiose schemes (which also involved Napoleon's visionary Rue Impérial further along the axis) had materialized in full, this would have taken the recreation of Rome's triumphal route and ritual to unparalleled heights.

The Louvre-Tuileries complex was integral to Napoleon's imperial visions, as is apparent in the relationship between the area as Napoleonic 'forum' and the symbolic display in the Emperor's *nouveau Capitole* of the treasures he and his armies had seized during the Italian campaigns. These symbolic spoils had been the focus of the absentee *triumphator*, Bonaparte's *Entrée triomphale* of 1798, and their later display in the Louvre's *Musée Napoléon* was used both to legitimize the regime and to disseminate Napoleon's image as universal dominator. This is recognized by scholars, as is the importance of the *spolia* in demonstrating Napoleon's transfer of Rome's power and cultural heritage to Paris. In this book, emphasis has also been placed on the area's conflicting pasts and how this influenced the ways it was exploited by Napoleon as the centre of his 'new Rome'. The Louvre had been a symbol of monarchical authority until space associated with it and the Tuileries was re-baptized as a 'republican forum' and the epicentre of revolutionary Paris. The conflicting ideologies of monarchical autocracy and republican fanaticism in this politically charged area give heightened meaning to the contradictory language of Lefebvre's 'monument' and that of Paris' layers of space. This allows for a deeper understanding both of Napoleon's re-appropriation of the Louvre-Tuileries and of antiquity's underlying role in the diffusion of his new and unique form of power.

These factors reaffirm the importance of evaluating the ways in which this area was exploited as a didactic arena for the dissemination of the Sun-King's *gloire* and Roman image. During the Grand Carrousel of 1662, it was used as a 'public' stage upon which Louis had re-enacted Roman spectacle as a modern Caesar. Claude Perrault's acclaimed eastern façade of the Louvre typifies the way Vitruvian architecture was reinvented under Louis XIV to create a 'new Rome' that was to challenge and surpass that of Augustus. The creation of Lebrun's Gallery of Apollo in the Louvre also established explicit links between Louis, Augustus and Augustan Rome, and was employed as a similarly powerful device to broadcast the King's rhetoric. We have seen the parallels between the Louvre (and the royal capital in general) and the palace and gardens at Versailles, in which the diffusion of the Sun-King's omnipotence and also his desire to surpass Augustus and the antique, were equally explicit. While Napoleon's visions of a palace that would rival Versailles and those of Imperial Rome remained little more than a grandiose (and a potentially catastrophic) fantasy, the exhibition in his *nouveau Capitole* of the treasures (above), also illustrated his ability to out-do the Sun-King's 'new Rome(s)'. This, too, was apparent in Napoleon's revamping of the King's influential *Académie de France à Rome*, in his symbolic resurrection of the *Forum Romanum* and also in the language and the topographical relationships of the architecture erected (and transformed) for the Emperor's magnificent 'triumphal' entrance in 1810, in the company of his empress, Marie-Louise. These important episodes in Napoleon's reign were to demonstrate further his incomparable authority and the new role of Paris, his 'first city', as *caput mundi*.

Much of the analysis presented here draws inspiration from the ideas and thoughts of Lefebvre on monuments and their interpretation. What this French philosopher did not elaborate upon, however, was the intersection between 'the monument' and its antique predecessor. This book leads to the conclusion that Lefebvre's comments on the monument can also be applied to the reception of antiquity. Both the monument and earlier exploitations of the antique were reinvented under Napoleon to create new meanings that would embody a new ideology of Paris as the centre of modern culture. In this way, we may understand the ideals from antiquity and the interpretations of the antique as fundamental features of a Napoleonic idiom found in the monuments (and the buildings he transformed) across his city. The (existing) themes displayed on these structures appear timeless and can be related to antiquity and to both the Revolution and the *ancien régime*. The ability of 'the monument' *and* antiquity to present 'the characteristics of a society' and to 'embody a sense of transcendence, a sense of being *elsewhere*',[6] provided a powerful vehicle for the re-articulation of Napoleonic Paris as a 'new Rome'. Perhaps we should also see the relevance of these considerations in relation to Napoleon himself, who, like his monuments, would become timeless and transcend the temporal and ideological divisions between the *ancien régime* and the Revolution through a recourse to antiquity.

These observations have a bearing on our understanding of the presentation of Napoleon's Roman image(s): antiquity's prototypes provided him with an additional tool with which to promote a new and an unmatched era that would eclipse the chasm between the *ancien régime* and the Revolution. Consequently, we should not take at face value the diffusion of Napoleon as a 'new Augustus' or even a 'new Caesar', but instead see these and other antique prototypes as vehicles to articulate the image of Napoleon as a modern and an exclusive exemplar in his own right. This is shown in the interrelationships of Augustus, Louis XIV, the Revolution and Napoleon: Augustus' image as an heroic warrior bringing peace by conquest; a builder and a patron of arts, sciences and letters, was particularly appealing to Louis XIV. As a monarch able to broadcast his absolute power, he had no need to reinvent Augustus' egalitarian traits – the people, after all, were perceived by the King and his inner circle more as adoring subjects, whose very existence merely accentuated his uniqueness. Napoleon's post-revolutionary rule, however, was such that he realized the advantages of Augustus' populist front as Rome's first emperor. The influential nature of the Sun-King's own Golden Age, and Napoleon's relentless efforts to create a cultural capital and an empire of unprecedented magnitude also had a pivotal part to play. Here we must reconsider the weight of Voltaire's four Golden Ages of civilization in his *Le Siècle de Louis XIV*, in which the King's era was seen as the most impressive and placed above that of Augustus. Although Voltaire envisaged Louis as a *grand homme par excellence* in his role as patron, he not only inferred that in other respects the King was less exemplary, but he also separated the monarch from the greatness of his century. On the one hand, it was highly beneficial to proclaim Napoleon the new patron *par excellence*, and his era a fifth and an ultimately superior Golden Age. Alternatively, the regime's post-revolutionary hindsight served as a warning of the dangers of allowing a link between Napoleon and the King. Although certain French historians had emphasized Augustus' astute disguise of sole power and condemned him even as a 'scheming tyrant',[7] an association between the Augustan Age and Napoleon's new superior era enabled the Emperor to display his universal pre-eminence without being likened to Louis XIV.

The speed and dexterity with which Napoleon manipulated both fact and his image(s) to suit the politics of the moment, also goes some way in explaining the number and mixture of prototypes he – and his publicists – chose to exploit. This brings to mind the manner in which both Napoleon and Augustus cleverly manipulated the past, and used to their advantage an influential body of broadcasters to disseminate their image(s). Importantly, neither emperor was alone in this respect: Louis XIV, too, was a forcible politician and an ingenious publicist who not only understood the benefits of a talented entourage, but also the power of the antique past. An investigation of the respective systems of representation under Louis XIV and Napoleon has allowed us a deeper understanding of the ways in which the Emperor fabricated and diffused his Roman image. Here, too, we return inevitably to the conflicting ideologies of the King and the Revolution (and also to the 'horizon of meaning' in Lefebvre's monuments), but with reference to their combined impact upon both the creation of Napoleon's Roman image(s) *and* the audience he and his broadcasters targeted. In this study, I have explored how Napoleon's Roman images, like those of Louis, spoke to 'himself' and his inner circle, as well as to those with power and to posterity. This audience (with the possible exception of posterity) finds parallels with 'negative' aspects of Lefebvre's 'monument' and with the pervasive manner in which the King and his entourage perpetuated his image. I have also stressed the importance of distinguishing between the persuasive and propagandist language of Napoleon's imagery, and that of Louis XIV, whose Roman image was simply an expression of his supreme power as an exceptional being, born to kingship. When viewed through *this* lens, the Sun-King's 'new Rome' may be equated with more positive aspects of Lefebvre's 'monument', while Napoleon's imperial capital, again, is seen to be lacking. By ensuring that the citizens, both as players and recipients of his image, were a part of the equation, however, Napoleon could legitimize his position and distance his ideology from that of Louis XIV. In this way, he could simultaneously recreate a 'new Rome' which would embody its benefactor's new, improved and exclusive form of power.

This is indicated in newspaper coverage of Napoleon's 1810 *entrée*, in which we find an emphasis both on crowd participation and the event's unequalled magnificence, and also an emphatic dismissal of a link between his *entrée* and that of Louis XIV in 1660. By 1810, Napoleon's rule, imperial capital and triumphal spectacle were such that it would not have been difficult to envisage parallels between the two sovereigns. Indeed, there was little resemblance between this grandiose emperor and the French Republic's (absentee) *triumphator* of 1798 who had been likened to Aemilius Paullus. Even though Napoleon harboured great personal respect for Louis XIV, it was crucial both that he distance his image and 'new Rome' from those of the King, and that the media continue to promote the role of the citizenry during the Emperor's elaborate Imperial 'triumphs'. This is reaffirmed by newspaper coverage of French Republican spectacle, through which it is possible to gauge not only the salient role of the citizenry, but also how the impassioned language of the Revolution's 'radical triumphs' served as poignant reminders to Napoleon of the dangers of his being branded an absolute *triumphator*, akin to those of France's despotic past. Media coverage of triumphal spectacle during the Revolution also allows valuable insight into the ways in which the organizers of these events, in striving to disassociate Republican ideology from that of the *ancien régime*, drew heavily both on the Roman *and* the post-antique triumph. This brings into focus not only how former appropriations of *Romanitas* were used either to ally or separate one regime's ideology from another, but, linked intricately to this, also the versatility and the power of the classical world and its figures as political media of persuasion.

Within these relationships, we have explored the influence of the magnificent absolute triumphs re-enacted by Charles V, in which antique *triumphators* such as Augustus and especially the military exemplar, *César*, were central to the imagery. To clarify the revolutionaries' slighting of the 'tyrannical' Caesar, but also the projection of Napoleon as a reinvented *triumphator* whose heroic qualities and military prowess were to surpass Caesar, it is crucial that we comprehend the cultivation of *la gloire césarienne* as an expression of power (and empire) during the *ancien régime*. Equally significant is the manner in which the quasi-divine imagery of Augustus was recreated, not least by the mighty *triumphator*, Louis XIV, and the impact this had upon the presentation of Napoleon as a new *triumphator* of unrivalled magnitude. These observations reinforce the value of exploring a wider pattern to reception: without an awareness of the diverse ways in which ancient Rome, its triumphal landscape and historical figures were exploited prior to Napoleon's rule, his Roman image(s) and the reinvention of Napoleonic Paris as a 'new Rome' remain hazy. In my study of this relationship, with the emphasis placed on the projection and the multifarious receptions of the 'new Rome(s)' of Louis XIV, I hope to have shown how we may bridge this scholarly gap and enhance our understanding of Napoleon's recreation(s) of ancient Rome.

Napoleon and his Roman monuments became, and are still, very much a part of the Parisian landscape, and as such, are themselves a subject for reception. Both Mussolini and Hitler were fascinated by Napoleon and his influential legacies. As dictators whose own visions of universal domination were also embedded in 'conquering' both the modern *and* the antique world, these subjects are worthy of a detailed study in the future. There is great scope for an investigation of the triumphal landscapes of Napoleon's 'new Rome' and those of Mussolini, whose manipulation of Rome's own multidimensional pasts was translated into the construction of the Via dell'Impero as part of a monumental route for the Fascist 'triumph'.[8] In June 1940, Hitler's troops paraded in triumph down the Champs-Élysées from Napoleon's Arc de Triomphe. Further, these symbolic landmarks were essential components of Hitler's official sightseeing tour of occupied Paris, as was the tomb of Napoleon. By conquering Paris, the Führer was also able to overcome Napoleon, whose final 'triumphal' entrance into Paris now found parallels with the route taken by Hitler's victorious troops: a century earlier on a cold winter's day in 1840, Napoleon's funeral *cortège*, after its passage through the Arc de Triomphe, continued down the Champs-Élysées to his final resting place beneath the golden dome of Les Invalides.[9] The tangible links between the living emperor Napoleon and *his* 'rival', Louis XIV, were cemented in death, for the major route he followed during his final 'triumph', and Les Invalides, had been important landmarks of the Sun-King's 'new Rome'. In death, Napoleon also managed to vie with the great rulers of the antique past: the immense sarcophagus emblazoned with his symbols and pulled by sixteen horses, in a similar fashion to the plans for Augustus' funeral procession in Rome, passed beneath the Napoleonic capital's magnificent (and now complete) *porta triumphalis*.[10] Napoleon's Arc de Triomphe no longer defines the limits of Paris, having been superseded by Mitterrand's Grande Arche de la Défense. Through further manipulation of the antique via the employment of monuments as powerful emblems of authority and change, Mitterrand seems to better Napoleon, adding a further 'horizon of meaning' to the landscape(s) of Paris.

Appendices

Appendix I

The first section of the song composed for the 1798 *Entrée triomphale*

Jadis à Rome en pélérins
Quant nous faifions vifite,
C'étoit pour voir les dieux, les faints,
Ou les héros qu'on cite;
Enfin chacun d'eux, polimont,
Nous rend notre vifite,
Nous rend,
Nous rend notre vifite.

Du plus beau de nos palais,
Que la porte s'ouvre;
Qu'ils reçoivent des Français
Les honneurs du LOUVRE.
Oui, mais, oui, mais,
Ils n'en fortisont jamais.

Honneur aux fils de la Victoire!
Honneur à nos vaillans guerriers!
MINERVE fourit à leur gloire.
APOLLON chérit leurs lauriers.
Différens
Des tyrans
Dont les ars redoutoient l'empire,
Ces vainqueurs,
Dans leurs cœurs,
N'afpirent qu'à les cultiver.
D'autres combattent pour détruire,
Nous triomphons pour conferver.

En marche triomphale,
Voyez-vous L'APOLLON,
L'HERCULE & LA VESTALE,
Et VÉNUS & CATON?
Tout héros, tout grand homme
A changé de pays;
Rome n'eft plus dans Rome,
Tout héros, tout grand homme
A changé de pays;
Rome n'eft plus dans Rome,
Elle eft toute à Paris.

Journal de Paris, No. 309, 27 July 1798: 1295 (9 Thermidor An VI)

Appendix II

It is possible to divide the 1789 French Revolution into three very general phases.

The first phase, once the Revolution had been declared officially, witnessed a certain continuity with the monarchical past where, for the most part, Louis XVI was still recognized as King (in name at least). What authority he had, nonetheless, was rapidly diminishing, as was that of the nobility. By the time the constitutional monarchy was abolished and the Republic proclaimed, a systematic suppression of social differences was certainly in the making. With the introduction of the Convention in September 1792, came the beginning of the most disruptive and influential phase of the Revolution's convoluted history. The quest for the total annihilation of hierarchy and the simultaneous eradication of the past was typified by the execution of the King in January 1793. The period which was soon to follow – known as the 'Reign of Terror' (September 1793–July 1794) – not only witnessed the abolition of Christianity, but also saw Marie-Antoinette, along with thousands of nobles and counter-revolutionaries, fall victim to the guillotine. During the official 'Reign of Terror', Paris alone witnessed around 2,700 executions (this is only an approximation). The third phase – once the infamous Committee of Public Safety had become ineffective – may be characterized by a less radical form of government and a period of transition. This final 'phase' was neither trouble-free nor static, and the establishment in 1795 of the less than stable Directory did not signal a definite end to the disquiet. With the passage of time, however, France saw a gradual decrease in internal strife and an increase in military activity abroad which, in turn, paved the way for the 1799 *coup d'état* and the beginning of the Consulate.

Appendix III

'Qui veut voir le Panorama de Paris et de ses environs, ne peut choisir un autre lieu que la galerie qui domine la Colonne. Là, l'œil de l'admirateur des beaux-arts y contemple avec plaisir les Palais des Tuileries, du Louvre et du Luxembourg, les Invalides, le Panthéon . . . des Champs-Élysées . . . Mais, ce que l'œil de l'un et de l'autre ne se fatigue point d'admirer, c'est le mouvement perpétuel du passage des Tuileries aux Boulevards, qui fait de la rue de la Paix un vrai spectacle en miniature.'

Anonymous 1818: 18, *Description de la Colonne de la Place Vendôme.*

Glossary

Ancien régime. Political and social system in France before the 1789 Revolution.

Appian (c.95–165 CE). Alexandrian author of a *History of Rome*.

Auctoritas. Roughly translated as 'authority', although its meaning was more complex in Roman antiquity: also suggestive of the ability to provide political *and* moral leadership.

Bernini. See Fontana de Trevi.

Blondel (1618–86). Author of the *Cours d'architecture*. In 1671, he became director of the Royal Academy of Architecture and official controller-general of Parisian works by the Crown.

***Campus Martius* (Field of Mars).** An area close to the Tiber which served originally as antique Rome's military training ground for the young.

Canova (1757–1822). Italian sculptor and a leading exponent of 'neoclassicism'. See Quatremère de Quincy.

Caput mundi. May be translated as 'capital of the world'.

Cato the Elder (234–149 BCE). Roman statesman (consul of 195 BCE), orator and writer, not to be confused with his great-grandson, Cato the Younger.

***Champs-de-Mars* (Field of Mars: see *Campus Martius*).** A Parisian space created as a parade ground for Louis XV's École Militaire. The area's symbolic importance was also linked to the Frankish kings of the distant past, notably Charlemagne.

Chapelain (1595–1674). French poet and literary critic.

Charles V. Influential French monarch whose reign saw the rebuilding of the Louvre and the (part) replacement of Philippe Auguste's *enceinte* with a new fortification (1365–1420) circling Paris' Right Bank.

Charles V (1500–58). Holy Roman Emperor, King of Spain and archduke of Austria who inherited a Spanish and a Habsburg empire covering extensive domains in Central, Western and Southern Europe, as well as Spanish colonies in the Americas and elsewhere.

Cicero (106–43 BCE). Politician, philosopher and author of numerous works – also considered as one of Rome's greatest orators.

Colonna (*c.*1433–1527). Italian monk credited with *Le songe de Poliphile*: a novel inspired by Vitruvius' *De architectura* and Alberti's *De re aedeficatoria* recounting an imaginary dream that focuses on Poliphile's walk through a garden punctuated with classical themes.

Colosseum (the). Originally the *Amphitheatrum Flavium*. Begun (*c.*72 CE) by Vespasian and completed (in main) by Titus. Its building (under a new dynasty of Roman emperors) is often associated with Rome's 'Bread and Circuses' (see below).

Compartmentalization of Roman emperors ('Good' vs 'Bad'). The former category – including Augustus, Vespasian and Trajan – were portrayed generally as rulers who fed and entertained the people ('Bread and Circuses'). Rome's 'bad' emperors – notably, Caligula, Nero and Domitian – were seen as thinking only of themselves and of their own glory.

Consul. The highest annually elected office of the Roman Republic with two elected every year, under the Empire an appointive office (four per year).

Dionysius (of Halicarnassus). Greek author of the first-century BCE – best known for his *Roman Antiquities*.

***Domus Aurea* (Golden House).** Nero's infamous and immense palace built in the centre of Rome after the Great Fire of 64 CE. The *Colossus* – a towering gilded bronze statue of the Emperor in the guise of the sun-god Helios – was built at the entrance to this extravagant dwelling.

Enlightenment (the). European intellectual movement of the seventeenth and eighteenth centuries which also infiltrated America. The philosopher and writer, Rousseau (1712–78), was one of its most prominent figures in France: the ideas of the Enlightenment and its criticism of government and the Church fuelled revolutionary thinking.

Fontana di Trevi (1732–62). Monumental fountain located in the Trevi district of Rome. Today's fountain by Nicola Salvi was realized a century later after the design of the Italian sculptor, architect and artist, Bernini (1598–1680).

***Forum Romanum* (Roman Forum).** From the Middle Ages also known as the *campo vaccino*. Multifunctional locus of activity which became an essentially political space. Established in the Republic, not to be confused with ancient Rome's *fora* built under Julius Caesar and the Roman emperors Augustus, Nerva and Trajan.

François I. Reigned from 1515 to 1547. Known for his sponsorship of the arts – often referred to as France's original 'Renaissance monarch'.

Gaul. An ancient region – settled by groups of Celts – corresponding to modern France and neighbouring countries: roughly, Belgium, the south Netherlands, south-west Germany and northern Italy. In essence, the three Roman Gauls (divided into multiple provinces) consisted of *Gallia Cisalpina*, *Gallia Transalpina* (including present-day Provence) and *Gallia Comata*.

Gracchi (the). Roman brothers from the second-century BCE whose names are synonymous with radical social and economic legislation.

Henri II. Heir of Francois I. King of France from 1547 to 1559.

***Historia Augusta*.** A collection of incomplete biographies on Rome's emperors and figures of note. Possibly written by six authors – its date is questionable, as is its credibility.

Horace (65–8 BCE). Poet of the Augustan age whose works include the *Ars Poetica*.

Hôtel des Invalides (also known as Les Invalides). Founded by Louis XIV in c.1671 as a home (and hospital) for injured and aged war veterans. This extensive Parisian complex was restored by Napoleon I, who now rests beneath its majestic dome.

Hymen. Greek God of marriage and attendant of Venus.

La Fontaine (1621–95). French poet remembered especially for his *Fables*, which drew (in part) from the antique.

Laocoön **(the).** Discovered by a farmer in Rome and considered the most famous sculpture from antiquity at the time of the 1798 *Entrée triomphale*.

Le Nôtre (1613–1700). Acclaimed for his landscape designs at Versailles – also designed the Champs-Élysées and the Tuileries gardens, as well as those of châteaux such as Chantilly, Marly, Saint-Cloud and Vaux-le-Vicomte.

Le Vau (1612–70). French architect famous for his many designs, not least those for the palaces of Versailles and the Louvre.

Livy (59 BCE–17 CE). Roman historian and writer of *Ab Urbe Condita*: a monumental history of Rome and its people from the city's legendary foundation to 9 BCE.

Louis-Philippe I. Reigned from 1830 to 1848 (the 'July Monarchy'). The last king of France, as opposed to France's last sovereign, Napoleon III.

Machiavelli (1469–1527). Influential Italian statesman and philosopher of the Renaissance.

Maecenas (c.70–8 BCE). Roman statesman, influential adviser to Octavian and patron of Augustan poets.

Marcellus (88–40 BCE). Senator and five times consul of the Roman Republic.

Medici (the). Powerful Italian family of bankers and merchants whose influence in Florence began in the late fourteenth century – in 1569 the Medici became grand dukes of Tuscany. They produced four popes and the regent queens of France, Catherine and Marie de Medici. Their most famous and influential member, Lorenzo de Medici (1449–92), is known especially for his contribution to the early Italian Renaissance and the Golden Age of Florence.

Minerva (Greek Athena). Goddess of wisdom. With Juno and the chief god of the Roman state, Jupiter, she formed part of the Capitoline triad.

Molière (1622–73). French dramatist and author of major works such as *Tartuffe*.

Montesquieu. His Rome inspired works – notably, *De l'esprit des lois* (1748) – were to have a significant impact upon French (and especially American) republican ideology.

Napoleon III. Emperor of France (1852–70: Second Empire). His name – with that of the eminent city planner Baron Haussmann – is synonymous with the most striking transformation of Paris and the city's *re*-creation as a 'new' Rome.

Ovid (*c*.43 BCE–17 CE). Augustan poet famous for works such as the *Amores*, *Fasti* and the epic, *Metamorphoses*.

Petrarch (1304–74). Italian scholar, poet and humanist – an important figure in the rediscovery of classical antiquity.

Pliny the Elder (*c*.23–79 CE). Roman senator and author of the fascinating encyclopaedic *Natural History*. Died during the eruption of Vesuvius.

Pliny the Younger (*c*.61–112 CE). Senator and nephew of the elder Pliny. Known for his *Letters* and a panegyric of Trajan.

Plutarch (*c*.46–120 CE). Greek philosopher and biographer known especially for his *Parallel Lives* – only two biographies of Rome's emperors survive (Galba and Otho).

Polybius (*c*.200–118 BCE). Greek historian whose partially extant work describes Rome and its rise to power from 220–146 BCE.

Pompey the Great (106–48 BCE). Roman general and statesman whose achievements include the defeat of the Mediterranean pirates.

Propertius (*c*.50–16 BCE). Poet – certain works written under Augustus.

Quadriga. A chariot drawn by four horses.

Quatremère de Quincy (1755–1849). French philosopher *and* architectural theorist *cum* armchair archaeologist. Like Canova, known also for his concern regarding the treatment of antiquity's material culture under Napoleon.

Racine (1639–99). Influential French dramatist. His classically inspired works include *Phèdre* and *Andromaque*.

Renaissance (the). Although it appears to have begun in Florence in the early fourteenth century and was to reach its apex (in Florence, Rome and Venice) from the end of the fifteenth century, it did not reach France and the rest of Western Europe until the early sixteenth century – it then thrived for a century or more.

Republican Calendar. Technically it began in Year I of the French Republic (September 1792) but was only in use from 1793 (Year II). It then lived on for 12 years until 1805 (and was readopted for several days by the Paris Commune in 1871).

Romanitas. A term used in this book to imply 'Romanness' within a generalized context, not to be confused with the Fascist ideal of *romanità* and the heritage of ancient Rome during the leadership of Benito Mussolini (1922–43).

Rousseau. See Enlightenment (the).

Rubicon (the). The shallow river (and ancient frontier between Gaul and Italy) that Caesar led his army across in 49 BCE.

Salutatio. In ancient Roman society, a daily ritual whereby a wealthy patron received clients in his house.

Sans-culottes. Radical republicans from the lower classes during the 1789 French Revolution (literally, those without silk knee-breeches).

Scipio Aemilianus (*c.*185–129 BCE). Distinguished Roman general and politician, and adopted son of Scipio Africanus.

Scipio Africanus (236–184 BCE). General and politician, famous for his military prowess and defeat of Hannibal.

Senator. Member of the Roman Senate: political institution (with varying levels of power) which began with the traditional foundation of Rome (753 BCE) and spanned the monarchical period, and the Republican and Imperial periods.

Senatus PopulusQue Romanus. SPQR (the Senate and People of Rome). See Senator.

Serlio (1475–1554). Renowned Italian architect and theorist whose multivolume treatise on architecture, *Tutte l'opere d'architettura et prospettiva*, included classically inspired visual stimuli and also passages on the sociopolitical role of spectacle *all'antica*.

Strabo. Geographer, historian and philosopher from Amaesia in modern Turkey. His most famous work, *Geography*, described many aspects of the places and people of the world he knew in the first-century CE.

Suetonius (*c.*70–130 CE). Biographer and author of the animated *Lives of the Caesars* (from Julius Caesar to Domitian).

Surintendant des bâtiments. The title attributed to the official in charge of royal buildings.

Tacitus (*c.* 56–118 CE). Roman senator and author of works such as the *Annals* and *Histories* of the Roman Empire.

Tarquinius Priscus. According to tradition, the fifth of early Rome's seven kings.

Thermae. Large and complex Roman baths within which were the *frigidarium* (an unheated room with cold pool), the *tepidarium* (a warm room with or without tepid pool), the *caldarium* (the hottest room and pool) and additional public spaces, such as the *palaestra* (a colonnaded exercise area).

Tribune. A collective title for elected officials whose powers during the Roman Republic included the right of veto and more.

Valerius Maximus. Latin author under the Emperor Tiberius. His anecdotal *Facta et Dicta Memorabilia*, for example, attempts to unravel certain complexities of the Republican triumph.

Varro (*c.*116–27 BCE). Roman scholar and satirist whose many works covered subjects such as philosophy, the Latin language and agriculture.

Vasari (1511–74). Italian painter, architect and biographer.

Venus (Greek Aphrodite). Goddess of love and divine mother of Aeneas.

Virgil (c.70–19 BCE). Prolific poet of the Augustan age whose works include the *Aeneid*, the *Eclogues* and the *Georgics*.

Virtus. May be translated as 'virtue', 'courage' or 'manliness'. Ancient writers who place emphasis on Roman *virtus* include Livy and Pliny the Elder.

Vitruvius (c.80–18 BCE). Roman engineer and architect whose *De architectura* – the only surviving treatise on architecture from antiquity – was composed during the later part of Augustan rule.

Notes

Introduction

1. Bonaparte 1798: Hautecoeur 1953:149, Vol. V. All translations are my own, unless stated otherwise. When speaking of Napoleon before his Coronation in 1804, I refer to him generally as 'Bonaparte'.
2. Fundamental to Charlemagne's favourable reception under Napoleon was an underlying perception of the sovereign as a national saviour free from associations with France's deposed monarchy.
3. The term 'Capitol' is ambiguous: Edwards 1996:69–70. In this book the Capitol and the Temple(s) of Jupiter are synonymous, while the hill upon which the temple(s) stood is referred to as the Capitoline (or *Capitolium*).
4. For example, see Versnel 1970:388–9.
5. Montesquieu 1999:123.
6. See Jenkins 1995.
7. Huet 1999:53–69. For thought-provoking discussion of Napoleon as a 'new Augustus', as well as that of a direct link between Napoleon's 'new Rome' and his later affiliation with the Emperor Trajan, see Tollfree 1999. Less detailed analyses include Driault 1942:134–5; Edwards 1999:11; Wyke 2008:80–157.
8. Huet 1999, esp. 64.
9. An inscription beneath a portrait of Henri IV read: 'During the reign of this great king, very clement, very valiant, very just, Paris is as Rome was under Augustus, the wonder of the world'. Trans. Ballon 1991:231.
10. Equally essential to an understanding of this topic is Wyke 2008. See also Griffin ed. 2009 (esp. Ch. 27). Further scholarship on reception within Classics includes Hardwick 2003; Mardindale and Thomas eds 2006; Kallendorf ed. 2007; Hardwick and Stray eds 2008; Brockliss, Chaudhuri, Haimson Lushkov and Wasdin eds 2012.
11. The many tantalisingly brief references to the interrelationship of Napoleon, antiquity and pre-1789 receptions of antiquity include Haskell and Penny 1981:5; Huet 1996:13; Tollfree 1999.
12. Hemmerle 2006:300.
13. 'Revolutions and "progressive movements" which break with the past, by definition, have their own relevant past, though it may be cut off at a certain date, such as 1789'. Hobsbawm 1983:2.

14 See endnote 13. Hobsbawm 1983:14, however, does emphasize the 'curious, but understandable, paradox' that the ideology of 'modern nations' is generally embedded in 'the remotest antiquity'.
15 Horne 2002:207.
16 Hazareesingh 2004a:175 for discussion. Also, see Bury and Tombs 1986.
17 For instance, Lowrie 2003:57 explores the implications of Rome's many 'layers'. For Rome's 'multiple' and 'conflicting signification' see Edwards 1999:3.
18 Lefebvre 2003:21–2, trans. Bononno.
19 Legrand and Landon 1818:17–18, Vol. I – although I have drawn on the later 1818 edition, the first was published in 1806 (during Napoleon's rule).
20 Legrand and Landon 1818:18, Vol. 1.
21 Stirling 2006:77.
22 Strabo, *Geography*: 5.3.8.

Chapter 1

1 *Journal de Paris*, No. 309, 27 July 1798:1295: see Appendix I for the *version originale*. When newspapers from the French Republic are employed in this book, the dates supplied are translated into a Gregorian format. Of the works addressing the etymology of symbolism associated with the 'new' Republican calendar see, for example, Gombrich 1999:169–70.
2 Mercier 1979:230, Vol. X.
3 On the *Laöcoon* see Pliny the Elder, *Natural History*: 36.37.
4 MacKendrick 1972:215.
5 See Honour 1991:43–50. Cooley 2003 provides a revealing account of the antique city's rather dubious 'reawakening' both prior to and during Napoleonic rule.
6 Similarly, volume II of Winckelmann's seminal *The History of the Art of Antiquity* (1764) was translated from German into French, and published in 1802 and 1803 (Volume I had been published in 1794).
7 Chateaubriand 1995:145–7: this edition includes his journal and a selection of letters he sent from Italy between 1803 and 1804.
8 Discussed in Johns 1998:194, from whom I borrow the term 'decontextualized'.
9 See Las Cases 1983:453, *Mémorial I*.
10 Goalen 1995:181–90 for discussion.
11 Cooley 2003:74–9.
12 See Hibbert 1985:200–2.
13 Dolan 2001:51–2.
14 Seta (de) 1996:18. Dolan 2001: Chapter 7 discusses additional factors contributing to the death of the Grand Tour. This is not to say that Rome did not continue

Notes 179

to fascinate certain travellers, as Salmon's comprehensive English guide (1800) demonstrates.
15 MacKendrick 1972:234.
16 See Caillat 2005:223-41.
17 Gaillard 1998:8.
18 On the Roman 'language of power' see Wallace-Hadrill 1990:143-81.
19 Recent works on Roman structures as 'speaking' monuments include Brilliant 2007; Hölscher 2004; Stirling 2006.
20 MacDonald 1986:83-4.
21 Ibid. 80, 84.
22 Discussion and examples of these categories are supplied in Dupavillon and Lacloche 1989:15-16, 26; MacDonald 1986:75-99.
23 Bausset (de) 1829:175-6, 179, Vol. IV.
24 Ibid.
25 On the (Tiberian?) Arc d'Orange see Ferris 2011:192-6; D. Kleiner 1992:154; F. Kleiner 1989:204-6; Stirling 2006:76.
26 Hazareesingh 2004a:151, 153-4 addresses the Wimille column (on which work began in 1810).
27 From the wealth of material on Augustus see Matyszak 2006: esp. Ch. 4; Raaflaub and Toher eds 1990; Syme 1960; Zanker 1988. For an extensive bibliography and wide-ranging discussions including those by Wallace-Hadrill and Favro see Galinsky ed. 2005. Of the many works on Caesar see Canforo 2007; P. Freeman 2008; Matyszak 2006:esp. Ch. 3; Wyke ed. 2006 and Wyke 2008.
28 *CIL* 5. 7817: Espérandieu 1907:10.
29 Suetonius, *Augustus*: 28: trans. Graves.
30 See Driault 1942:134-5; Perouse de Montclose 1969a:78.
31 On the implications of 'tourism' in pre- and post-modern societies see Urry 1990.
32 Dwyer 2004b:402. Additionally, Dwyer 2007: Ch. 1-2; also Forrest 2011 esp. Ch. 2: an equally informative introduction to Bonaparte's youth and 'Corsican beginnings'.
33 See Lyons 1994:186-7.
34 Discussed by Ellis 1997:11-13.
35 Detail in Ellis 1997: Ch. 2, esp. 13.
36 For example, Tulard ed. 2001: esp. Ch. 13 examines Bonaparte's notes on Rollin's eighteenth-century *Histoire ancienne*. On Bonaparte's earlier pieces see Dwyer 2004b. The appendix of Healey 1957 includes a table with the titles and dates of all relevant manuscripts from 1786-95.
37 Tulard ed. 2001:91.
38 Works on Bonaparte's earlier military activity include Broers 2005: Emsley 2003:9-31; Forrest 2011: esp. Ch. 3-4.
39 On the division of the *epoca francese* in 'Italy' into two distinct phases: the revolutionary triennium (1796-9) and the Napoleonic period (1800-15) see Grab

2004:4, 6. For those placed in charge of the First Empire's kingdoms and satellite kingdoms see Tulard 2002:18–25.
40 For instance, *Le Moniteur Universel*, No. 56, 25 February 1810.
41 Ridley 1992:5–8.
42 Tournon (de) 1855:259, Vol. II. The less savoury side to Napoleonic rule, however, is apparent in his reference to the regime's 'injustice flagrante' Ibid.
43 Vandiver Nicassio 2005:35 for discussion (the author's *Imperial City: Rome under Napoleon* differs only in that it was published in 2009 with The University of Chicago Press). The project, nevertheless, remained unfinished under Napoleon.
44 On Roman *horti* and the concept of 'Country in Town' see Purcell 1987.
45 Tournon (de) 1855:262, Vol. II.
46 Johns 1998:78–9.
47 Ibid.
48 Vandiver Nicassio 2005:35, 184. Also, see Ridley 1992: for example, 64, 68–70, 86, 143–4.
49 Part of a decree dating to 17 February 1810 announced: 'The city of Rome is the second city of the Empire': Driault 1942:153.
50 Tournon (de) 1855:156–7, Vol. II.
51 By 1812, external complications and the reserve felt by a portion of French society combined to undermine Napoleon's position. The possession of Rome by the King of Naples in 1814 and the reinstatement of Pius VII marked the end of Napoleonic control.
52 Leith 1991:307; Vaulchier (de) 1989:255–9. For a brief overview of the 1789 French Revolution see Appendix II.
53 Connelly 2006:19–20.
54 Johns 1998:1.
55 See Leith 1991:173; also Etlin 1994:18–21.
56 Interestingly, Lee 1999:5 comments that the term 'Neoclassicism' was not used until the 1880s, and that David would have viewed his works in the Grand Manner style.
57 Discussed by Honour 1991:71–2; Lee 1999:87–95.
58 Porterfield and Siegried 2006:118.
59 On the appropriation of Republican Rome in the revolutionaries' quest to project a new beginning see Edwards 1999:8–9; Leigh 1979:155–60.
60 Shovlin 2006:24–5.
61 Ibid.
62 Malamud 2006:148–54 for discussion. Edwards 1999:9 also notes that soon after the 'revolutions' of America and France, like-minded regimes sought to exploit Democratic Athens rather than Republican Rome. On the adoption of the former in revolutionary America (and France) see C. Freeman 1996:558–60, though he remarks that Rome still remained *the* popular model for most Republicans.

63 Malamud 2006:148–54.
64 See Leigh 1979:156–60; also Lee 1999:184.
65 Huet 1999:53.
66 See Huet 1999:53; Tulard 1971:188–9.
67 C. Freeman 1996:558 notes the inscription and its relevance to the link between the transformation of Paris under Louis XIV and that of Augustan Rome. Also, see Burke 1992:195.
68 Apostolidès 1981:67–8.
69 It should therefore be understood that whenever I refer to either Louis XIV or to Napoleon as a 'new', a 'modern' or an 'improved' Augustus, that I do so with these considerations in mind.
70 Hazareesingh 2004a:4. Scholars who envisage the Napoleonic myth and legend as a singular phenomenon include Tulard 1971.
71 Hazareesingh Ibid. 4–7.
72 On Rousseau's works and the 'myth of antiquity' see Leigh 1979. The monthly series of *Studies on Voltaire and the Eighteenth Century (SVEC)* provides many relevant references to Rousseau.
73 Discussed by Martindale 9–11 in Martindale and Thomas eds 2006.
74 Huet 1999:56. Additionally, see Ellis 1997:227–8 who argues that Napoleon's own hand testifies to the interrelated influence both of Charlemagne and Rome, and also that such parallels reinforced his ultimate superiority over history's most celebrated heroes. Siegfried's argument (Porterfield and Siegfried 2006:80) that Charlemagne became increasingly less popular as a Napoleonic model – as related symbolism decreased after 1806 – underlines how the 'Carolingian analogy' remains a hotbed of scholarly debate. See also Jourdan 2004:26; Ruiz 2004:26–9.
75 Amaury-Duval in Baltard 1802: opening page.
76 Tulard 1971:34. Names of note from a more recent past include the military strategist and patron of the arts, 'Frederick the Great' of Prussia (1712–86) and also Lorenzo de Medici.
77 Dwyer 2004b:389 notes that the royalist *Messager du Soir* had been warning against Bonaparte's dictatorial ambitions. He cites an excerpt from 1797, in which unfavourable links between the two dictators were explicit: 'Is the Rubicon already crossed . . . will we avoid a military Republic by going to prostrate ourselves at the feet of the dictator?'
78 Canforo 2007:xii; Mackenzie 2006:131–2 for discussion.
79 Canforo 2007:xii.
80 Wintjes 2006:277–9. See also Wyke 2008: esp. 79–80, 156–66.
81 For instance, Las Cases 1983:575, *Mémorial II*.
82 See Canforo 2007:xiii; Hemmerle 2006:286–7; Tulard 1965:219.
83 Plutarch, *Caesar*: 15, trans. Perrin.

84 Anonymous 1800:10–11. Although this politically motivated pamphlet was circulated anonymously, it has been attributed to Bonaparte's brother, Lucien. See, for example, Wyke 2008:157.
85 Thibaudeau 1913:27.
86 Norvins (de) 1896:221, Vol. II.
87 Ibid. 251.
88 Ibid. 225.
89 See Zanker 1998, in which the interrelationship between Augustus' political agenda and the media used to project his image is explored to great effect.
90 Noted by Lyons 1994:178; also Forrest 2004.
91 For instance, Dwyer 2004a:350 and 2004b:381; Jourdan 2004:17.
92 Discussion includes Bosséno 1998:449–65 and his article in the exhibition catalogue for *1796-1797 – Da Montenotte a Campoformio: la rapida marcia di Napoleone Bonaparte* 1997:54–7. Bosséno also addresses the 'role' played by Bonaparte in similar paintings from this period, as does Mazzocca Ibid. 49–53.
93 Dwyer 2004b:381.
94 Lee 1999:233.
95 Boime 1990:39–40, 43–4.
96 See Laird Kleine-Ahlbrandt 2004:95–6.
97 Additional analyses of the painting include Lee 1999:233; Hazareesingh 2004a:174.
98 Discussed by Porterfield and Siegfried 2006:25–114; Ruiz 2004:26.
99 On the propagandist nature of these paintings see Lee 1999:239–68; Lyons 1994:192–3. On the Roman imagery and references to Charlemagne in David's *Coronation* see Porterfield and Siegfried 2006:115–72.
100 Healey 1957:16.
101 Ellis 1997:158.
102 Napoleon's address to the *Conseil d'État*: Regenbogen 1998:123.
103 Ribner 1993:30–5 for discussion.
104 See Ribner 1993:30.
105 Lyons 1994:193. This painting, however, was not commissioned by Napoleon.
106 Noted in Driskel 1993; Hazareesingh 2004a.
107 See Hazareesingh 2004a; Tulard 1965 and 1971. Jourdan 2004:204 also includes more recent examples, including the links created between Napoleon and Adolf Hitler (1889–1945) though, as she rightly remarks, 'En tant que dictateur, Napoléon n'a rien a voir avec les monstres enfantés par le xxe siècle'.
108 Discussed by Boudon 2004:22–5; Hazareesingh 2004a:167. On Charlet's 1842 frontispiece see Driskel 1993:68–70.
109 This was manifest in the ritual of *passaggiata*, and also in an emperor's presence at the *thermae* and public spectacles: for instance, Suetonius, *Titus*: 8. Relevant scholarly works include Stirling 2006:76–9; also Wallace-Hadrill 1990 on Rome and the 'language of power'.

110 Gregory 1994:83–4.
111 Plutarch, *Marcellus*: 8.
112 Östenberg 2009:10 notes the impact of the triumphal procession on the senses and its importance as a 'boiling-pot of full emotions'.
113 The first French newspaper – *La Gazette* – appeared under Louis XIII. Roche 1989: esp. pp. 5–7 discusses the heightened accent on censorship under Louis XIV.
114 'La Liberté de la Presse' was proclaimed in June 1789 and abolished in August 1792.
115 The printed word, theatre, opera and art were also subject to Napoleon's strict censorship. Drama had the added advantage of appealing to the lower classes (and did not necessitate literacy): Forrest 2004:427, 441–2.
116 Mazedier 1945:53. Additionally, see Hanley 2008: a detailed study of Bonaparte and the press from 1796–9.
117 *Le Moniteur Universel*, No. 86, 27 March 1810:343; No. 89, 30 March 1810:353–5, 360.
118 *Journal de l'Empire*, 1 April 1810:1.
119 Ibid.
120 Ibid.
121 Ibid.
122 Ibid.
123 Ibid.

Chapter 2

1 Amaury-Duval 1802:1 in the 'description historique' to Baltard's *Paris et ses monuments*.
2 For instance, Loyer's *Histoire de l'architecture française* . . . 1999.
3 Etlin 1994:1.
4 Lefebvre 1991:222, trans. Nicholson-Smith.
5 Napoleon's Austerlitz victory took place on 2 December 1805.
6 On the use of the Arc de Triomphe and Champs-Élysées as backdrops for triumphal activity see Gaillard 1998:106–15: examples include the role played by arch and avenue following the liberation of Paris (1944).
7 For instance, see Bausset (de) 1829:175–6, Vol. IV.
8 Lyons 1994:188.
9 Suetonius, *Domitian*: 13, trans. Graves.
10 Herein the avenue is referred to as the Champs-Élysées.
11 Rome's tallest extant triumphal arch, the Arch of Constantine, stands at 21.10 m: Derderian 1991:86. Paris' Arc de Triomphe is 49.54 m. high, its length is 44.82 m. and width 22.21 m.

12 Bourrienne (de) 1829:38–9, Vol. IV – although invaluable as a source, these memoirs should be read with caution and could also be apocryphal.
13 On the trouble-ridden construction of the Arc de Triomphe see Muratori-Philip 2007:3–11.
14 Works addressing Napoleon's camouflage of the arch as a celebration of his *gloire personelle* include Hautecoeur 1953:148, Vol. V.
15 *Correspondance de Napoléon Ier*, No. 10235, 14 May 1806: Lanzac de Laborie 1905:251–2, Vol. II.
16 Garraffoni and Stoiani 2006:218 supply additional examples.
17 For contemporary newspaper coverage of the event see notes 117–23 of ch. 1.
18 Lefebvre 1991:244. Lefebvre mistakenly names Romulus' brother, Remus, as Rome's (legendary) founder and the individual who 'described a circle with his plough'.
19 Lefebvre 1991:244.
20 Ibid. 245: trans. Nicholson-Smith.
21 Etlin 1994:2–3 speaks of Paris in general.
22 Reported in Jouin, *Inventaire Général des Richesses d'Art de la France . . .* 1879:166, Vol. I.
23 MacDonald 1986:75, Vol. II.
24 Kostof 1991:263–4; MacDonald 1986:75–7, Vol. II.
25 Kostof 1991:263.
26 MacDonald 1986:77, Vol. II.
27 Reported in Jouin, *Inventaire Général des Richesses d'Art de la France . . .* 1879: 165–6, Vol. I.
28 Ibid.
29 Ibid. 166.
30 Pure (de) 1972:123–4, 120. For reference to the pivotal role of the Arc de Triomphe in Napoleon's 'revival of Roman imperial iconography' see Kostof 1991:268.
31 Lefebvre 1991:244–5.
32 Claridge 1998:116–18. See also Arce in *LTUR*, Vol. I (A–C), Steinby ed. 1993:109–11. For reference to the influence of the Arch of Titus upon the Arc de Triomphe see Fernandes et al. 2000:6 and especially Bausset (de) 1829:175–6; 179.
33 Kostof 1991:271–2.
34 Las Cases 1983:125, *Mémorial II*.
35 Ibid.; Ovid, *Fasti*: 2.683–4: Östenberg 2009:292.
36 Östenberg Ibid.
37 Ibid.
38 See Wisch 1990.
39 Detail in Kostof 1991:272; Etlin 1994:4.
40 Ironically, war with Napoleon put paid to the building of London's processional route.

41 Reported in Bausset (de) 1829:179, Vol. IV.
42 On the symbolic link between the Arc de Triomphe as a marker signalling the entrance to Imperial Paris and the Porte Saint-Denis heralding the entrance to the royal city, see Perouse de Montclos 1969a:70.
43 Lowrie 2003:57.
44 For instance, Soja 1996:72; Lefebvre 1991 and 2003.
45 Etlin 1994; Leith 1991.
46 Etlin 1994:1 as noted in the introduction to this chapter.
47 Lowrie 2003:57. Lowrie's argument finds parallels with Lefebvre and Soja (above) whose more complex analyses explore to great effect the interplay between physical and cognitive aspects of space.
48 See especially the introduction to Marrinan 2009:1–3; also his comment that 'Napoléon used monuments to forge memories that would *shape* history, not simply challenge it': Marrinan 2009:45.
49 See Kostof 1991:226.
50 Year II began on 22 September 1793.
51 See Szambien 1986:53–4.
52 Poyet 1799:8.
53 The *barrières* were also known as *Propylées* in imitation of the entrance pavilions to the Acropolis.
54 Discussed by Etlin 1994:35.
55 Trans. Etlin 1994:35. Discussion also includes Chadych and Leborgne 1999:108.
56 Earlier classically inspired projects associated with this space are discussed by Etlin 1994:33 and Perouse de Montclos 1969b:169.
57 Legrand and Landon 1809:47, Vol. II, Section III. Also, see an 1818 edition of Vol. II:118.
58 Quoted in Driault 1942:96–7.
59 On Napoleon's personal wishes regarding the unification of the palaces see Percier and Fontaine: *Parallèle* 1833a: especially the section starting on p. 53 (1973 edition), in which we see the difficulties of the buildings' slightly different axes. Napoleon's orders concerning the erection of the arch and the implementation of further alterations to the complex are discussed by Bausset (de) 1829:126–9, Vol. IV.
60 Plutarch, *Marcellus*: 8.
61 Ibid.
62 See *Le Moniteur Universel*, No. 2, 2 January 1806:10. Scholarly discussion of the link includes Duncan and Wallach 1980:449, 459; Leith 1991:26; Tollfree 1999: for example, 98, 150.
63 Amaury-Duval in Baltard 1802:41. See also Bausset (de) 1829:233, Vol. IV.
64 Mainardi 1989:155. Equally, see Miles 2008:323.
65 Mainardi Ibid.

66 Johns 1998:11,194. On the regime's justification of the looting, as well as the (part) restitution of these treasures once Napoleon was no longer in power see especially Mainardi 1989:156-7;160-1; also Miles 2008:326-7.
67 Works on the Severan arch include Brilliant in *LTUR*, Vol. I (A–C), Steinby ed. 1993:103-5; Claridge 1998:75-6; Hannestad 1986:262-7; F. Kleiner 2007:238-40; Ramage and Ramage 2009:287-9.
68 See Driault 1942:147. Tollfree 1999:164-205 provides a fuller discussion of the Arc du Carrousel: its function, siting and iconography are combined with an analysis of Napoleon's 'forum' and that of Rome. The additional relevance of Milan's Forum Bonaparte (1806) is broached: on the project's arena and Arco del Sempione see also Perouse de Montclos 1969a:74.
69 The (then) Place de la Révolution (originally Place Louis XV) received its present name under Napoleon.
70 Poyet 1799:3.
71 It is unclear whether the group – which might be attributed to the Greek sculptor, Lysippos – was Roman booty, or which of Rome's triumphal arches it had adorned.
72 *Le Patriote Français*, No. 304, 22 July 1798:1219.
73 Legrand and Landon 1809:20, Vol. II.
74 Constans and Salmon eds 1998:39-40 for discussion: additional plans included an amphitheatre resembling the Colosseum and the Theatre of Marcellus.
75 On the National Palace and the Republic's transformation of Paris' political centre: Leith 1991:154-5.
76 The link between Napoleon, the area's symbolic language and antique Rome is discussed by Tollfree 1999:175.
77 The origins of this stretch beyond Roman times and can be traced to the fortifications of Mesopotamia, Palestine and Egypt: Baldwin Smith 1978:11. Man's basic desire to display his status through his dwelling and its entrance also predates Roman times and this, too, was translated into a contemporary context by the Romans in, for example, the ritual of *salutatio*.
78 Quoted in Gaillard 1996:94.
79 See Bausset (de) 1829:119, 172-3, 187-8, Vol. IV.
80 Fontaine: n.p., reproduced in Baltard's *Arc de triomphe du Carrousel* (folio edition 1875). This and subsequent references to the work are cited as 'Fontaine in Baltard 1875'. Jouin also provides a fund of relevant information in *Inventaire Général des Richesses d'Art* ... 1879:245-59, Vol. I.
81 For the inscriptions see *CIL* 6.1033=*ILS* 425; *CIL* 6.31230.
82 Works on the Arch of Constantine include Brilliant 2007:9-10; Capodiferro in *LTUR*, Vol. I (A-C), Steinby ed. 1993:86-91; Claridge 1998:272-6; F. Kleiner 2007:294-6; Ramage and Ramage 2009:344-9. For the inscriptions see *CIL* 6. 1139=*ILS* 694.

Notes

83 Discussed by Legrand and Landon 1809:49, Vol. II, Section III. Also, Fouché 1907:93.
84 Of the many scholars who highlight the antique group's importance see Lanzac de Laborie 1905:180, Vol. II; Poisson 2002:115–17.
85 Legrand and Landon 1809:49, Vol. II, Section III.
86 In his capacity as Director of Museums, Denon 'acquired' numerous treasures from Europe (and Italy) with which to furnish the Louvre's *Musée Napoléon*.
87 Fontaine in Baltard 1875:7.
88 Montesquieu 1999:122–3.
89 Tollfree 1999:150, 164–205. The only doubtful aspect of this compelling (and detailed) study of the 'forum Napoléon' (in which Napoleon's wish to be considered the 'Empereur des Français' is recognized) lies with the underlying argument that the redevelopment of this area be seen as a deliberate ploy both to recreate Augustan Rome and underscore Napoleon's affiliation with Augustus.
90 For instance, *Le Moniteur Universel*, No. 89, 1810:355.
91 Percier and Fontaine 1833b:42. See also Fontaine in Baltard 1875:10.
92 Percier and Fontaine 1833b:42. The inscriptions were never realized under Napoleon; those visible today date to the reign of Louis-Philippe.
93 Percier and Fontaine 1833b:42.
94 Napoleon's return to power before his second abdication on 22 June 1815 is known as 'les Cent-Jours'.
95 See Varner in Varner ed. 2001:19 and Flower in Varner Ibid.:65, within which are similarly illustrative examples of Rome's *damnatio memoriae* – 'a modern umbrella term' which covers various post-mortem actions taken against an individual's memory and/or monuments: Varner ed. 2001: footnote 4.
96 Fontaine in Baltard 1875:11.
97 Enough of the original iconographical programme has been restored to allow a more than adequate analysis of the monument. Further, Baltard 1875:1–16 provides a fascinating overview of the alterations and also exquisite pictorial representations of the original reliefs.
98 See note 31 of this chapter and the associated text.
99 The ceremonial route created by the building of the Rue de Rivoli does not follow a totally straight line: once reaching the Place de la Concorde, it meets a staggered junction of sorts, and then continues its course along the Champs-Élysées. The Tuileries gardens also lead onto the Place de la Concorde, but join the square at a central point, thus forming part of the perspective (and *axe historique*) which today begins at the Louvre's 'La cour Napoléon' and stretches to the Arc de Triomphe and beyond.
100 On the Rue de Rivoli and its environs see Gaillard 1996:110–16; Poisson 2002:68–71.
101 Leith 1991:95–9 for discussion.

102 For example, detail in Brilliant 1984; Claridge 1993:8–22; Galinier 2007; Lepper and Frere 1988. Works on Roman imagery which address Trajan's Column include Brilliant 2007:12; F. Kleiner 2007:159–62; Ramage and Ramage 2009:213–20; Stirling 2006:76; Veyne 2002:3–4.
103 *Le Moniteur Universel*, No. 2, 2 January 1806. The relationship between the Vendôme Column and Napoleon's image as a 'modern' emperor is noted by Huet 1999:64. See also Huet 1996:9–24; Grell 1998:251.
104 *Le Moniteur Universel*, No. 2, 2 January 1806:11.
105 For glowing accounts of the links between the two structures see Cally 1810a:1–5; Legrand and Landon 1809:18, Vol. II, Section III.
106 A collection of Percier's *Envois* – including Antoine-Laurent-Thomas Vaudoyer's *Mémoire historique* (1839) – is provided in *Restaurations des monuments antiques par les architectes pensionnaires de l'Académie de France à Rome depuis 1788 jusqu'à nos jours* (1877).
107 See Agosti, Farinella, Morel and Simoncini eds 1988: the exhibition catalogue for *La colonna Traiana e gli artisti francesi da Luigi XIV a Napoleoni I* (Villa Medici); also Haskell and Penny 1981:6, 46–7; Galinier 2007:69.
108 Noted by Grell 1988:251.
109 Chambray (de) 2005:139.
110 Tollfree 1999:208. See also Huet 1996:13, and Ibid. 1999:63, in which she comments on the cast undertaken under Napoleon III who, like Napoleon I, and both Louis XIV and François I, went to great lengths to reinvent the ideology and symbolism of Imperial Rome.
111 See Leith 1991:157–8; Szambien 1986:59–60.
112 Leith 1991:68–9. Similar plans are supplied in Leith Ibid.; Folliot 1989:305–22; Hautecoeur 1953:138–9, Vol. V.
113 Trajan's Column is 39.8 m. high (with its statue); the Vendôme Column stands at 43.50 m.
114 See *Article III*, 1 October 1803 (*Archives Nationales*): Saint-Simon (de) 1982:122–3. Bonaparte had been responsible for the removal of the statue from Aix-la-Chapelle – once the seat of Charlemagne's great empire.
115 For instance, see Siegfried in Porterfield and Siegfried 2006:79–80.
116 Pliny, *Natural History*: 34.27.
117 Lefebvre 1991:236, 262, 287.
118 The panels' composition of captured canon was proposed by Denon. This calls to mind the influential role he played in the acquisition and transfer from Rome to the *Musée Napoléon* of the famous Borghese collection of antiquities. For a lively account of the column: Marrinan 2009: 114-22. On the Borghese treasures, Denon (and Ennio Quirino Visconti): Huet 1999: 61-3.
119 Pliny, *Natural History*: 34.43.
120 See Van Zanten 1994:109.

121 For instance, Bonaparte, *Article I*, 1 October 1803 (*Archives Nationales*): Poisson 2002:102. On the column see also Jouin in *Inventaire Général des Richesses d'Art . . .* 1879:343–65, Vol. I.
122 Tollfree examines the ideological and topographical implications of the square and column in relation to Napoleon's 'new Rome'. Bound intricately to this, however, is her argument that the column's construction was based on Napoleon's deliberate presentation as the 'new Trajan': for example, 1999:233–5.
123 The ceremony was also part of a national festival marking the first anniversary of the 'Consulat': it involved a second station at Place de la Concorde, a third at Les Invalides and a fourth in the Champ-de-Mars: Norvins (de) 1896:252–6, Vol. II.
124 Bausset (de) 1829:235. See also Norvins (de) 1896:221, 243, 245–55, Vol. II.
125 Various editions of *Le Moniteur Universel* published after Napoleon's victories reveal lengthy articles which glorify his heroic exploits abroad: for example, 2 January edition, No. 2, 1806:7.
126 See Cally 1810a:1.
127 Thibaudeau 1913:27 reaffirms the importance attached to the Place du Carrousel as a finishing point for the victorious troops on their return to Paris.
128 This is reinforced by analogies drawn between ancient Rome and the Napoleonic Empire in *Le Moniteur Universel*. Observe also, the reference to Napoleon's 'triomphe' and his subsequent image as '*triomphateur*' in Ibid., No 2, 2 January 1806:10–11.
129 See *Le Moniteur Universel*, No. 2, 2 January 1806:7. Norvins (de) 1896:245, 254–5, Vol. II supplies a personal account of Paris' celebrations after Napoleon's Marengo victory. Both he and Thibadeau provide vivid testimonies with which to substantiate my reconstruction. Their accounts also reinforce the 'Roman' nature of triumphal spectacle at this time.
130 Chaumont (de) 1854:3.
131 The monument (referred to mistakenly as a copy of Rome's 'Colonne Antonine') was open from 9 a.m. to 6 p.m. in the summer, and midday to 4 p.m. during the winter: anonymous 1818:3, 18.
132 Ibid. 18. See Appendix III.
133 Levebvre 1991:221. See also Cally 1810a:2.
134 Lefebvre Ibid.
135 For instance, Pliny *Natural History*: 34.27.
136 See Etlin 1994:37. Unsurprisingly, this subject has generated immense interest: discussion includes Lefebvre 1991:308; Van Zanten 1994 and Vaulchier (de) 1989:257.
137 On the fate of Chaudet's statue see Krief 2004:116–23.
138 Detail in Christ, Léri and Fierro 2002:132–3.
139 Only six of the column's bronze panels had to be remade from scratch: discussion in Saint-Simon (de) 1982:154. Also, see Driskel 1993:37–42; Haskell 1993, esp. Ch. 9.
140 Lefebvre 1991:222.

141 Harvey 1985:200–28. Also, see Southhall 1998:342–3.
142 Harvey 1985:215: discussion also includes the Communards' toppling of the Vendôme Column.
143 Ibid. 225.
144 One can only assume that Napoleon's visions in 1808 were linked to one of the three temples at S. Nicola in Carcere. Ancient references to Janus (the god of gates) and/or the illusive temple include Plutarch, *Life of Numa*: 20; Suetonius, *Life of Nero*: 13; Virgil, *Aeneid*: 7.595–625.
145 Bourrienne (de) 1829:52, Vol. IV. Although there is no date fixing when exactly Napoleon is recorded to have expressed these views, it would appear it was in (or just before) 1809.
146 Quoted in the introduction to this book.
147 Percier and Fontaine: Lanzac de Labori 1905:179, Vol. II.
148 Discussed in Gaillard 1996:16–17; Poisson 2002:131–3.
149 Under Napoleon III, additional Egyptian motifs such as the sphinxes were added. To make way for Baron Haussmann's redesign of the square, the structure was moved to the east by about 12 m.
150 Pliny, *Natural History*: 31.1–3; 36.121–4.
151 Quoted in Lavedan 1993:346.
152 For discussion of Napoleon's elephant project see especially Poisson 2002:203–10. On the symbolic history of the elephant see Capuano 1997:76–9.
153 Pliny, *Natural History*: 8.4. See also Plutarch, *Life of Pompey*: 14.6.
154 For discussion of the 1758 project: Gaillard 1998:23–4.
155 See Leith 1991:156–7; Szambien 1986:54–5.
156 Chateaubriand 1831: Poisson 2002:206. Victor Hugo's novel, *Les Misérables* (1862), was set in 1832: it provides a vivid impression of how the elephant fountain was perceived some years after Napoleon's death.
157 The elephant project was abandoned completely towards 1817–18. The Place de la Bastille remained empty until the erection of Louis-Philippe's Colonne de Juillet (1840–1) to commemorate the deaths incurred by the riots in July, 1830.
158 See Lavedan 1993:345–6; detail also supplied on pages 41–2 of this chapter.
159 On the relationship between Napoleon's visions for an arch in the Place de la Bastille and the location of Louis XIV's triumphal arch see Derderian 1991:86.
160 Detail in Jordan 1995:30–1.
161 For discussion of the reasons behind this change in route see Bryant 1986:211. On the prestige today attached to the east-west axis – notably the area related topographically to the triumphal way leading westward from the Louvre – see Lefebvre 2003:126–7.
162 Inevitably, there were exceptions to the rule, not least Louis XVIII's symbolic re-appropriation of the traditional kingly entrance into Paris via the Porte Saint-Denis (May 1814) as France's first post-revolutionary monarch: Marrinan 2009:47.
163 The pyramid is not quite in line with the exact path of the axis.

164 Discussion of the arch and earlier designs for the western section of the monumental perspective is provided in Dupavillon and Lacloche 1989.
165 The Grande Arche de la Défense is 110 m. high. The Arc de Triomphe stands at 49.54 m. and is over double the height of Rome's highest arch, the Arch of Constantine.
166 Driault 1942:92.
167 For a comprehensive analysis of Hitler's classically inspired visions and architectural projects see Scobie 1990. Losemann 1999:221–35 examines the 'Nazi concept' of ancient Rome.
168 Vuillaume n.d: quoted in Christ, Léri and Fierro 2002:133. Given the title of the work, 'Mes cahiers rouges au temps de la Commune', we may assume that it was written around 1871.
169 Lefebvre 1991:386–7, trans. Nicholson-Smith.

Chapter 3

1 Colbert 1669, trans. Ballon 1991:255.
2 Couture 1852:5.
3 Ibid. 6–7, 9. See also Black 1999:178 who notes that while the Napoleonic system became essentially monarchical, a major difference between it and pre-revolutionary France lay with the accent now placed upon obtaining a favourable opinion from the public.
4 Forrest 2011:232.
5 This is still more surprising given the number of studies devoted to Louis and an even greater number of works on Napoleon, not least those by eminent French historians, notably, Tulard, Lentz and Bély. In 2004 there was a heightened flood of French and non-French publications that coincided with the Bicentenary of Napoleon's Coronation and the founding of his empire: many of these stimulating works (such as those by Dwyer, Forrest, Jourdan and Hazareesingh) focus on the creation of Napoleon's legend and include aspects relating to his 'Roman' imagery, and yet the potential of developing this relationship with a view to the 'Roman' legacy of Louis XIV, remains largely unexplored. This is in stark contrast to the number of works on Napoleon and Charlemagne, and the major role played by Carolingian symbolism in the 1804 Coronation.
6 As demonstrated in Lister's *A Journey to Paris in the Year 1698*:1823:38, 69.
7 Leon 1970:287. Also, see Berger 1994:74.
8 Van Zanten 1994:113.
9 For instance, Lyons 1994:188.
10 Of the multitude of generalized references to Napoleon as the child (or heir) of the 1789 Revolution see Arnaud 2012:60.

11 Bluche 1984:100–5. See also Roudil 1984:106–7.
12 See Charles Perrault's *Mémoires de ma vie*:1993:254–5. Billaut's article 2011:44–9 is aptly entitled 'Jean-Baptiste Colbert: Le ministre absolu'.
13 Vasari: Haskell and Penny 1981:5. On the presentation of François I as a Roman emperor see Cleary 1999:134; for discussion of the capitals of Henri IV and Louis XIV: Ballon 1991:255.
14 For instance, Desgodetz 1682: Chs XVII, XVIII, XX.
15 Ibid. Chs XI, XVII, XVIII, XX.
16 See Apostolidès 1981:79, 87.
17 Burke 1992:195.
18 See Cleary 1999:135, 284.
19 Ibid. 135.
20 Discussed by Haskell and Penny 1981:43–5.
21 Burke 1992:49. See also Bluche 1984:102 who envisages Colbert as a 'nouveau Mécène' and Louis as a 'nouvel Auguste'. Barchiesi 2005:281 emphasizes the appropriation of Augustan models at the King's Court.
22 For example, Virgil, *Aeneid*: 8. 682–731.
23 Apostolidès 1981:116 and Burke 1992:126 observe the work's importance as a demonstration of the ongoing conflict between the 'ancients' and the 'moderns'.
24 See the introduction to the 1968 Loeb edition of *De re publica*: 1–8.
25 For example, Perrault 1979:18; Ibid. 79 for the citation of the poem. Similarly: Vertron (de) 1685:53 in which the age of Louis XIV is also seen to improve upon that of Augustus.
26 Burke 1992:59.
27 *Le Moniteur Universel*, No. 89, 30 March 1810:355.
28 The link between Colbert and Denon in their respective roles as managers of their patron's artistic and cultural policy is discussed by Forrest 2004:439.
29 Barker 2001:34–5.
30 Ibid. 42.
31 Ibid. 68.
32 Perrault 1979:20.
33 A letter to Colbert from Charles Perrault expressed the King's wishes that painting and sculpture make a special contribution to 'the transmission of his name to posterity': Burke 1992:153.
34 For example, Perrault 1979:94.
35 For instance, Perrault 1979:17. The text includes the *Epistre au Roy*, within which is further reference to the King's immortality and the future.
36 Of the many works on Voltaire and *Le Siècle de Louis XIV* see Pierse 2008:151–3. Also, the collection of papers in *SVEC 2006:10* including Mortgat-Longuet's analysis of the respective 'centuries' of Augustus and Louis:97–116.

Notes

37 On Napoleon's fifth 'Golden Age' of civilization see Broers 2005:15. On Voltaire's distinction between the King and the wonders of his age: Pierse 2008:151–2.
38 Similarities include the preponderance (and variety) of publicists and also the sovereigns' respective image-diffusing devices, while the differences include Augustus' post-Republic rise to power and the more populist front to his image: Burke 1992:195–7. Interestingly, the only reference made to Napoleon is in conjunction with both his and Louis' images as sovereigns who watched over their people while they rested: Ibid. 200.
39 Ibid. 4.
40 Ibid. 4–5; Veyne 2002:4.
41 For instance, see Napoleon, *Correspondance* No. 13358, 1807:164, Vol. 16.
42 Barker 2001:5.
43 *Le Moniteur Universel*, No. 73, 4 December 1804:280.
44 *Journal de l'Empire*, 1 April 1810:1–4. Newspapers such as the *Le Moniteur Universel* provide equally detailed pre-event information: No. 86, 27 March 1810:343; No. 89, 30 March 1810:353–60.
45 *Journal de l'Empire*, 1 April 1810:1.
46 Ibid.
47 For instance, Burke 1992:76 notes how the plain language of the *Gazette* tended to deviate from its somewhat cool tone only when it published special issues commemorating events such as the King's military victories and extraordinary spectacles.
48 *Le Moniteur Universel*, No. 73, 4 December 1804:280.
49 For instance, see Napoleon *Correspondance*, No.12415, 1807:97, Vol. 15.
50 See note 42 and accompanying text of this chapter; also Barker 2001:52, 83.
51 The compartmentalization of Rome's 'good' and 'bad' emperors is discussed by Varner 2001:9–10.
52 Observe, for example, the Arch of Constantine's inscription: *P(io) F(elici) Augusto S(enatus) P(opulus) Q(ue) R(omanus)*.
53 For example, Brice 1971:17, Vol. I: reproduced from the 9th edition (published posthumously in 1752). Certain other editions – such as those of 1687 and 1688 – had been translated into English.
54 Ibid.
55 Ibid. 233–4, Vol. II.
56 Gady 1999:50 for discussion.
57 Brice 1971:97–8, Vol. I.
58 See Dectot 1999:70–1. Also, Brice 1971:198, Vol. II for reference to other statues influenced by the Aurelian prototype, notably those of Henri IV and Louis XIII.
59 The former Porte Saint-Denis (the second of this name) had formed part of Charles V's *enceinte*. Works on Blondel's arch include Gady 1999:53–4; Chadych and Leborgne

1999:82–3; Saurat and Devignac 1990:90–1. Also, see Cally 1810b:1–2; Legrand and Landon 1809:41–4, Vol. II; Sauval 1724:105–6, Vol. I.
60　Brice 1971:164, Vol. II.
61　Thiéry 1786:513, Vol. I.
62　The high regard Louis XIV held for Caesar is reflected in his *Mémoires pour l'instruction du Dauphin*, 1992:74.
63　As the arch underwent later alterations, my observations consider contemporary works including Brice's pictorial representation of the structure.
64　The Porte Saint-Denis' inscriptions are supplied in Brice 1971:164, Vol. II.
65　On Perrault's comment and the importance of the Arch of Constantine as a model see Burke 1992:194, in which reference is also made to modern weaponry in the iconographical detail of Blondel's structures.
66　See Brice 1971:174–6, Vol. II.
67　Detail in Berger 1994:82–3; Gady 1999:54–6.
68　See Mattingly and Sydenham 1926:288, No. 620, Vol. II.
69　Brice 1971:229–31, 260–2, Vol. II; Sauval 1724:105–6, Vol. I.
70　The Porte Saint-Bernard stood on the Left Bank and therefore did not form part of the *Nouveau Cours*.
71　Rome's Aurelianic walls (271–5 CE) were added to by later emperors.
72　The symbolism of Hellenistic and Roman gateways is discussed by Baldwin Smith 1978:13 who, for instance, notes a reference by Homer to the 'Gate of the Sun' and that of Virgil to 'The Ivory Gate'. Equally, see Burke 1992:197 on the French monarchy's knowledge of the Egyptian cult of the sun.
73　On the map see Berger 1994:81, 83; Leon 1970:284. For aspects relating to Rome's history of cartography: Vout 2007:295–322.
74　Brice 1971:17, Vol. I. Although the city's exact population eludes us as there was no census until 1801, by 1700 it had become the most populous urban centre in Europe with an estimated population of half a million: Berger 1994:73.
75　Brice 1971:231, Vol. II. Also noted in Piganiol de la Force 1765:53–4, Vol. V.
76　Tacitus, *Annals*: 12.23–4: Stambaugh 1988:69–70.
77　Cleary 1999:135.
78　In his *Mémoires de ma vie* Charles Perrault donates considerable space to his brother's triumphal arch design:1993:254–5. Claude Perrault's quest to display the superiority of the present age over antiquity is discussed by Picon in the related text Ibid. 55.
79　See note 55 and the associated text of this chapter.
80　See also Benevelo 1978:740 who notes how the programmes of Paris and Versailles developed in a parallel fashion and were connected politically, economically and stylistically. Of relevance, too, is Louis' royal retreat of Marly, seen by Cleary 1999:136 as a 'modern incarnation of the villa and gardens of Augustus'.
81　Burke 1992:18.

82 For instance, Pliny the Younger's delineation of his Laurentine residence: *Letters*, 2. 17.
83 Perrault 1979:18, 43, 94.
84 Elias 1983:41 – the chapter in general serves as an excellent introduction to the social structure of dwellings under the nobility of the *ancien régime*.
85 Burke 1992:152.
86 See Edwards 1993: for example, 150–8 inc. footnote 37. Additionally, Wallace-Hadrill 1994:12. On the social structure of the Roman house: especially Wallace-Hadrill 1988:43–97. See also Laurence 1994: a stimulating account of 'Space and Society' in Pompeii.
87 For reference to Apollo and gold: Pliny, *Natural History*: 33. 83.
88 Earlier monarchical associations with Apollo are discussed by Burke 1992:175, 180–1, 187.
89 Petzet 2000:66–7 for discussion.
90 Although extensive excavations of the site were not carried out until the 1960s, Petzet Ibid. notes the relevance of Etienne Du Pérac's 'Disegni de le ruine di Roma' (1574).
91 Berger 1994:27.
92 Sauval 1724:48–9, Vol. III. See Suetonius, *Augustus*: 28.
93 Relevant works include Berger 1994:83; Cole 1994:95; Leon 1970:3. Although Louis' employment of the sun and Apollo remained, both it and associations drawn between his person and classical models, such as Augustus, lost some of their impetus over time: Black 1999:25. Also, see notes 68–9 (ch. 1) of this book and the related text.
94 Discussion of the Hall of Mirrors and the decoration of its ceiling: Milovanovic 2007:34–51. Also, see Constans and Salmon eds 1998:102–3.
95 Ménestrier 1975:254.
96 Ibid. 3.
97 Haskell and Penny 1981:39.
98 See Pliny, *Natural History*: 31.1–63, 36.2 and Pliny the Younger's letter to Domitius Apollinaris: *Letters* 5. 6. For discussion of the hydraulics at Versailles: Bultez 2005:88–91.
99 See Constans and Salmon eds 1998:94.
100 For instance, Kostof 1991:251 observes the parallels between the layout of the three converging avenues in the gardens at Versailles and the *trivium* of those at Les Invalides.
101 Lister 1823:45. The work was first published in 1698.
102 Ibid. 38.
103 Ibid. 50–1.
104 Ibid. 51.

105 Ibid. 54. At the time of Lister's visit, the statue was still standing where it had been cast.
106 Ibid.
107 Detail in Burke 1992: for example, Ch. 10.
108 When elaborating upon Louis' equestrian statue, Lister 1823:55 inadvertently emphasizes the inventiveness of the King's broadcasters: 'It seems as if the people of the present time are ashamed of the stile of their dress, yet no one will venture to affirm that the equestrian statues of Henri IV and Louis XIII are the less valued for being arrayed in the true dress of their times'.
109 Dectot 1999:69 for discussion.
110 Sauval 1724:106, Vol. I.
111 Thiéry 1786:513, Vol. I.
112 Ibid. 121–3, 327–31, 395–403. Strangely, however, this particular edition was published only a few years before the 1789 Revolution.
113 Piganiol de la Force 1765:51, Vol. V: this multivolume guide was first published in 1742.
114 Mercier 1979:122, Vol. XI; 6, Vol. X. On Mercier, his politics and many literary works: Astbury 2007:133–42.
115 Mercier 1979:2, Vol. II; 103–4, Vol. X. For similarly derogatory remarks: Ibid. 1, Vol. XI; 6, Vol. X.
116 Ibid. 93, Vol. X.
117 Napoleon 1806: Regenbogen 1998:142.
118 For instance, Nero's *Domus Aurea* and *Colossus*: Suetonius, *Nero*: 31; Pliny, *Natural History*: 33.53, 34.43, 36.111. Works on Nero include Holland 2000: an enlightening (and an alternative) analysis of the Emperor; also Coleman 2005:545–50; Smith 2000:532–42.
119 See Bourrienne (de) 1885:14–15 and Lyons 1994:182. On the circulation of similar works including *Le Néron corse, Du Néron du XIXe siècle* and Chateaubriand's famous *De Buonaparte et des Bourbons* see Tulard 1965:252; 1971:46, 135.
120 Napoleon 1816. *Dicté* Las Cases: Dinfreville 1977:265.
121 Las Cases 1983:120, *Mémorial II*.
122 Legrand and Landon 1806: xx, Vol. I.
123 Legrand and Landon 1809:42, Vol. II.
124 Ibid. 41.
125 Ibid. 10.
126 Mercier 1979:227, Vol. IV. Legrand and Landon 1809:10, Vol. II.
127 For reference to the interrelationships of antiquity, Louis XIV, Napoleon and the adoption of the title *le Grand*: Horne 2004:59.
128 Haskell and Penny 1981:5.
129 Colbert: Haskell and Penny 1981:37.

130 Haskell and Penny 1981:37–42.
131 On Napoleon's comment see Dunlop 1999:299. On the duc de Saint-Simon and his *Mémoires*: Bély 2005:3–5. See also Weerdt-Pilorge (de) 2006:117–32 who compares and contrasts the ways in which the King's rule was treated by Saint-Simon and Voltaire.
132 See Denon, *Correspondance administrative (1802–1815)* 15 October 1804, Arch. nat. O2 150 n° 467a. (www.napoleonica.org) accessed: 19 August 2011. The statue was still in its plaster form at this stage, for the question of whether 'Desaix' was to be clothed or not had yet to be decided! Once Napoleon was no longer in power, the statue was removed to be replaced later by Bosio's equestrian statue of a 'Roman' Louis XIV: Krief 2004:182–7; Poisson 2002:41–2 for discussion.
133 Denon, *Correspondance administrative (1802–1815)* 9 February 1806, Arch. nat. AF IV 1050 dr 2 n° 5. (www.napoleonica.org) accessed: 19 August 2011.
134 Cleary 1999:137–41.
135 Ibid. 137. On the nature and magnificence of the initial project; also the reasons for the modification of these plans and how the new square (Place Louis-le-Grand) was largely residential, rather than imperial in character see also Rochell and Ziskin 1999: Ch. 1.
136 Denon, *Correspondance administrative (1802–1815)* 9 February 1806, Arch. nat. AF IV 1050 dr 2 n° 5. (www.napoleonica.org) accessed: 19 August 2011.
137 For discussion of Rome's French Academy and the King's interrelated role as Patron of Architecture see Berger 1994; Burke 1992:50, 188.
138 In 1793 the National Convention abolished the *Académie de France à Rome* and similar institutions which then were reinitiated (in part) before the end of the Revolution.
139 On Durand's *Précis des leçons d'architecture* . . . and also his ealier *Recueil et parallèle des édifices de tous genres,* see Hitchcock 1958: Ch. 2; Szambien 1984.
140 *Mercure Galant* 1682: original citation in Haskell and Penny 1981:42.
141 *Recüeil des Gazettes nouvelles ordinaires et extraordinares,* No. 28, 1662:221–36.
142 For instance, *Le Moniteur Universel,* No. 58, 27 February 1810; No. 61, 2 March 1810:243; No. 81, 25 March 1810:325.
143 Napoleon's son (Napoleon II) was born in 1811. See also Johns 1998:11.
144 See Bourrienne (de) 1829:51, Vol. IV.
145 For instance, Cally 1810b:1–2. See also notes 123–4 of this chapter and the associated text.
146 Reported in Bausset (de) 1829:179, Vol. IV.
147 The dating and authorship of Louis XIV's *Mémoires* continue to be a subject of dispute.
148 Amaury-Duval in Baltard 1805:17, Vol. II.
149 Percier and Fontaine 1833a:33.

150 Fontaine, *Journal 1799–1824*, Vol. I: 1987:289–90.
151 Horne 2004:76. The author also notes that the palace was to be bigger than Versailles and that the project was reminiscent of Napoleon and Louis' respective preoccupation with *la gloire*: 75–6. Equally, see Poisson 2002:212–20.
152 Pliny, *Natural History*: 36. 111; Suetonius, *Nero*: 31.
153 Royou 1826:91–4, Vol. I.
154 Horne 2004:76–7.
155 Detail in notes 118–19 of this chapter and the associated text.
156 Las Cases 1983:124, *Mémorial II*.
157 Discussed by Vandiver Nicassio 2005:31–3.
158 On Napoleon's love for immense monuments see Bourrienne (de) 1829:40, 52, 54, Vol. IV; Bausset (de) 1829:201, Vol. IV.
159 Additional figures of note include François I and Louis XIII.

Chapter 4

1 Machiavelli, *The Discourses on the First Decad of Titus Livy*, I.25.1: Wisch 1990: xv.
2 For example, *La Gazette de France*, No. 103, 3 September 1660:805, 806.
3 Ibid. 806.
4 Ibid. 805–36.
5 Beard 2007:61–7 for discussion.
6 See Beard 2007:19–20, 91.
7 Pure (de) 1972:154.
8 For instance, the evolution of the Roman Forum from the archaic period through to the Empire is an area that has become clearer only in more recent years. See Purcell in Steinby *LTUR* II, 1995 (a and b):325–6; 336–42; Scott 2000:183–91. Also, Coarelli in Steinby *LTUR* IV, 1999:223–8, as well as Beard 2007:104 who emphasizes the problems involved in ascertaining the route(s) that any triumphal procession followed.
9 *CIL*: 6.1139=*ILS* 694.
10 Desgodetz 1682:174–91, Ch. XVII.
11 See F. Kleiner 2007:129–31; Ramage and Ramage 2009:176–9. Kleiner 2007: 129–31 emphasizes the posthumous nature of the dedication – this has bearing on the depiction of the arch in the first relief: whether it was the *porta triumphalis* or an idealized image of Titus passing beneath 'his' triumphal arch are but two possibilities.
12 Montfaucon (de) 1719:167, Ch. X; Ibid. 189–90, Ch. XV.
13 Additional works include Serlio's sixteenth-century appraisal of the arches; Palladio's *Quattro Libri dell'Architettura* (1570); Piranesi's eighteenth-century series (known later as the *Archi Trionfali*) and also Gibbon's essay: *Sur les triomphes des Romains* (1764).

14 Desgodetz 1682:174–91 and Lalande (de) 1769:314, Ch. XV, Vol. IV respectively.
15 On the monument's iconography see Beard 2007:46–7, 126–8; D. Kleiner 1992, esp. 227–8. For Jupiter as the 'Greatest and Best': Suetonius, *Augustus*: 23.
16 Pure (de) 1972:111.
17 Ibid. 123–4.
18 Ibid. 112–14, 120, 123. See also Livy, *Early History of Rome*: 3.63–4; Suetonius, *Caesar*: 45.
19 Pure (de) 1972:154.
20 Ibid. 147. See also Ménestrier 1975:44–6. Additionally, Pliny, *Natural History*: 33.16.
21 Pure (de) 1972:111–14. See Plutarch, *Marcellus*: 22; Suetonius, *Augustus*: 22.
22 Pure (de) 1972:128–9. The triumphal garments were known as the *tunica palmata* and *toga picta* (also worn by the Capitoline statue of Jupiter).
23 Plutarch, *Marcellus*: 22.
24 Pure (de) 1972:126. On the laurel and also its link with Jupiter Optimus Maximus see Pliny, *Natural History*: 15.125, 127, 133–4. For the eagle-crowned ivory staff and additional aspects of the triumph: Juvenal, *Satires*: 10.27–55, 56–82, 111–39 and 14.77–104.
25 Pliny, *Natural History*: 10.15–17.
26 Ancient references to Rome's four-horse *currus triumphalis* include Livy, *Rome and Italy*: 10.23.
27 For the *triumphator*'s purple robe: Suetonius, *Caesar*: 80.
28 Ordinarily the horses were dark, although there were exceptions such as the white horses pulling Caesar's chariot: Weinstock 1971:68, 71–6.
29 For the link between Jupiter and thunderbolts: Pliny *Natural History*: 2.138.
30 Briant 2011:91.
31 Virgil, *Aeneid*: 12.158–91.
32 On the radiate crown, its solar connotations and association with the 'Golden Ages' of Augustus' successors see Smith 2000:532–42.
33 Pure (de) 1972:144. While describing the procession's course, Pure equates the 'Marché couvert' with the Velabrum. He based his understanding of the processions' passage through the Velabrum (the valley between the Capitoline and the Palatine that joins the Forum to the Forum Boarium) on the reference by Suetonius (*Caesar*: 37) to Caesar's Gallic triumph (46 BCE). On today's various (and often conflicting) interpretations of this 'evidence' see Beard 2007:102–5.
34 Pure (de) 1972:145–6.
35 Lalande (de) 1769:238, Ch. X, Vol. IV.
36 Ibid. 237. See Plutarch, *Marcellus*: 8. Also, Winckelmann 1802:181–7, Vol. II, Book V: a French edition of the *History of the Art of Antiquity*.
37 Royou 1809:33, Vol. I.
38 Edwards 1996:69, 86.

39 Ibid. 71.
40 Anonymous 1783:273, Vol. II. The title of this guide, *La ville de Rome, ou description abrégée de cette superbe ville*, is identical to that of Dominique Magnan (1778).
41 Gibbon 1805:390, Vol. III. For discussion of the seminal part the Capitoline played in Gibbon's *The Decline and Fall of the Roman Empire* (1776–88) and the influence ancient texts had upon conceptions of the link between the Capitoline and Roman imperial power see Edwards 1996:69, 71–2.
42 See also Edwards 1996:90 on the description of the Capitoline as *caput mundi* in the twelfth-century *Mirabilia urbus Romae*.
43 Bryant 1986:15.
44 Silver 1990:293 uses the term 'image politics' in his analysis of Germany's sixteenth-century entries *all'antica*.
45 On the *adventus* (or *Adventus Augusti*) and, for example, the building of monumental gateways to mark the ceremonial entrances to Augustus' provincial cities, see Baldwin Smith 1978:5, 10–11, 21–9. Also, MacCormack 1981:17–92.
46 The significance of the ancient imperial *adventus* is noted by Giesey 1985:53.
47 For instance, see Bryant 1986:66.
48 R. Strong 1984:42, 48. See also Giesey 1985.
49 Schneider 1913:106.
50 Ibid.
51 See R. Strong 1984:45,66. The term 'humanistic' is borrowed from Giesey 1985:51: 'The characteristic feature of what I call "humanistic" kingship is the great authority provided by models derived from human history, especially classical antiquity, and from pagan mythology regarded as a historical (not religious) phenomenon'.
52 Although the work by Specchi post-dates France's early *entrées*, such ritual had long been an intrinsic part of Papal Rome's history.
53 For example, see the exhibition catalogue for the Museo di Roma (Palazzo Braschi): Leone, Pirani, Tittoni and Tozzi eds 2002, and also Cimino and Nota Santi eds 1998.
54 Baldwin Smith 1978:7.
55 In my discussion of the Italian entry *all'antica*, I draw from R. Strong 1984:44–5. On Petrarch's *I Trionfi* (and a French translation of 1503) see also Wyke 2008:99–101, 132–3.
56 R. Strong 1984:76.
57 Ibid. 66, 74, 86: Strong also discusses Erasmus' sixteenth-century work, in which the virtues of Roman prototypes were examined and linked to those of Charles V.
58 See Hibbert 1985:165 on the 'clearing' of the Roman Forum. On the elaborately decorated triumphal arches (both antique and modern): R. Strong 1984:83.
59 Detail in Guibbert 2000:27–36 in the exhibition catalogue: *Hypnerotomachia Poliphili ou: le Songe de Poliphile le plus beau livre du monde, Venise 1499, Paris 1546*.
60 See Audebrand 1999:29; Bryant 1986:65–6.
61 Henri II's official Parisian *entrée* was accompanied by lavish entries *à l'antique* into cities such as Lyon (1548) and indeed Rouen (1550).

62 Giesey 1985:52–3.
63 See notes 152–4 (ch. 2) and the associated texts; also note 155 (ch. 2) on the 1789 Revolution's exploitation of the elephant.
64 Suetonius, *Caesar*: 37.
65 Wyke 2008:139, 135–8, 140–3. Similarly, see R. Strong 1984:46–7; Wisch 1990: xvi. It appears Mantegna also drew from Flavio Biondo's *Roma triumphans* (1457–9) and Roberto Valturio's *De re militari* (1460).
66 See R. Strong 1984:46–7. On the complexities of Caesarian imagery at these (and other) royal entry festivals see especially Wyke 2008:140–4. Interestingly, the significance of the elephant reappears, for these powerful creatures were also portrayed in Mantegna's masterpiece.
67 Thibaudeau 1913:26–7. The citation is supplied on p. 29 of this book.
68 Saunier n.d:2.
69 Ibid.
70 R. Strong 1984:75: Virgil, *Aeneid*: 6. 785–817.
71 See Virgil, *Aeneid*: 6.255–87, 879–901; 8.649–81. Ovid, *Metamorphoses*: 14.356–7; 15.425. For instance, Ovid's *Metamorphoses* was printed by the *Imprimerie Royale* (1676) and recognized as *the* model upon which to base 'les décors monarchiques' under Louis XIV: Apostolidès 1981:79, 87.
72 Etlin 1975:27: a stimulating analysis of the festival's Roman flavour, its architecture and purpose. Additionally, see Vaulchier (de) 1989:258–9 and especially Leith 1991:36–55.
73 Bordes 1992:61.
74 Etlin 1975:28; Leith 1991:48–9.
75 Leith 1991:46–8 for discussion.
76 The 'unifying' symbolism of the festival's temporary bridge is noted by Leith 1991:46.
77 See *Journal de Paris National*, No. 222, 10 August 1793:892. Also, Leith 1991:132.
78 Leith 1991:132. On the 1793 festival in general see also McClellan 1994:95–9.
79 Reference to these monarchical 'tyrants' is supplied in *Journal de Paris National*, No. 222, 10 August 1793:893.
80 Refer to *Journal de Paris National*, No. 222, 10 August 1793:893. On the omnipresence of Hercules as a forceful emblem of revolutionary ideology see Leith 1991:216: examples embrace a proposal for a statue of Hercules as a 'devourer of kings' who grasps a monarch about to be bludgeoned to death with the demi-god's club.
81 See *Journal de Paris National*, No. 222, 10 August 1793:892.
82 Discussion in Leith 1991:212–13; Szambien 1986:8–9.
83 Hibbert 1985:231.
84 Discussion includes Haskell and Penny 1981:109–10; Vandiver Nicassio 2005:20–3. See also Tittoni 1997:101–7 in the exhibition catalogue:*1796-1797 – Da Montenotte a Campoformio: la rapida marcia di Napoleone Bonaparte*. Miles 2008:319–27 provides a particularly vibrant account of the extensive plundering by Bonaparte and his republican armies.

85 Mainardi 1989:157.
86 For discussion see Capon ed. 1986:48–9; Giardina and Vauchez 2000:94–5, 97, 113–16; Hibbert 1985:230–37; Madelin 1906 and also Gorgone and Tittoni eds 1997: the exhibition catalogue for *Da Montenotte a Campoformio* (above).
87 On the festival, the imagery of Giuseppe Barberi's arch and its structural likeness to the Arch of Constantine see Faldi 1955:14–18. Relevant works also include Giardina and Vauchez 2000:130–1. A painting of the arch by Felice Giani is housed in the Museo di Roma (Palazzo Braschi).
88 The Altar to the Fatherland was depicted by Felice Giani and it, too, is housed in the Museo di Roma.
89 In reality, the Capitoline Tree of Liberty was a wooden pole: Johns 1998:72.
90 See Edwards 1996:94.
91 See Livy, *Rome and Italy*: 10.23; Pliny, *Natural History*: 15.77.
92 Discussed by Tollfree 2004:38.
93 Discussion includes Giardina and Vauchez 2000:97–8; Tollfree 2004:38.
94 *Le Patriote Francais*, No. 311, 29 July 1798:1246.
95 *Le Moniteur*, No. 309, 27 July 1798 in *Réimpression de l'Ancien moniteur* 1863:322, Vol. 29.
96 Plutarch, *Aemilius Paullus*: 32: trans. Perrin.
97 Mainardi 1989:156–7.
98 For instance, Giardina and Vauchez 2000:114–16; Tittoni 1997:104–5; Loyer 1999:25. The display of the treasures as museum pieces also renders the subject relevant to the evolution of the Louvre as a cultural, an ideological and a political billboard: for example, Duncan and Wallach 1980:448–69; McClellan 1984:438–64 and 1994, esp. Chs 3–4.
99 Mainardi 1989:158. Similarly insightful works examining the links between the 1798 *fête* and antiquity include Miles 2008:321–4; Tollfree 1999:88–100.
100 See Hanley 2008: Ch. 4 whose enlightening work, while not orientated to an investigation of the festival's 'Roman' character, reinforces the advantages of employing newspapers as a source.
101 For example, Plutarch, *Aemilius Paullus*: 34.
102 *Journal de Paris*, No. 309, 27 July 1798:1295. See Appendix I.
103 *Le Patriote Français*, No. 311, 29 July 1798:1247.
104 *Gazette de France*, No. 23, 24 February 1660:176 in *Recüeil de Toutes les Gazettes Nouvelles Ordinaires & Extraordinaires* 1661.
105 *Le Patriote Français*, No. 304, 22 July 1798:1219. *Journal de Paris*, No. 308, 24 July 1798:1287.
106 *Le Patriote Français*, No. 311, 29 July 1798:1246.
107 See Mainardi, 1989:156 and p. 49 of this book.
108 *Journal de Paris*, No. 308, 24 July 1798: 1295–6.
109 Quoted in *Journal de Paris*, No. 308, 26 July 1798:1290.

110 *Journal de Paris*, No. 308, 26 July 1798:1289–91.
111 See Haskell and Penny 1981:111.
112 See *Le Patriote Français*, No. 312, 30 July 1798:1249.
113 *Journal de Paris*, No. 308, 26 July 1798:1290.
114 This is alluded to by Tollfree 1999:99.
115 Livy, *Early History of Rome*: 2.1.
116 For example, Plutarch, *Brutus*: 1. For reference to 'Brutus the Liberator' see Livy, *Early History of Rome*: 1.60.
117 *Le Patriote Françias*, No. 312, 30 July 1798:1249. See also *Journal de Paris*, No. 309, 27 July 1798:1295.
118 On the Republic's 'temple magique' see *Le Patriote Français*, No. 312, 30 July 1798:1249.
119 For instance, *Le Patriote Français*, No. 304, 22 July 1798:1219; *Journal de Paris*, No. 308, 26 July 1798:1290.
120 *Le Patriote Français*, No. 304, 22 July 1798:1219.
121 The irony of this is reinforced by Chateaubriand's critique of Napoleonic rule: 'Towards the end of the Empire everyone detested imperial despotism' *Mémoires* 1998:273.
122 *Journal de Paris*, No. 308, 26 July 1798:1289–90.
123 *Le Moniteur Universel*, No. 2, 2 January 1806:10.
124 Ibid. 7. For a more critical – though no less subjective – version of the crowds' reaction to Napoleonic spectacle (and Napoleon's inner indifference to the crowd) see Bourrienne (de) 1829:227, Vol. IV.
125 *Le Moniteur Universel*, No. 2, 2 January 1806:7.
126 Kostof 1991:271–2.
127 Relevant works include Audebrand 1999; Bryant 1986; Giesey 1985; Scobie 1990; R. Strong 1984 and also Wisch in Munshower and Wisch eds 1990: see note 138 of this chapter.
128 Bryant 1986:212.
129 On the equation between France's increase in external power and decrease in internal freedom, especially after Napoleon's marriage to Marie-Louise, see Thibaudeau 1913:258.
130 *Journal de l'Empire*, 5 April 1810:1–2. The celebration of Napoleon's civil marriage took place on 1 April at the Palais de Saint-Cloud, while the 2 April was given to the *entrée* and the religious ceremony in the Louvre. Louis' marriage dates to June 1660, while the *entrée* was staged on 26 August.
131 For instance, *La Gazette de France*, No. 103, 3 September 1660:810; *Journal de Paris*, 5 April 1810:2.
132 *Entrée triomphante* 1662:4: 'Preparitifs dans la ville de Paris'. This exquisite work (housed in the BnF, Estampes) also includes a wealth of visual stimuli detailing the architecture and epigraphy of the 1660 *entrée*. For an inscription on the Marché Neuf

arch referring to the 'Pax Augusta' see *Entrée triomphante* 1662:23: 'Preparitifs dans la ville de Paris'. For this and a further inscription, in which parallels between Augustus and Louis are equally clear, see Loyson 1660:18–19. On the Senate and the People of Rome's wish that Augustus become 'Father of his Country': Suetonius, *Augustus*: 58.

133 *Le Moniteur Universel*, No. 89, 30 March 1810:355. See also *Journal de Paris* 5 April 1810:2.
134 *Journal de l'Empire*, 3–4 April 1810:1.
135 On the resemblance between the Queen's 'Caléche' and antique Rome's triumphal chariots: *Entrée triomphante* 1662:27: 'Suites de l'entrée de leurs Majeftez'.
136 The imperial couple rode in a carriage to the Tuileries Palace, from where the procession (on foot) continued to the Louvre.
137 R. Strong 1984:47.
138 Wisch 1990: xv: the author addresses aspects of self-presentation at festivities during the Renaissance and Baroque periods.
139 *Entrée triomphante* 1662:24: 'Preparitifs dans la ville de Paris'.
140 Roy 1981:318; Tapie 1957:176.
141 Discussed by Roy 1981:318.
142 See *La Gazette de France*, No. 103, 3 September 1660:808–11. On Napoleonic iconography: for example, the temporary bas-reliefs of the Étoile arch see *Journal de Paris*, 1 April 1810:1.
143 For instance, *Journal de l'Empire*, 3–4 April 1810:1.
144 Rumeau-Dieudonné 2007:26 notes the relationship between the 1660 *entrée* and the triumphs of the '*imperatores* romains' in her comprehensive overview of the event and its decoration.
145 Trans. Bryant 1986:210. For contemporary details of the bridge: *La Gazette de France*, No. 103, 3 September 1660: 809; *Entrée triomphante* 1662:11–20: 'Preparitifs dans la ville de Paris'.
146 See Bryant 1986:211. The equestrian statue of Henri IV was built shortly after his assassination by a fanatic in 1610.
147 *Entrée triomphante* 1662:29: 'Preparitifs dans la ville de Paris'.
148 Loyson 1660:19.
149 Pliny, *Natural History*: 2.92, 100–1. Ovid, *Metamorphoses*: 15.749–52 comments on the star in relation to Caesar's deification and his achievements as the 'father' of Octavian.
150 See *Journal de Paris*, 5 April 1810:2.
151 *Entrée triomphante* 1662:1: 'Preparitifs dans la ville de Paris'.
152 I have borrowed this expression from Zanger 1997:8 who refers to marriage as 'a ritual of transition or passage' which 'joins two bodies or two nation-states'.
153 *Entrée triomphante* 1662:3: 'Preparitifs dans la ville de Paris'.

154 We might remember from chapter 2, however, that a gradual shift in emphasis from Paris' traditional north-south route to the city's east-west route was already in place before 1660.
155 This and similar etchings are housed in the BnF, Estampes.
156 Lalande (de) 1769:237, Ch. X, Vol. IV.
157 Detail in Miles 2008:324. The vase, 'L'entrée à Paris des oeuvres destinées au Musée Napoléon', is held at the Musée national de la Céramique de Sèvres.

Conclusion

1 Horace, *Satires*: 1.6.20–40: trans. Rushton Fairclough.
2 Victor Hugo 1912:752, section XL, III. The ode forms part of a collection of poems, *Les Orientales*, first published in 1829. Additionally, see Tulard 1971:127.
3 The reference to Bonaparte by Pascal Paoli is reported in Las Cases 1983:98, *Mémorial II*. See also Hazareesingh 2004a:298.
4 Las Cases 1983:233, *Mémorial II*: trans. Hazareesingh 2004a:170.
5 The 'horizon of meaning' and 'subcodes' of Lefebvre's 'monument' are quoted on pp. 37–8 of this study.
6 Lefebvre 2003:22.
7 For example, Montesquieu 1999:123.
8 Studies of the association between *romanità* and Mussolini's 'heritage' of ancient Rome include Nelis 2007:391–415.
9 Of the numerous pieces on the return of Napoleon's ashes to Paris (a number of years after his death in 1821) see Driskel 1993:30–5; Gaillard 1998:106–8; Muratori-Philip 1992:92–113.
10 On the plans involving the passage of Augustus' funeral procession beneath Rome's 'Triumphal Gate' see Suetonius, *Augustus*: 100.

Select Bibliography

For reasons of clarity, this bibliography is divided into two main sections: the first deals with works that were composed before the twentieth century (including newspaper entries), while the second section details those of post-1900 published authors. For similar reasons, I have chosen to cite volume numbers only when they have been consulted – although I cannot profess to have read every volume of Napoleon's *Correspondance* from cover to cover! A final word: publisher name details relating to the first section are provided only for post-1900 editions of earlier works.

Pre-twentieth-century authors

Baltard, L.-P. 1802 and 1805. *Paris et ses monumens, mesurés, dessinés et gravés par Baltard, Architecte, avec des descriptions historiques par le cit. Amaury-Duval* (Paris).
— 1875. *Arc de triomphe du Carrousel, édifié par Percier et Fontaine, . . . gravé d'après leurs dessins par Louis-Pierre Baltard, précédé d'un aperçu sur les monuments triomphaux, rédigé par Fontaine, et d'une notice sur l'arc du Carrousel, tirée presque entièrement de ses mémoires manuscrits* (Paris).
Bausset (de), L. F. J. 1829. *Mémoires anecdotiques sur l'intérieur du palais et sur quelques événemens de l'Empire depius 1805 jusqu'en Ier mai 1814, pour servir à l'hisoire de Napoléon*, Vol. IV (Paris).
Bourrienne (de), L.-A. F. 1829. *Mémoires de M. de Bourrienne, Ministre d'État; sur Napoléon, le Directoire, le Consulat, l'Empire et la Restauration*, Vol. IV (Paris).
— 1885. *Memoirs of Napoleon Bonaparte by Louis Antoine Fauvelet de Bourrienne, his private secretary*, Vols I–III, ed. R. W. Phipps (London).
Brice, G. 1971. *Description de la ville de Paris et de tout ce qu'elle contient de plus remarquable* (1752 edn), Vols I and II (Paris: Librairie Minard).
Cally, P.-J. 1810a. *La superbe Colonne de la place Vendôme, sur laquelle est posée la statue en pied de Napoléon le Grand, érigée en l'honneur et la gloire de la grande ARMÈE par S. M. l'Empereur des français et Roi d'Italie. Description historique de ce monument et de celui élevé sur la place des Victoires, à la mémoire du Général Desaix . . .* (Paris).
— 1810b. *Description générale de la porte St. Denis et des bas-reliefs qui décorent ce monument, depuis qu'elle a été débrunie et restaurée* (Paris).
Carême, A. 1980. *Le Pâtissier pittoresque*, with extracts from J.-M. Durand's *Parallèle des monuments antiques et modernes* (1828 edn) (Marseille: Laffitte).

Chambray (de), R. F. 2005. *'Parallèle de l'architecture antique avec la moderne'* (1650), suivi de *'Idée de la perfection de la peinture'* (1662), ed. F. Lemerle-Pauwels and M. Stanić (Paris: École nationale supérieure des Beaux-Arts).

Chas, J. 1805. *Parallèle de Napoléon Ier, avec Charlemagne* (Paris).

Chateaubriand (vicomte de), F.-A.-R. 1995. *Voyage en Italie* (Lausanne: La Bibliothèque des Arts).

— 1998. *Napoléon: livres XIX à XIV des Mémoires d'outre-tombe* (Paris: La Table Ronde).

Chaumont (de), L. C. 1854. *Les monuments et embellissements de Paris: la rue de Rivoli. Curieux détails sur le tour St. Jacques – la Boucherie. Decouvertes qu'on vient de faire en touillant aux pieds de la tour* . . . (Paris).

Colbert, J.-B. 1868. *Lettres, Instructions et Mémoires de Colbert* (*publiés d'après les ordres de l'Empereur*), Vol. V, ed. P. Clément (Paris).

Couture, L. 1852. *Parallèles Historiques: Napoléon-Louis XIV-Cromwell-Washington: Extrait du Bonapartisme dans l'histoire de France* (Paris).

Denon, D.-V. (baron de), 1804 and 1806. 'Correspondance administrative (1802–15)'. In *Fondation Napoléon: Bibliothèque Numérique Napoleonienne*.

Desgodetz, A. 1682. *Les édifices antiques de Rome dessinés et mesurés très exactement par Antoine Desgodetz, Architecte* (Paris).

Durand, J. M. See Câreme, A.

Fontaine, P.-F.-L. 1987. *Journal, 1799–1853*, Vol. I: 1799–1824 (Paris: École nationale supérieure des Beaux-Arts).

Garnier, C. 1621. *Parallèle de Louys le victorieux et d'Alexandre le Grand* (Paris).

Gibbon, E. 1805. *Histoire de la décadence et de la chute de l'empire romain* (*abrégée et réduite par Adam*), Vols I–III, ed. and trans. P. C. Briand (Paris).

— 1909. *The History of the Decline and Fall of the Roman Empire*, Vol. I, ed. J. B. Bury (London: Methuen & Co).

Hippolyte, C. 1858. *Parallèle entre César, Charlemagne et Napoléon: l'empire et la démocratie. Philosophie de la légende impériale* (Paris).

Hugo, V. 1912. *Les Orientales* (Paris: Librairie Ollendorff).

Jouin, H. 1879. '"Arc de Triomphe de l'Étoile"; "Arc de Triomphe du Carrousel"; "Colonne de la Grande Armée"'. In *Inventaire Général des Richesses d'Art de la France: Paris, Monuments Civils*, Vol. I (Paris), pp.159–84; 245–59; 343–65.

Lalande (de), J. J. 1769. *Voyage d'un françois en Italie, faites dans les années 1765 et 1766: contenant l'histoire & les anecdotes les plus singulières de l'Italie* . . . , Vols III and IV (Venise).

Las Cases, M.-J.-E.-D. (comte de), 1983. *Le Mémorial de Sainte-Hélène I & II. Première édition intégrale et critique* (Paris: Flammarion).

Legrand, J.-G. and Landon, C.-P. 1806 and 1809. *Description de Paris et de ses édifices, avec un précis historique et des observations sur le caractère de leur architecture et sur les principaux objets d'art et de curiosité qu'ils renferment*, 2 vols (Paris).

— 1808 and 1818. *Description de Paris et de ses édifices, avec un précis historique et des observations sur le caractère de leur architecture et sur les principaux objets d'art et de curiosité qu'ils renferment*, 2 vols (Paris).

Lenoir, A. 1798. *Description Historique et chronique des monumens de sculpture, réunis au Musée des Monumens Français par Alexandre Lenoir, Conservateur de ce Musée, suivi d'un traité-historique de la peinture sur verre, par le même auteur* (Paris).

Lister, M. 1823. *A Journey to Paris in the Year 1698. An Account of Paris at the close of the Seventeenth Century: Relating to the Buildings of that City, Its Libraries, Gardens, Natural and Artificial Curiosities, the Manners and Customs of the People, Their Arts, Manufactures, & c.*, ed. G. Henning (London).

Louis XIV. 1992. *Mémoires pour l'instruction du Dauphin: 1661–1668*, ed. G. Duby (Paris: Impr. nationale Éditions).

Loyson, J.-B. 1660. *Les devis générales et particulières des tableaux, figures en relief... qui sont aux portes et portiques des arcs de triomphe élevés à la gloire de Louis XIV, roi de France et de Navarre, et de Marie-Thérèse d'Autriche..., aux faubourg et porte Saint-Antoine, cimetière Saint-Jean, pont Notre-Dame, Marché-Neuf et Place Dauphine...* (Paris).

Ménestrier, C.-F. 1975. *Traité des tournois, joustes, carrousels et autres spectacles publics* (1669) (Lyon: Éditions Horwath).

Mercier, L.-S. 1979. *Tableau de Paris* (1782), Vols II–IV, rpt Slatkine (Geneva).

— 1979. *Tableau de Paris* (1788), Vols IX–XII, rpt Slatkine (Geneva).

Michelet, M. 1845. *History of France, from the Earliest Period to the Present Time*, Vols I and II, trans. G.-H. Smith (New York).

Montesquieu, C.-L. (baron de), 1999. *Considerations on the Causes of the Greatness of the Romans and Their Decline* (1748 edn), ed. and trans. D. Lowenthal (Indianapolis: Hacket Publishing Company).

Montfaucon (de), B. 1719. *L'Antiquité expliquée et représentée en figures*, Vols I–III (Paris).

Napoléon, I. 1859–69. *Correspondance de Napoléon Ier*, 32 vols (Paris).

— 1885. See Bourrienne (de).

— 1983. See Las Cases (comte de).

— 1998. *Napoleon on Napoleon: An Autobiography of the Emperor*, ed. Somerset de Chair (London: Brockhampton Press).

Norvins (de), J. 1896. *Mémorial de J. de Norvins 1793–1802*, Vol. II, ed. L. Lanzac de Laborie (Paris).

Patte, M. 1973. *Mémoires sur les objets les plus importans de l'architecture* (1769 edn), rpt Minkoff (Geneva).

Percier, C. See Vaudoyer, A.-L.-T.

Percier, C. and Fontaine, P.-F.-L. 1833a. *Résidences de souverains. Parallèle entre plusieurs résidences de souverains de France, d'Allemagne, de Suède, de Russie, d'Espagne, et d'Italie* (Hildesheim: G. Olms Verlag) 1973.

— 1833b (July–August). 'Napoléon Architecte'. *Revue de Paris* 52–53, 33–45.

— 1875. See Baltard, L.-P.

Perrault, Ch. 1670. *Courses de Testes et de Bague, faites par le Roy et par les princes et seigneurs de sa cour en l'année 1662* (Paris).

— 1979. *Parallèle des anciens et des modernes en ce qui regarde les arts et les sciences: dialogues avec le poème du siècle de Louis-le-Grand et une épître en vers sur le génie*, Vols I–IV, 1692–7, rpt Slatkine (Geneva).

— 1993. *Mémoires de ma vie. Précédé d'un essai d'Antoine Picon: 'un moderne paradoxal'* (Paris: Macula).

Piganiol de La Force, J.-A. 1765. *Description historique de la ville de Paris et de ses environs*, Vols IV and V (Paris).

Poyet, B. 1799. *Projets de monumens à ériger pour la gloire et l'utilité de la République* (Paris).

Pure (de), M. 1972. *Idée des spectacles anciens et nouveaux* (1668), rpt Minkoff (Geneva).

Royou, J.-C. 1803. *Précis de l'histoire ancienne, d'après Rollin*, Vol. I (Paris).

— 1809. *Histoire Romaine, depuis la fondation de Rome jusqu'au règne d'Auguste*, Vol. I (Paris).

— 1826. *Histoire des Empereurs Romains, suivre d'une Notice sur la vie des impératrices romaines*, Vol. I (Paris).

Salmon, J. 1800. *An Historical Description of Ancient & Modern Rome; also of the works of Art, particularly in Architecture, Sculpture, and Painting: to which are added, a tour through the cities & towns in the environs of that Metropolis, and an Account of the Antiquities found at Gabia*, Vols I and II (London).

Saunier, P.-M. (n.d.). *Réjouissez-vous, voilà la paix. Arrivée du consul Bonaparte à Paris: apportant les articles de la paix conclue avec S.M. l'empereur, roi de Bohême et de Hongrie* (Paris).

Sauval, H. 1724. *Histoire et recherches des antiquités de la ville de Paris*, Vols I–III (Paris).

Thibaudeau, A.-C. 1913. *Mémoires de A.-C. Thibaudeau, 1799–1815* (Paris: Librairie Plon).

Thiéry, L.-V. 1786. *Guide des amateurs et des étrangers voyageurs à Paris. Almanach du voyageur à Paris, contenant une description de tous les monumens, chef-d'œuvres des arts, établissemens utiles et autres objets de curiosité*, Vol. I (Paris).

Tournon (comte de), C. 1855. *Études statistiques sur Rome et la partie occidentale des états romains . . .* , Vol. II, 2nd edn (Paris).

Vaudoyer, A.-L.-T. 1877. *Restaurations des monuments antiques par les architectes pensionnaires de l'Académie de France à Rome depuis 1788 jusqu'à nos jours: Mémoire Historique rédigé en 1839 par Thomas Vaudoyer sur le projet de restauration de la Colonne Trajane exécuté en 1788 par Charles Percier* (Paris).

Vertron (de), C.-C. G. 1685. *Parallèle de Louis le Grand, avec les princes qui ont efté furnommez Grands: dedié a monseigneur le Dauphin* (Paris).

Voltaire (de), F.-M. A. 1910. *Le Siècle de Louis XIV*, ed. E. Bourgeois (Paris: Librairie Hachette).

— 1930. *Voltaire: Œuvres Choisies*, ed. L. Flandrin (Paris: Librairie A. Hatier).

Winckelmann, J. J. 1784. *Recueil de lettres de M. Winckelmann, sur les découvertes faites à Herculanum, à Pompeii, à Stabia, à Caferte & à Rome* (Paris).

— 1794. *Histoire de l'art chez les anciens par Winckelmann*, Vol. I, trans. various (Paris).
— 1802. *Histoire de l'art chez les anciens par Winckelmann*, Vol. II, trans. various (Paris).
— 1808. *Monumens inédits de l'antiquité: statues, peintures antiques, pierres gravées, bas-reliefs de marbre et de terre cuite, expliqués par Winckelmann*, Vols I and II, trans. A. F. Désodoards (Paris).
— 1809. *Monumens inédits de l'antiquité: statues, peintures antiques, pierres gravées, bas-reliefs de marbre et de terre cuite, expliqués par Winckelmann*, Vol. III, trans. A. F. Désodoards (Paris).

Anonymous. 1662. *l'Entrée triomphante de leurs maiestez Louis XIV Roy de France et de Navarre et Marie Thérèse d'Autriche, son épouse, dans la ville de Paris, capitale de leurs Royaumes, au retour de la signature de la Paix générale et de leur heureux mariage* . . . (Paris).
— 1783. *La ville de Rome, ou description abrégée de cette superbe ville*, Vols I, II and IV (n.p.).
— 1800. *Parallèle entre César, Cromwell, Monck et Bonaparte* (Paris).
— 1818. *Description de la Colonne de la Place Vendôme* (Paris).

Newspaper articles

Lemaire. 1798 (29 July, Year IV). *Le Patriote Français*, No. 311.
Napoleon. 1810 (10 February). *Gazette Nationale ou Le Moniteur Universel* (section: Décrets Impériaux), No. 41.
— 1811 (12 January). *Gazette Nationale ou Le Moniteur Universel* (section: Décrets Impériaux), No. 12.
Talleyrand. 1804 (4 December, Year X). *Gazette Nationale ou Le Moniteur Universel*, No. 73.

Anonymous newspaper articles

1660. *La Gazette de France*. (Recüeil des Gazettes nouvelles ordinaires et extraordinaires: 1661), Nos 18, 20, 23, 86, 89, 92, 103 (Paris).
1661. *La Gazette de France*. (Recüeil des Gazettes nouvelles ordinaires et extraordinaires: 1662), Nos 19, 28, 39, 68 (Paris).
1798 (27 July, Year VI). *Gazette Nationale ou Le Moniteur Universel*, No. 309. Reproduced in 1863 (Paris).
1806 (2 January). *Gazette Nationale ou Le Moniteur Universel*, No. 2.
1810 (26 January). *Gazette Nationale ou Le Moniteur Universel*, No. 26.
1810 (25 February). *Gazette Nationale ou Le Moniteur Universel*, No. 56.
1810 (2, 15, 24, 25, 27, 28 March). *Gazette Nationale ou Le Moniteur Universel*, Nos 61, 74, 80, 81, 86, 87.
1810 (30 March). *Gazette Nationale ou le Moniteur Universel*, No. 89.

All relevant bibliographical references relating to anonymous articles from the *Journal de Paris National*, *Le Patriote Français*, the *Journal de Paris* and *Journal de l'Empire* are supplied in the appropriate notes.

Post-1900 authors

Agosti, G., Farinella, V., Morel, P. and Simoncini, G. eds, 1988. *La colonna Traiana e gli artisti francesi da Luigi XIV a Napoleone I*, catalogue for the exhibition held at the Villa Medici, 12 April–12 June, 1988 (Rome: Edizioni Carte Segrete).

Agulton, M. 1985. 'Politics, Images, and Symbolism in Post-Revolutionary France'. In *Rites of Power: Symbolism, Ritual, and Politics since the Middle Ages*, ed. S. Wilentz (Pennsylvania: University of Pennsylvania Press), pp. 177–205.

Andia (de), B., Bacha, M. and Chassel, J.-L. et al. 2001. *Larousse: Paris. Monuments; Districts; Parisian Life*, ed. E. Ybert and A. Luthaud (Paris: Larousse).

Andrieux, M. 1968. *Daily Life in Papal Rome in the Eighteenth Century*, trans. M. Fitton (London: George Allen and Unwin).

Apostolidès, J.-M. 1981. *Le roi-machine. Spectacle et politique au temps de Louis XIV* (Paris: Éditions de Minuit).

— 1985. *Le prince sacrifié. Théâtre et politique au temps de Louis XIV* (Paris: Éditions de Minuit).

Arce, J. 1993. 'Arcus Titi (Via Sacra)'. In *Lexicon Topographicum Urbis Romae* Vol. I, A–C, ed. E. M. Steinby (Rome: Edizioni Quasar), pp. 109–11.

Arnaud, J.-C. 2012 (January–February). 'Les plus grands stratèges et conquérants'. *Les Dossiers: Comprendre l'Histoire*, Vol. II, ed. ESI (Paris).

Astbury, K. 2007. 'Reacting to the Revolution: The Example of Marmontel and Mercier'. *Studies on Voltaire and the Eighteenth Century* (SVEC 2007: 06), 133–42.

Audebrand, F. 1999. 'Entrées royales'. In *Art ou politique? Arcs, statues et colonnes de Paris*, ed. Action artistique de la Ville de Paris (Paris: Action artistique de la Ville de Paris), pp. 29–33.

Baldwin, Smith E. 1978. *Architectural Symbolism of Imperial Rome and the Middle Ages* (New York: Hacker Art Books).

Ballon, H. 1991. *The Paris of Henri IV. Architecture and Urbanism* (Cambridge, MA: MIT Press).

Barchiesi, A. 2005. 'Learned Eyes: Poets, Viewers, Image Makers'. In *The Cambridge Companion to the Age of Augustus*, ed. K. Galinsky (Cambridge: Cambridge University Press), pp. 281–305.

Barker, R. 2001. *Legitimating Identities: The Self-Presentations of Rulers and Subjects* (Cambridge: Cambridge University Press).

Beard, M. 2007. *The Roman Triumph* (Cambridge, MA: The Belknap Press of Harvard University Press).

Bély, L. 1990. *Louis XIV* (Rennes: Ouest-France).

— 2001. *The History of France*, trans. A. Moyon (Paris: Éditions J.-P. Gisserot).
— 2005. *Louis XIV: le plus grand roi du monde* (Paris: Éditions J.-P. Gisserot).
Benevolo, L. 1978. *The Architecture of the Renaissance*, Vol. II (London: Routledge & Kegan Paul).
Berger, R. W. 1994. *A Royal Passion: Louis XIV as Patron of Architecture* (Cambridge: Cambridge University Pres).
Bignamini, I. and Jenkins, I. 1996. 'The Antique'. In *Grand Tour: The Lure of Italy in the Eighteenth Century*, ed. A. Wilton and I. Bignamini (London: Tate Gallery Publishing), pp. 203–70.
Billaut, F. 2011 (September–November) 'Jean-Baptiste Colbert: le ministre absolu'. *Histoire 9*, 44–9.
Biver, M.-L. 1963. *Le Paris de Napoléon* (Paris: Librairie Plon).
— 1964. *Pierre Fontaine, premier architecte de l'Empereur* (Paris: Librairie Plon).
Black, J. 1999. *From Louis XIV to Napoleon. The Fate of a Great Power* (London: UCL Press).
Blanchard, J. 2003 (July). 'Le spectacle du rite: les entrées royales'. *Revue Historique 627*, 475–519.
Blevins, J. 2007. 'Staging Rome: The Renaissance, Rome, and the Humanism's Classical Crisis'. In *The Sites of Rome. Time, Space, Memory*, ed. D. H. J. Larmour and D. Spencer (Oxford: Oxford University Press), pp. 271–94.
Blond, A. 2008. *A Brief History of the Private Lives of the Roman Emperors* (London: Robinson).
Bluche, F. 1984 (May). 'Arrêtez de démolir Louis XIV!' *Historama-Histoire Magazine 3*, 100–5.
Boime, A. 1990. *Art in the Age of Bonapartism 1800–1815* (Chicago, IL: University of Chicago Press).
Bonney, R. 2007 (June). 'Vindication of the Fronde? The Cost of Louis XIV's Versailles Building programme'. *French History 21(2)*, 205–25.
Bordes, P. 1992 (October). 'Da la satire sociale à la change contre Burke: la cour d'Auberge à Calais (1790) de F. G. Bryon'. *Revue du Louvre 4*, 57–64.
Bosséno, C.-M. 1997. 'Bonaparte ad Arcole ovvero come "vedersi nella storia"'. In *1796–1797 – Da Montenotte a Campoformio: la rapida marcia di Napoleone Bonaparte*, catalogue for the exhibition held at the Museo Napoleonico, 4 February–27 April 1997, ed. G. Gorgone and M. E. Tittoni (Rome: "L'Erma" di Bretschneider), pp. 54–7.
— 1998. '"Je me vis dans l'histoire" Bonaparte, de Lodi à Arcole: généalogie d'une image de légende'. *Annales Historiques de la Révolution Française 3*, 449–65.
— 1999 (July-August). 'Le rêve romain de Napoléon'. *L'Histoire. Numéro Spécial: Rome, capitale du monde 234*, 72–3.
Boudon, J.-O. 2004 (February). 'Que la plume remplace l'épée!' *Notre Histoire 218*, 22–5.
Bouyer, C. 2005 (July–August). 'L'amoureux des fêtes'. *Historia Thématique. Louis XIV, ombres et lumières 96*, 28–31.

Bowman, C. ed., 2005. *Essays on the Philosophy and History of Art*, Vol. II (London: Continuum International Publishing Group).

Bresc-Bautier, G. 1999. 'Le triomphe des Bourbons; Utopies royals; Louis XIV, place des Victoires; Desaix, héros de Marengo'. In *Art ou politique? Arcs, statues et colonnes de Paris*, ed. Action artistique de la Ville de Paris (Paris: Action artistique de la Ville de Paris), pp. 46–8; 61–3; 64–8; 90.

Briant, B. 2011 (October–December). 'Le miroir de l'Occident'. *Les Collections de L'Histoire. Alexandre le Grand: quinze ans qui ont bouleversé le monde* 53, 88–92.

Brilliant, R. 1967. 'The Arch of Septimius Severus in the Roman Forum'. *Memoirs of the American Academy in Rome* 29, 29–90.

— 1984. *Visual Narratives. Story Telling in Etruscan and Roman Art* (Ithaca, NY: Cornell University Press).

— 1993. 'Arcus: Septimius Severus (Forum)'. In *Lexicon Topographicum Urbis Romae* Vol. I, A–C, ed. E. M. Steinby (Rome: Edizioni Quasar), pp. 103–5.

— 1994. 'Roman Art'. In *History of Western Art*, ed. D. Hooker (New York: Barnes & Noble Books), pp. 34–57.

— 2007. 'Forwards and Backwards in the Historiography of Roman Art'. *Journal of Roman Archaeology* 20, 7–24.

Brockliss, W., Chaudhuri, P., Haimson Lushkov, A. and Wasdin, K. eds, 2012. *Reception and the Classics: An Interdisciplinary Approach to the Classical Tradition. Yale Classical Studies* 36 (Cambridge: Cambridge University Press).

Broers, M. 2005. *The Napoleonic Empire in Italy, 1796–1814: Cultural Imperialism in a European Context?* (Basingstoke: Palgrave Macmillan).

Bryant, L. M. 1986. *The King and the City in the Parisian Royal Entry Ceremony: Politics, Ritual, and Art in the Renaissance* (Geneva: Librairie Droz).

Bultez, G. 2005. 'L'Hydraulique des jardins'. *Monumental. Revue Scientifique et Technique des Monuments Historiques: Dossier Versailles*, 88–91.

Burke, P. 1992. *The Fabrication of Louis XIV* (New Haven, CT: Yale University Press).

Bury, J. P. T. and Tombs, R. P. 1986. *Thiers 1797–1877: A Political Life* (London: Allen & Unwin).

Caillat, G. 2005. 'La première restauration de la Maison Carrée de Nîmes (1670–1691): documents inédits'. *Bulletin Monumental* 163, 223–41.

Canforo, L. 2007. *Julius Caesar. The People's Dictator*, trans. M. Hill and K. Windle (Edinburgh: Edinburgh University Press).

Capidiferro, A. 1993. 'Arcus Constantini'. In *Lexicon Topographicum Urbis Romae* Vol. I, A–C, ed. E. M. Steinby (Rome: Edizioni Quasar), pp. 86–91.

Capon, L. ed., 1986. *Il Museo Napoleonico* (Rome: Fratelli Palombi Editori).

Capuano, A. 1997 (November). 'La saga degli elefanti'. *Capitolium* 1, 3, 76–9.

Chadych, D. and Leborgne, D. 1999. *Atlas de Paris: évolution d'un paysage urbain* (Paris: Parigramme).

— 2000 (October). 'Les sept murailles de Paris'. *Les Collections de l'Histoire. Paris la traversée des siècles* 9, 40–3.

Chaney, E. 1996. 'The Grand Tour and the Evolution of the Travel Book'. In *Grand Tour: The Lure of Italy in the Eighteenth Century*, ed. A. Wilton and I. Bignamini (London: Tate Gallery Publishing), pp. 95–7.

Chaslin, F. and Picon-Lefebvre, V. 1989. *La Grande Arche de la Défense* (Paris: Electa Moniteur).

Chastel, A. 1974. 'Cortèges et paysage de la Fête'. In *Les fêtes de la Révolution*, catalogue for the exhibition held at the Musée Bargoin, Clermont-Ferrand, 15 June–15 September, 1974, ed. J.-P. Bouillon, M. Mosser and D. Rabreau (Clermont-Ferrand: Impr. Clermont-Ferrand), pp. 7–9.

Chevé, J. 2005 (July–August). 'Le grand régisseur dans ses œuvres'. *Historia Thématique. Louis XIV, ombres et lumières* 96, 60–5.

Christ, Y., Léri, J.-M. and Fierro, A. et al., 2002. *Vie et histoire du 1er arrondissement: Saint-Germain l'Auxerrois – Halles – Place Royal – Place Vendôme*, ed. J. Colson and M.-C. Bellanger (Paris: Éditions Hervas).

Cimino M.-G. and Nota Santi, M., eds, 1998. *Corso Vittorio Emanuele II tra urbanistica e archeologia. Storia di uno sventramento* (Naples: Electa).

Claridge, A. 1993. 'Hadrian's Column of Trajan'. *Journal of Roman Archaeology* 6, 8–22.

— 1998 and 2010. *Rome: An Oxford Archaeological Guide* (Oxford: Oxford University Press).

Cleary, R. L. 1999. *The Place Royale and Urban Design in the Ancien Régime* (Cambridge: Cambridge University Press).

Coarelli, F. 1999. 'La *Sacra via*'. In *Lexicon Topographicum Urbis Romae* Vol. IV, P–S, ed. E. M. Steinby (Rome: Edizioni Quasar), pp. 223–8.

— 2007. *Rome and Environs: An Archaeological Guide*, trans. J. J. Clauss and D. P. Harmon (Berkeley, CA: University of California Press).

Cole, R. 1994. *A Traveller's History of Paris* (Gloucestershire: Windrush Press).

Coleman, K. 2005. 'One Man in His Time plays many Parts: The Rôles of Nero'. *Journal of Roman Archaeology* 18, 545–50.

Connelly, O. 2006. *The Wars of the French Revolution and Napoleon, 1792–1815* (London: Routledge).

Constans, C. and Salmon, X. eds, 1998. *Splendors of Versailles*, catalogue for the exhibition held at the Mississippi Arts Pavilion, Jackson, Mississippi, April 1–August 31, 1998 (New York: Welcome Enterprises).

Cooley, A. E. 2003. *Pompeii* (London: Duckworth).

Cornette, J. 2000 (October). 'De François 1er à Louis XVI: le roi et sa ville'. *Les Collections de l'Histoire. Paris la traversée des siècles* 9, 46–51.

— 2004 (July–August). 'Louis XIV ou la religion royale'. *L'Histoire. Dieu et la politique* 289, 30–3.

Darlow, M. 2007. 'The Role of the Listener in the Musical Aesthetics of the Revolution'. *Studies on Voltaire and the Eighteenth Century* (SVEC 2007:06), 143–57.

Dectot, X. 1999. 'Louis XIV, place Vendôme; La colonne Vendôme'. In *Art ou politique? Arcs, statues et colonnes de Paris*, ed. Action artistique de la Ville de Paris (Paris: Action artistique de la Ville de Paris), pp. 69–71; 156–7.

Denby, D. J. 1995. 'Individual, Universal, National: A French Revolutionary Trilogy?' *Studies on Voltaire & the Eighteenth Century* (SVEC 1995:335), 27–35.

Derderian, V. 1991 (May). 'Un arc pour quel triomphe?' *Historama* 87, 86–9.

Dinfreville, J. 1977. *Louis XIV: les saisons d'un grand règne* (Paris: Éditions Albatros).

Dolan, B. 2001. *Ladies of the Grand Tour* (London: HarperCollins Publishers).

Driault, E. 1918. 'Rome et Napoléon'. *Revue des études napoléoniennes* 13, 5–43.

— 1942. *Napoléon architecte* (Paris).

Driskel, M. P. 1993. *As Befits a Legend. Building a Tomb for Napoleon 1840–1861* (Kent, OH: Kent State University Press).

Duncan, C. 1993. *The Aesthetics of Power: Essays in Critical Art History* (Cambridge: Cambridge University Press).

Duncan, C. and Wallach, A. 1980 (December). 'The Universal Survey Museum'. *Art History* 3(4), 448–69.

Dunlop, I. 1999. *Louis XIV* (London: Pimlico).

Dupavillon, C. and Lacloche, F. 1989. *Le triomphe des arcs* (Paris: Gallimard).

Dwyer, P. G. 2004a (December). 'Introduction: Images of Napoleon and the Empire'. *French History* 18(4), 349–53.

— 2004b (December). 'Napoleon Bonaparte as Hero and Saviour: Image, Rhetoric and Behaviour in the Construction of a Legend'. *French History* 18(4), 379–403.

— 2007. *Napoleon: The Path to Power, 1769–1799* (London: Bloomsbury Publishing Plc.).

Eder, W. 2005. 'Augustus and the Power of Tradition'. In *The Cambridge Companion to the Age of Augustus*, ed. and trans. K. Galinsky (Cambridge: Cambridge University Press), pp. 13–32.

Edwards, C. 1993. *The Politics of Immorality in Ancient Rome* (Cambridge: Cambridge University Press).

— 1996. *Writing Rome: Textual Approaches to the City* (Cambridge: Cambridge University Press).

— 1999. 'Introduction: Shadows and Fragments'. In *Roman Presences: Receptions of Rome in European Culture, 1789–1945*, ed. C. Edwards (Cambridge: Cambridge University Press), pp. 1–18.

— 2008. 'Possessing Rome: The Politics of Ruins in *Roma capitale*'. In *A Companion to Classical Receptions*, ed. L. Hardwick and C. Stray (Oxford: Blackwell), pp. 345–59.

Elias, N. 1983. *The Court Society*, trans. E. Jephcott (Oxford: Blackwell).

Ellis, G. 1997. *Napoleon* (London: Longman).

Emsley, C. 2003. *Napoleon. Conquest, Reform and Reorganisation: Seminar Studies in History* (Harlow: Pearson-Longman).

Espérandieu, E. 1907. *Collection de documents inédits sur l'histoire de France: recueil Général des bas-reliefs de la Gaule Romaine*, Vol. I (Paris: Impr. Nationale).

Etlin, R.A. 1975. 'Architecture and the Festival of Federation, Paris, 1790'. *Architectural History* 18, 23–42.

— 1994. *Symbolic Space: French Enlightenment Architecture and Its Legacy* (Chicago, IL: University of Chicago Press).

Faldi, I. 1955. 'La Festa Patriottica della Federazione in due dipinti di Felice Giani'. *Bollettino dei Musei Comunali di Roma, Anno II, 1–2*, 14–18.

Favro, D. 2005. 'Making Rome a World City'. In *The Cambridge Companion to the Age of Augustus*, ed. K. Galinsky (Cambridge: Cambridge University Press), pp. 234–63.

Fernandes, D., Plum, G. and Rouge-Ducos, I. 2000 (April). *Arc de Triomphe de l'Étoile* (Paris: Éditions du patrimoine).

Ferris, I. M. 2011. 'The Pity of War: Representations of Gauls and Germans in Roman Art'. In *Cultural Identity in the Ancient Mediterranean*, ed. E. S. Gruen (Los Angeles, CA: Getty Research Institute), pp. 185–201.

Fierro, A. 1996. *Histoire et dictionnaire de Paris* (Paris: Robert Laffont).

— 1998. *Dictionnaire du Paris disparu: sites et monuments* (Paris: Éditions Parigramme).

Flower, H. I. 2001. '*Damnatio Memoriae* and Epigraphy'. In *From Caligula to Constantine: Tyranny & Transformation in Roman Portraiture*, ed. E. R. Varner (Atlanta, GA: Michael C. Carlos Museum), pp. 58–69.

— 2004. 'Spectacle and Political Culture in the Roman Republic'. In *The Cambridge Companion to the Roman Republic*, ed. H. I. Flower (Cambridge: Cambridge University Press), pp. 322–43.

Folliot, F. 1989. 'Des Colonnes pour les héros'. In *Les Architectes de la Liberté 1789–1799*, catalogue for the exhibition held at the École nationale supérieure des Beaux-Arts, 4 October, 1989–7 January, 1990 (Paris: École nationale supérieure des Beaux-Arts), pp. 305–22.

Formica, M. 2004. 'The Protagonists and the Principal Phases of the Roman Republic of 1798 to 1799'. In *Tosca's Prism. Three Moments of Western Cultural History*, ed. D. Burton, S. Vandiver Nicassio and A. Ziino (Boston, MA: Northeastern University Press), pp. 67–81.

Forrest, A. 2004 (December). 'Propaganda and the Legitimation of Power in Napoleonic France'. *French History 18 (4)*, 426–45.

— 2011. *Napoleon* (London: Quercus).

Fouché, M. 1907. *Les grands artistes: Percier et Fontaine* (Paris: Librairie Renouard).

Freeman, C. 1996. *Egypt, Greece and Rome: Civilizations of the Ancient Mediterranean* (Oxford: Oxford University Press).

Freeman, P. 2008. *Julius Caesar* (London: JR Books).

Gady, A. 1999. 'Les portes du Soleil'. In *Art ou politique? Arcs, statues et colonnes de Paris*, ed. Action artistique de la Ville de Paris (Paris: Action artistique de la Ville de Paris), pp. 49–60.

Gaillard, M. 1996. *Paris: de l'Hôtel de Ville à la Défense. Guide de l'Axe Historique* (Amiens: Martelle Editions).

— 1998 (July). *The 'Arc de Triomphe'*, trans. N. Randall (Amiens: Martelle Editions).

Galinier, M. 2007. 'La Colonne Trajane et les forums impériaux'. *Collection de l'École française de Rome 382* (Rome).

Galinsky, K. ed., 2005. *The Cambridge Companion to the Age of Augustus* (Cambridge: Cambridge University Press).

Garraffoni, R. S. and Stoiani, R. 2006 (December). 'To Excavate the Past, To (Re-) Construct the Present: The symbolic Uses of Classical Antiquity by Napoleon Bonaparte'. *Revista de História da Arte e Arqueologia 6*, 214–22.

Giardina A. and Vauchez, A. 2000. *Rome: l'idée et le mythe du moyen âge à nos jours* (Paris: Librairie Arthème Fayard).

Giesey, R. E. 1985. 'Models of Rulership in French Royal Ceremonial'. In *Rites of Power: Symbolism, Ritual, and Politics since the Middle Ages*, ed. S. Wilentz (Pennsylvania State University: University of Pennsylvania Press), pp. 41–64.

Goalen, M. 1995. 'The Idea of the City and the Excavations at Pompeii'. In *Urban Society in Roman Italy*, ed. T. J. Cornell and K. Lomas (London: UCL Press), pp. 181–202.

Gombrich, E. H. 1989. *The Story of Art* (London: Phaidon).

— 1999. *The Uses of Images: Studies in the Social Function of Art and Visual Communication* (London: Phaidon).

Gorgone, G. and Tittoni, M. E. eds, 1997. *1796–1797 – Da Montenotte a Campoformio: la rapida marcia di Napoleone Bonaparte*, catalogue for the exhibition held at the Museo Napoleonico, 4 February–27 April, 1997 (Rome: 'L'Erma' di Bretschneider).

Grab, A. 2003. *Napoleon and the Transformation of Europe: European History in Perspective* (Basingstoke: Palgrave Macmillan).

— 2004. 'The Napoleonic Legacy in Italy'. In *Tosca's Prism. Three Moments of Western Cultural History*, ed. D. Burton, S. Vandiver Nicassio and A. Ziino (Boston, MA: Northeastern University Press), pp. 3–18.

Gregory, A. P. 1994. '"Powerful Images": Responses to Portraits and the Political uses of Images in Rome'. *Journal of Roman Archaeology 7*, 80–99.

Grell, C. 1988. 'La renommée de Trajan au XVIIe et au XVIIIe s'. In *La colonna Traiana e gli artisti francesi da Luigi XIV a Napoleone I*, catalogue for the exhibition held at the Villa Medici, 12 April–12 June, 1988, ed. G. Agosti, V. Farinella, P. Morel and G. Simoncini (Rome: Edizioni Carte Segrete), pp. 244–52.

Griffin, M. ed., 2009. *A Companion to Julius Caesar. Blackwell Companions to the Ancient World* (Oxford: Wiley-Blackwell).

Guibbert, J.-P. 2000. 'Poliphile et son temps'. In *Hypnerotomachia Poliphili ou: le Songe de Poliphile le plus beau livre du monde, Venise 1499, Paris 1546*, catalogue for the exhibition held at la Bibliothèque municipale d'Auxerre, 17 June–24 September, 2000, ed. Bibliothèque municipale d'Auxerre (Auxerre: Bibliothèque municipale), pp. 27–36.

Guigon, C. 2000a (October). 'A la découverte de Lutèce'. *Les Collections d'Histoire. Paris la traversée des siècles 9*, 10–11.

— 2000b (October). 'Sous le Louvre, huit siècles d'histoire: entretien avec Jean-Pierre Babelon (Membre de l'Institut)'. *Les Collections d'Histoire. Paris la traversée des siècles 9*, 34–9.

Hanley, S. 1983. *The 'Lit de Justice' of the Kings of France. Constitutional Ideology in Legend, Ritual, and Discourse* (Princeton, NJ: Princeton University Press).

Hanley, W. 2008. *The Genesis of Napoleonic Propaganda, 1796–1799* (New York: Colombia University Press).

Hannestad, N. 1986. *Roman Art and Imperial Policy* (Aarhus: Aarhus University Press).

Hardwick, L. 2003. *Reception Studies. Greece and Rome: New Surveys in the Classics No. 33* (Oxford).

Hardwick, L. and Stray, C. eds, 2008. *A Companion to Classical Receptions. Blackwell Companions to the Ancient World* (Oxford: Blackwell).

Harvey, D. 1985. *Consciousness and the Urban Experience* (Oxford: Blackwell).

Haskell, F. 1993. *History and Its Images. Art and the Interpretation of the Past* (New Haven, CT: Yale University Press).

Haskell, F. and Penny, N. 1981. *Taste and the Antique: The Lure of Classical Sculpture, 1500–1900* (New Haven, CT: Yale University Press).

Hautecoeur, L. 1914. 'Études sur l'art du premier empire'. *Revue des études Napoléoniennes* 6, 122–37.

— 1953. *Histoire de l'Architecture classique en France*, Vols IV and V (Paris: Éditions A. et J. Picard).

Hazareesingh, S. 2004a. *The Legend of Napoleon* (London: Granta Books).

— 2004b (December). 'Memory and Political Imagination: The Legend of Napoleon Revisited'. *French History* 18(4), 463–83.

Healey, F. G. 1957. *Rousseau et Napoléon* (Paris: Librairie Minard).

Hemmerle, O. B. 2006. 'Crossing the Rubicon into Paris: Caesarian Comparisons from Napoleon to de Gaulle'. In *Julius Caesar in Western Culture*, ed. M. Wyke (Oxford: Blackwell), pp. 285–302.

Hesse, C. 1989. 'Economic Upheavals in Publishing'. In *Revolution in Print. The Press in France 1775–1800*, ed. R. Darnton and D. Roche (Berkeley, CA: University of California Press), pp. 69–97.

Hibbert, C. 1969. *The Grand Tour* (London: Weidenfeld & Nicolson).

— 1985. *Rome: The Bibliography of a City* (Harmondsworth: Penguin Books).

Hitchcock, H. R. 1958. *Architecture, Nineteenth and Twentieth Centuries* (Harmondsworth: Penguin Books).

Hobsbawm, E. 1983. 'Introduction: Inventing Traditions'. In *The Invention of Tradition*, ed. E. Hobsbawm and T. Ranger (Cambridge: Cambridge University Press), pp. 1–14.

— 1996. *The Age of Revolution, 1789–1848* (New York: Vintage Books).

Holland, R. 2000. *Nero: The Man behind the Myth* (Gloucestershire: Sutton Publishing).

Hölscher, T. 2004. *The Language of Images in Roman Art*, trans. A. Snodgrass and A. Künzl-Snodgrass, with foreword by J. Elsner (Cambridge: Cambridge University Press).

Honour, H. 1991. *Neo-Classicism* (Harmondsworth: Penguin Books).

Horne, A. 2002. *Seven Ages of Paris: Portrait of a City* (London: Pan Books).

— 2004. *The Age of Napoleon* (London: Weidenfeld & Nicolson).

Hubert, G. 1999. 'L'arc du Carrousel; Les projets'. In *Art ou politique? Arcs, statues et colonnes de Paris*, ed. Action artistique de la Ville de Paris (Paris: Action artistique de la Ville de Paris), pp. 95–8; 110–13.

Huet, V. 1996. 'Stories One Might Tell of Roman Art: Reading Trajan's Column and the Tiberius Cup'. In *Art and Text in Roman Culture*, ed. J. Elsner (Cambridge: Cambridge University Press), pp. 8–31.

— 1999. 'Napoleon I: A New Augustus?' In *Roman Presences: Receptions of Rome in European Culture, 1789–1945*, ed. C. Edwards (Cambridge: Cambridge University Press), pp. 53–69.

Ingamells, J. 1996. 'Discovering Italy: British Travellers in the Eighteenth Century'. In *Grand Tour: The Lure of Italy in the Eighteenth Century*, ed. A. Wilton and I. Bignamini (London: Tate Gallery Publishing), pp. 21–30.

Itgenshorst, T. 2005. *Tota illa pompa: Der Triumph in der römischen Republik* (Göttingen: Vandenhoeck & Ruprecht).

Jenkins, K. 1995. *On 'What is History?'* (London: Routledge).

Jenkyns, R. ed., 1992. *The Legacy of Rome: A New Appraisal* (Oxford: Oxford University Press).

Johns, C. M. S. 1998. *Antonio Canova and the Politics of Patronage in Revolutionary and Napoleonic Europe* (Los Angeles, CA: University of California Press).

Jones, P. and Sidwell, K. eds, 1997. *The World of Rome. An Introduction to Roman Culture* (Cambridge: Cambridge University Press).

Jordan, D. P. 1995. *Transforming Paris. The Life and Labors of Baron Haussman* (New York: Free Press).

Jourdan, A. 2004. *Mythes et légendes de Napoléon. Un destin d'exception, entre rêve et réalité* (Toulouse: Éditions Privat).

Kallendorf, C. W. ed., 2007. *A Companion to the Classical Tradition* (Oxford: Blackwell).

Kleiner, D. E. E. 1992. *Roman Sculpture* (New Haven, CT: Yale University Press).

Kleiner, F. S. 1989. 'The Study of Roman Triumphal and Honorary Arches 50 Years after Kähler'. *Journal of Roman Archaeology* 2, 195–206.

— 2007. *The History of Roman Art* (Belmont, CA: Thomson Wadsworth).

Kostof, S. 1978. 'The Emperor and the Duce: The Planning of Piazzale Augusto Imperatore in Rome'. In *Art and Architecture in the Service of Politics*, ed. A. Millon and L. Nochlin (Cambridge, MA: MIT Press), pp. 270–325.

— 1991. *The City Shaped. Urban Patterns and Meanings through History* (London: Thames and Hudson).

Krautheimer, R. 1980. *Rome: Profile of a City, 312–1308* (Princeton, NJ: Princeton University Press).

Krief, P. 2004. *Paris Rive Droite: petites histoires & grands secrets* (Paris: Éditions Massin).

Künzl, E. 1988. *Der römische Triumph: siegesfeiern im antiken Rom* (Munich: Verlag C.H. Beck).

Kuttner, A. L. 2004. 'Roman Art during the Republic'. In *The Cambridge Companion to the Republic*, ed. H. I. Flower (Cambridge: Cambridge University Press), pp. 294–321.

Laird Kleine-Ahlbrandt, W. 2004. 'Victorien Sardou and the Legend of Marengo'. In *Tosca's Prism. Three Moments of Western Cultural History*, ed. D. Burton, S. Vandiver Nicassio and A. Ziino (Boston, MA: Northeastern University Press), pp. 94–113.

Lanzac de Laborie, L. 1905. *Paris sous Napoléon: Consulat provisoire et Consulat à temps; Paris sous Napoléon: administration grands travaux*, Vols I and II (Paris: Librairie Plon).

— 1913. *Paris sous Napoléon: spectacles et musées*, Vol. VIII (Paris: Librairie Plon).

Laurence, R. 1991. 'The Urban *vicus*: The Spatial Organisation of Power in the Roman City'. In *Papers of the Fourth Conference of Italian Archaeology: The Archaeology of Power 1*, ed. E. Herring, R. Whitehouse and J. Wilkins (London), pp. 145–52.

— 1994. *Roman Pompeii: Space and Society* (London: Routledge).

Lavedan, P. 1993. *Nouvelle histoire de Paris: histoire de l'urbanisme à Paris* (Paris: Librairie Hachette).

Ledbury, M. ed., 2007. *David after David. Essays on the Later Work* (New Haven, CT: Yale University Press).

Lee, S. 1999. *David* (London: Phaidon).

Lefebvre, G. 1969. *Napoleon: From Tilsit to Waterloo 1807–1815 (2)*, trans. J. E. Anderson (London: Routledge & Kegan Paul).

Lefebvre, H. 1991. *The Production of Space*, trans. D. Nicholson-Smith (Oxford: Blackwell).

— 2000. *La production de l'espace* (Paris: Anthropos).

— 2003. *The Urban Revolution*, trans. R. Bononno (Minneapolis, MN: University of Minnesota).

Leigh, R. A. 1979. 'Jean-Jacques Rousseau and the Myth of Antiquity in the Eighteenth Century'. In *Classical Influences on Western Thought A.D. 1650–1870*, ed. R. R. Bolgar (Cambridge: Cambridge University Press), pp. 155–68.

Leith, J. A. 1991. *Space and Revolution: Projects for Monuments, Squares, and Public Buildings in France 1789–1799* (Montreal: McGill-Queen's University Press).

Lenski, N. ed., 2006. *The Cambridge Companion to the Age of Constantine* (Cambridge: Cambridge University Press).

Lentz, T. 2004 (February). 'Napoléon, créateur de sa légende'. *Notre Histoire* 218, 18–21.

— 2007. *Nouvelle Histoire du Premier Empire: la France et l'Europe de Napoléon (1804–1814)*, Vol. III (Paris: Éditions Fayard).

Leon, B. 1970. *The Emerging City, Paris, in the Age of Louis XIV* (Durham, NC: Duke University Press).

Leone, R., Pirani, F., Tittoni, M. E. and Tozzi, S. eds, 2002. *Il Museo di Roma racconta la città*, catalogue for the exhibition held at the Palazzo Braschi, 4 May, 2002 (Rome: Gangemi Editore).

Lepper, F. and Frere, S. 1988. *Trajan's Column: A New Edition of the Chicorius plates* (Gloucester: Sutton Publishing).

Losemann, V. 1999. 'The Nazi Concept of Rome'. In *Roman Presences: Receptions of Rome in European Culture, 1789–1945*, ed. C. Edwards (Cambridge: Cambridge University Press), pp. 221–35.

Lossendiere (de), L. ed., 2008 (August). 'Napoléon 1ᵉʳ: despot ou génie?' *Les Chroniques de l'Histoire 1*, 3–81.

Lowrie, M. 2003 (Fall). 'Rome: City and Empire'. *Classical World 97(1)*, 57–68.

Loyer, F. 1999. *Histoire de l'architecture française: de la Révolution à nos jours* (Paris: Éditions Mengès).

Lyons, M. 1994. *Napoleon Bonaparte and the Legacy of the French Revolution* (London: Macmillan Press).

McClellan, A. L. 1984 (December). 'Aesthetics of Display: Museums in Paris 1750–1800'. *Art History 7(4)*, 438–64.

— 1994. *Inventing the Louvre. Art, Politics, and the Origins of the Modern Museum in Eighteenth-Century Paris* (Berekeley, CA: University of California Press).

MacCormack, S. G. 1981. *Art and Ceremony in Late Antiquity* (Berkeley, CA: University of California Press).

MacDonald, W. L. 1986. *The Architecture of the Roman Empire II: An Urban Appraisal* (New Haven, CT: Yale University Press).

MacKendrick, P. 1972. *Roman France* (New York: St Martin's Press).

Mackenzie, L. 2006. 'Imitation Gone Wrong: The "Pestilentially Ambitious" Figure of Julius Caesar in Michel de Montaigne's *Essais*'. In *Julius Caesar in Western Culture*, ed. M. Wyke (Oxford: Blackwell), pp. 131–47.

Madelin, L. 1906. *La Rome de Napoléon: la domination française à Rome de 1809–1814* (Paris: Plon-Nourrit et Cie).

Mader, G. 2006 (Summer). 'Triumphal Elephants and Political Circus at Plutarch, *Pomp.* 14.6'. *Classical World 99*, 397–403.

Mainardi, P. 1989. 'Assuring the Empire of the Future: The 1798 Fête de la Liberté'. *Art Journal 48(2)*, 155–63.

Malamud, M. 2006. 'Manifest Destiny and the Eclipse of Julius Caesar'. In *Julius Caesar in Western Culture*, ed. M. Wyke (Oxford: Blackwell), pp. 148–69.

Maria (da), S. 1988. *Gli Archi Onorari di Roma e dell'Italia Romana* (Rome: 'L'Erma' di Bretschneider).

Marrinan, M. 2009. *Romantic Paris. Histories of a Cultural Landscape, 1800–1850* (Stanford, CA: Stanford University Press).

Martindale, C. and Thomas, R. F. eds, 2006. *Classics and the Uses of Reception* (Oxford: Blackwell).

Mattingly, H. and Sydenham, E. A. 1926. *The Roman Imperial Coinage*, Vol. II: Vespasian to Hadrian (London: Spink & Son).

Mattusch, C. C. 2009. 'Herculaneum, Pompeii, and the French'. *Journal of Roman Archaeology 22*, 587–90.

Matyszak, P. 2006. *The Sons of Caesar: Imperial Rome's First Dynasty* (London: Thames and Hudson).

Mazedier, R. 1945. *Histoire de la presse parisienne, de Théophraste Renaudot à la IV République, 1631–1945* (Paris: Éditions du Pavois).

Mazzocca, F. 1997. 'L'iconografia di Napoleone e delle prima campagna d'Italia tra la realtà storica e la leggenda'. In *1796–1797 – Da Montenotte a Campoformio: la rapida marcia di Napoleone Bonaparte*, catalogue for the exhibition held at the Museo Napoleonico, 4 February–27 April, 1997, ed. G. Gorgone and M. E. Tittoni (Rome: "L'Erma" di Bretschneider), pp. 49–53.

Middleton, R. 1994. 'The Age of Reason'. In *History of Western Art*, ed. D. Hooker (New York: Barnes & Noble Books), pp. 270–93.

Miles, M. M. 2008. *Art as Plunder: The Ancient Origins of Debate about Cultural Property* (Cambridge: Cambridge University Press).

Millar, F. 1992. *The Emperor in the Roman World: 31 BC–AD 337* (London: Duckworth).

Millar, F. and Segal, E. eds, 1984. *Caesar Augustus: Seven Aspects* (Oxford: Clarendon Press).

Milovanovic, N. 2007 (June). 'Le décor peint de la Galerie des Glaces'. *Dossier de l'Art 142*, 34–51.

Mortgat-Longuet, E. 2006 (October). 'Du "siècle d'Auguste" au *Siècle de Louis XIV*: quelques réflexions sur le concept de "siècle" du début du dix-septième siècle à Voltaire'. *Studies on Voltaire and the Eighteenth Century* (SVEC 2006:10), 97–116.

Mourey, G. 1930. *Le livre des fêtes française* (Paris: Librairie de France).

Muratori-Philip, A. 1992. *La mémoire des lieux: l'Hôtel des Invalides* (Brussels: Éditions Complexe).

— 2007 (November). *Arc de Triomphe* (Paris: Éditions du patrimoine).

Nelis, J. 2007 (Summer). 'Constructing Fascist Identity: Benito Mussolini and the Myth of romanità'. *Classical World 100(4)*, 391–415.

Norma, P. 2002. *Napoléon* (Paris: Maxi-livres).

O'Brien, D. 1995 (October). 'Antoine-Jean Gros in Italy'. *The Burlington Magasine 137*, 651–60.

— 2004 (December). 'Antonio Canova's *Napoleon as Mars the Peacemaker* and the Limits of Imperial Portraiture'. *French History 18(4)*, 354–78.

Östenberg, I. 2009. *Staging the World: Spoils, Captives, and Representations in the Roman Triumphal Procession: Oxford Studies in Ancient Culture and Representation* (Oxford: Oxford University Press).

Ozouf, M. 1975 (July). 'Space and Time in the Festivals of the French Revolution'. *Comparative Studies in Society and History 17*, 372–84.

Pelling, C. 2006. 'Judging Julius Caesar'. In *Julius Caesar in Western Culture*, ed. M. Wyke (Oxford: Blackwell), pp. 3–26.

Pérouse de Montclos, J.-M. 1969a (October–December). 'La tradition classique et révolutionnaire dans l'urbanisme napoléonien'. *Les Monuments Historiques de la France 15*, 67–79.

— 1969b. *Etienne-Louis Boullée (1728–1799). De l'architecture classique à l'architecture révolutionnaire* (Paris: Arts et Métiers graphiques).

— 1989. *Histoire de l'architecture française. De la Renaissance à la Révolution* (Paris: Éditions Mengès).

Petiteau, N. 2004. *Napoléon, de la mythologie à l'histoire* (Paris: Éditions du seuil).

Petitfils, J.-C. 2005 (July-August). 'Le petit prince s'émancipe'. *Historia Thématique. Louis XIV, ombres et lumières* 96, 8–15.

Petzet, M. 2000. *Claude Perrault und die Architektur des Sonnenkönigs* (Munich: Deutscher Kunstverlag).

Picon, A. 1988. *Architectes et ingénieurs au Siècle des lumières* (Marseille: Éditions Parenthèses).

Pierse, S. 2008 (May). 'Voltaire Historiographer: Narrative Paradigms'. *Studies on Voltaire and the Eighteenth Century* (SVEC 2008:05).

Pinatel, C. 1988. 'Les moulages de la Colonne Trajane à Versailles, provenant de l'École des Beaux-Arts de Paris et antérieurs à 1800'. In *La colonna Traiana e gli artisti francesi da Luigi XIV a Napoleone I*, catalogue for the exhibition held at the Villa Medici, 12 April–12 June, 1988, ed. G. Agosti, V. Farinella, P. Morel and G. Simoncini (Rome: Edizioni Carte), pp. 274–80.

Pingeot, A. 1999. 'Triomphes éphémères'. In *Art ou politique? Arcs, statues et colonnes de Paris*, ed. Action artistique de la Ville de Paris (Paris: Action artistique de la Ville de Paris), pp. 145–55.

Poisson, G. 1999. 'L'Empereur, colonne Vendôme'. In *Art ou politique? Arcs, statues et colonnes de Paris*, ed. Action artistique de la Ville de Paris (Paris: Action artistique de la Ville de Paris), pp. 91–4.

— 2002. *Napoléon 1er et Paris* (Paris: Éditions Tallandier).

Porterfield, T. and Siegfried, S. L. 2006. *Staging Empire. Napoleon, Ingres, and David* (University Park, PA: Pennsylvania State University Press).

Punzi, R. 1999. 'Fonti documentarie per una rilettura delle vicende post-antiche dell'arco di Costantino'. In *Arco di Costantino. Tra archeologia e archeometria*, ed. P. Pensabene and C. Panella (Rome: "L'Erma" di Bretschneider), pp. 185–228.

Purcell, N. 1987. 'Town in Country and Country in Town'. In *Dumbarton Oaks Colloquium on the History of Landscape Architecture 10: Ancient Roman Villa Gardens*, ed. E. B. MacDougall (Washington, DC), pp. 185–203.

— 1989. 'Rediscovering the Roman Forum'. *Journal of Roman Archaeology* 2, 156–66.

— 1995a. 'Forum Romanum (The Imperial Period)'. In *Lexicon Topographicum Urbis Romae* Vol II, D–G, ed. E. M. Steinby (Rome: Edizioni Quasar), pp. 336–42.

— 1995b. 'Forum Romanum (The Republican Period)'. In *Lexicon Topographicum Urbis Romae* Vol II, D–G, ed. E. M. Steinby (Rome: Edizioni Quasar), pp. 325–6.

Raaflaub, K. A. and Toher, M. eds, 1990. *Between Republic and Empire: Interpretations of Augustus and His Principate* (Berkeley, CA: University of California Press).

Ramage, N. H. and Ramage, A. 2009. *Roman Art: Romulus to Constantine* (Upper Saddle River, NJ: Pearson Prentice Hall).

Regenbogen, L. 1998. *Napoléon a dit: aphorismes, citations et opinions* (Paris: Société d'Édition les Belles Lettres).

Ribner, J. P. 1993. *Broken Tablets: The Cult of the Law in French Art from David to Delacroix* (Berkeley, CA: University of California Press).

Ridley, R. T. 1992. *The Eagle and the Spade: The Archaeology in Rome during the Napoleonic Era 1809–1814* (Cambridge: Cambridge University Press).

Rioux, J.-P. 2000 (October). 'Les douze travaux de Mitterrand 1er'. *Les Collections de l'Histoire. Paris traversée des siècles 9*, 102–3.

Roche, D. 1989. 'Censorship and the Publishing Industry'. In *Revolution in Print. The Press in France 1775–1800*, ed. R. Darnton and D. Roche (Berkeley, CA: University of California Press), pp. 3–26.

Rochell and Ziskin, R. 1999. *The Place Vendôme: Architecture and Social Mobility in Eighteenth-Century Paris* (Cambridge: Cambridge University Press).

Roudil, P. 1984 (May). '"Il n'a jamais exercé un pouvoir absolu": entretien avec Michel Déon de l'Académie Française'. *Historama-Histoire Magazine 3*, 106–7.

Rouge, I. 1999. 'L'Arc de Triomphe de l'Etoile'. In *Art ou politique? Arcs, statues et colonnes de Paris*, ed. Action artistique de la Ville de Paris (Paris: Action artistique de la Ville de Paris), pp. 99–105; 122–6.

Roy, A. 1981. 'Pouvoir municipale et prestige monarchique: les entrées royales à Paris en 1660, à Strasbourg en 1681 et 1744'. In *Pouvoir, ville et société en Europe 1650–1750*, papers delivered at the Collogue Internationale du C. N. R. S., October 1981, ed. G. Livetet (Paris), pp. 317–20.

Ruiz, A. 2004 (February). 'Napoléon Magne'. *Notre Histoire 218*, 26–9.

Rumeau-Dieudonné, M.-H. 2007 (December). 'L'entrée triomphale de Louis XIV et Marie-Thérèse d'Autriche le 26 août 1660'. *La Cité: Société Historique et Archéologique des IIIe IVe XIe et XIIe Arrondissements de Paris 26*, 25–40.

Saint-Simon (de), F. 1982. *La place Vendôme* (Paris: Éditions Vendôme).

Saurat, P. and Devignac, H.-G. 1990. *La mémoire de Paris* (Paris: Éditions Saurat).

Scherer, M. R. 1955. *Marvels of Ancient Rome* (London: Phaidon).

Schneider, R. 1913 (January). 'Le thème du triomphe dans les entrées solennelles en France à la Renaissance'. *Gazette des Beaux-Arts 9*, 85–106.

Scobie, A. 1990. *Hitler's State Architecture: The Impact of Classical Antiquity* (University Park, PA: Pennsylvania State University Press).

Scott, R. T. 2000. 'The Triple Arch of Augustus and the Roman Triumph'. *Journal of Roman Archaeology 13*, 183–91.

Sellers. M. N. S. 2004. 'The Roman Republic and the French and American Revolutions'. In *The Cambridge Companion to the Roman Republic*, ed. H. I. Flower (Cambridge: Cambridge University Press), pp. 347–64.

Seta (de), C. 1996. 'Grand Tour: The Lure of Italy in the Eighteenth Century'. In *Grand Tour: The Lure of Italy in the Eighteenth Century*, ed. A. Wilton and I. Bignamini (London: Tate Gallery Publishing), pp. 13–19.

Shovlin, J. 2006. *The Political Economy of Virtue: Luxury, Patriotism, and the Origins of the French Revolution* (Ithaca, NY: Cornell University Press).

Silver, L. 1990. 'Paper Pageants: The Triumphs of Emperor Maximilian I'. In *'All the World's a Stage . . . ': Art and Pageantry in the Renaissance and Baroque*, Vols I and II, papers in Art History from the Pennsylvania State University, ed. S. S. Munshower, B. Wisch (University Park, PA: Pennsylvania State University Press), pp. 293–308.

Smith, R. R. R. 2000. 'Nero and the Sun-God: Divine Accessories and Political Symbols in Roman Imperial Images'. *Journal of Roman Archaeology 13*, 532–42.

Soja, E. W. 1996. *Thirdspace: Journeys to Los Angeles and Other Real-and-Imagined Places* (Oxford: Blackwell).
Southall, A. 1998. *The City in Time and Space* (Cambridge: Cambridge University Press).
Souza (de), P. 2011. 'War, Slavery, and Empire in Roman Imperial Iconography'. *Bulletin of the Institute of Classical Studies 54(1)*, 31–62.
Stambaugh, J. E. 1988. *The Ancient Roman City* (Baltimore, MD: John Hopkins University Press).
Steinby, E. M. ed., 1993. *Lexicon Topographicum Urbis Romae* Vol. I, A–C (Rome: Edizioni Quasar).
— 1995. *Lexicon Topographicum Urbis Romae* Vol. II, D–G (Rome: Edizioni Quasar).
— 1996. *Lexicon Topographicum Urbis Romae* Vol. III, H–O (Rome: Edizioni Quasar).
— 1999. *Lexicon Topographicum Urbis Romae* Vol. IV, P–S (Rome: Edizioni Quasar).
— 1999. *Lexicon Topographicum Urbis Romae* Vol. V, T–Z (Rome: Edizioni Quasar).
Stevens Curl, J. 2001. *Classical Architecture: An Introduction to Its Vocabulary and Essentials, with a Select Glossary of Terms* (London: B.T. Batsford).
Stewart, P. 2006. 'Roman Art'. *The Classical Review 56(1)*, 210–11.
Stirling, L. 2006. 'Art, Architecture, and Archaeology in the Roman Empire'. In *A Companion to the Roman Empire*, ed. D. S. Potter (Oxford: Blackwell), pp. 75–97.
Stone, M. 1999. 'A Flexible Rome: Fascism and the Cult of *romanità*'. In *Roman Presences: Receptions of Rome in European Culture, 1789–1945*, ed. C. Edwards (Cambridge: Cambridge University Press), pp. 205–20.
Strong, E. 1929. *Art in Ancient Rome*, Vol. II (London: William Heinemann).
— 1939. '*Romanità* through the Ages'. *Journal of Roman Studies 29*, 137–66.
Strong, R. 1984. *Art and Power: Renaissance Festivals 1450–1650* (Berkeley, CA: University of California Press).
Sutcliffe, A. 1993. *Paris: An Architectural History* (New Haven, CT: Yale University Press).
Syme, R. 1960. *The Roman Revolution* (Oxford: Oxford University Press).
Szambien, W. 1984. *J-N-L Durand 1760–1834: de l'imitation à la norme* (Paris: Picard).
— 1986. *Les projets de l'an II. Concours d'architecture de la période révolutionnaire* (Paris: École nationale supérieure des Beaux-Arts).
— 1989. 'Les Concours de l'an II'. In *Les Architectes de la Liberté 1789–1799*, catalogue for the exhibition held at the École nationale supérieure des Beaux-Arts, 4 October, 1989–7 January, 1990 (Paris: École nationale supérieure des Beaux-Arts), pp. 181–201.
— 1992. *De la rue des Colonnes à la rue de Rivoli* (Paris: Délégation à l'action artistique de la Ville de Paris).
Tapie, V. L. 1957. *Baroque et classicisme* (Paris: Librairie Plon).
Texier, S. 1999. 'Arche de la Défense'. In *Art ou politique? Arcs, statues et colonnes de Paris*, ed. Action artistique de la Ville de Paris (Paris: Action artistique de la Ville de Paris), pp. 216–25.
Tieder, I. 1993. 'Le calendrier républicain et ses incidences littéraires'. *Annales Historiques de la Révolution Française 2*, 259–67.

Tittoni, M. E. 1997. 'Le requisizioni delle opere d'arte nella prima campagna d'Italia'. In *1796–1797 – Da Montenotte a Campoformio: la rapida marcia di Napoleone Bonaparte*, catalogue for the exhibition held at the Museo Napoleonico, 4 February–27 April, 1997, ed. G. Gorgone and M. E. Tittoni (Rome: "L'Erma" di Bretschneider), pp. 101–7.

Toher, M. 2007. 'The Augustan Age'. *The Classical Review* 57(2), 472–4.

Tollfree, E. 1999 (September). *Napoleon and the 'New Rome': Rebuilding Imperial Rome in Late Eighteenth and Early Nineteenth-Century Paris*. PhD dissertation, University of Bristol.

— 2004 (January). 'Roman Republicans, Fasces and Festivals. The French Occupation of Rome, 1798–99, from the Archives of the Museo Napoleonico'. *Apollo: The International Magazine of the Arts*, 33–43.

Tulard, J. 1965. *L'anti-Napoléon: la légende noire de l'Empereur* (Paris: René Julliard).

— 1970. *Nouvelle histoire de Paris: Le Consulat et l'Empire, 1800–1815* (Paris: Librairie Hachette).

— 1971. *Le mythe de Napoléon* (Paris: Armand Colin).

— 1982. *Le Grand Empire, 1804–1815* (Paris: Éditions Albin Michel).

— 1993. *Napoléon: le Sacre. gravures et procès-verbal de la cérémonie du Sacre et du Couronnement de leurs Majestés Impériales, 1805*, ed. G. Duby (Paris: Impr. nationale Éditions).

— ed., 2001. *Napoléon Bonaparte: Œuvres littéraires et écrits militaires*. Vol. I (Paris: Bibliothèque des Introuvables).

Tulard, J. 2002 (July–August). 'Le grand chambardement des frontières'. *Historia Thématique* 78, 18–25.

Urry, J. 1990. *The Tourist Gaze: Leisure and Travel in Contemporary Societies* (London: Sage Publications).

Vandiver Nicassio, S. 2005. *Imperial City: Rome, Romans and Napoleon, 1796–1815* (Welwyn Garden City: Ravenhall Books).

— 2009. *Imperial City: Rome under Napoleon* (Chicago, IL: University of Chicago Press).

Van Zanten, D. 1994. *Building Paris: Architectural Institutions and the Transformation of the French Capital, 1830–1870* (Cambridge: Cambridge University Press).

Varner, E. R. 2001. 'Tyranny and the Transformation of the Roman Visual Landscape'. In *From Caligula to Constantine: Tyranny & Transformation in Roman Portraiture*, ed. E. R. Varner (Atlanta, GA: Michael C. Carlos Museum), pp. 9–26.

Vaulchier (de), C. 1989. 'La recherche d'un palais pour l'Assemblée nationale; Iconographie de décors révolutionnaires'. In *Les Architectes de la Liberté 1789–1799*, catalogue for the exhibition held at the École nationale supérieure des Beaux-Arts, 4 October, 1989 – 7 January, 1990 (Paris: École nationale supérieure des Beaux-Arts), pp. 137–62, 255–79.

Versnel, H. S. 1970. *'Triumphus': An Inquiry into the Origin, Development and Meaning of the Roman Triumph* (Leiden: E.J. Brill).

Veyne, P. 2002 (January–March). 'Lisibilité des images, propagande et apparat monarchique dans l'Empire romain'. *Revue Historique* 621, 3–30.

Vout, C. 2007. 'Sizing up Rome, or Theorizing the Overview'. In *The Sites of Rome. Time, Space, Memory*, ed. D. H. J. Larmour and D. Spencer (Oxford: Oxford University Press), pp. 295–322.

Walde, C. 2006. 'Caesar, Lucan's *Bellum Civile*, and Their Reception'. In *Julius Caesar in Western Culture*, ed. M. Wyke (Oxford: Blackwell), pp. 45–61.

Wallace-Hadrill, A. 1988. 'The Social Structure of the Roman House'. *Papers of the British School at Rome* 56, 43–97.

— 1990. 'Roman Arches and Greek Honours: The Language of Power at Rome'. *Proceedings of the Cambridge Philosophical Society* 36, 143–81.

— 1994. *Houses and Society in Pompeii and Herculaneum* (Princeton, NJ: Princeton University Press).

— 2005. '*Mutatas Formas*: The Augustan Transformation of Roman Knowledge'. In *The Cambridge Companion to the Age of Augustus*, ed. K. Galinsky (Cambridge: Cambridge University Press), pp. 55–84.

Weerdt-Pilorge (de), M.-P. 2006 (October). 'Saint-Simon et Voltaire: ombres et lumières d'un tableau du Grand Siècle'. *Studies on Voltaire and the Eighteenth Century* (*SVEC* 2006:10), 117–32.

Weinstock, S. 1971. *Divus Julius* (Oxford: Clarendon Press).

Wilson-Smith, T. 2002. *Napoleon. Man of War, Man of Peace* (London: Constable).

Wilton, A. and Bignamini, I. eds, 1996. *Grand Tour: The Lure of Italy in the Eighteenth Century* (London: Tate Gallery Publishing).

Wintjes, J. 2006. 'From "Capitano" to "Great Commander": The Military Reception of Caesar from the Sixteenth to the Twentieth Centuries'. In *Julius Caesar in Western Culture*, ed. M. Wyke (Oxford: Blackwell), pp. 269–84.

Wisch, B. 1990. Introduction. In *'All the World's a Stage . . .' Art and Pageantry in the Renaissance and Baroque*, Vols I and II, papers in Art History from the Pennsylvania State University, ed. S. S. Munshower and B. Wisch (University Park, PA: Pennsylvania State University Press).

Wright, D. G. 1984. *Napoleon and Europe* (London: Longman).

Wyke, M. 1999. 'Sawdust Caesar: Mussolini, Julius Caesar, and the Drama of Dictatorship'. In *The Uses and Abuses of Antiquity*, ed. M. Wyke and M. Biddiss (New York: Peter Lang), pp. 167–84.

— ed., 2006. *Julius Caesar in Western Culture* (Oxford: Blackwell).

— 2008. *Caesar: A Life in Western Culture* (Chicago, IL: University of Chicago Press).

Zadorojnyi, A. V. 2006. 'Plutarch's Statesmen'. *The Classical Review* 56(1), 74–6.

Zanger, A. E. 1997. *Scenes from the Marriage of Louis XIV: Nuptial Fictions and the Making of Absolutist Power* (Palo Alto, CA: Stanford University Press).

Zanker, P. 1988. *The Power of Images in the Age of Augustus* (Ann Arbor, MI: University of Michigan Press).

Index

Académie de France à Rome 12, 92, 118–19, 162
    Palazzo Mancini 12, 119
    Villa Medici 12, 119
Académie royale d'Architecture 92
adventus 131, 136
Aemilius Paullus 127, 133, 142–4, 164
Aeneas 93 *see also* Virgil
Alexander the Great 27, 66, 96, 129
Amaury-Duval 27, 37, 48, 121
American War of Independence 25
ancien régime 24, 35, 38, 54, 70, 157–8, 162, 164–5
Aphrodite 111
Apollo 106–7
    association with Louis XIV 106–7, 129
    gallery of (in Louvre) under Louis XIV 50, 107, 154, 161
    gallery of (in Louvre) under Napoleon 154
    salon of (at Versailles) 106–7
    see also Augustus; Nero
Apollo Belvedere 50, 116, 145
Apostolidès, J.-M. 26
Appian 125
aqueducts 66
    Aquéduc d'Arcueil 7
    Aquéduc de Maintenon 116
    Pont du Gard 17, 66
arch(es)
    Brandenburg Gate 44
    Carrousel, arc du 16–17, 38–40, 47–54, 55, 61–3, 68–70, 118, 120, 146, 159–60
    Constantine, arch of 16, 22, 51–2, 102, 111, 119, 126, 140
    Défense, Grande Arche de la 69–70, 166
    Entrée triomphale (1660), obelisk-topped arch 150–1
    Entrée triomphale (1660), Pont Notre-Dame arch 151
    Faubourg Saint-Antoine, arch of 101, 104–5, 112
    Festival of the Federation (Paris), arch for 137
    Festival of the Federation (Rome), arch for 140
    Festival of Unity and Indivisibility, arch for 138
    Glanum, arch at 15
    Janus, arch of 22
    Marble Arch 51
    Orange, arch at 16–18, 127
    Pantin arch 40
    S. Sebastiano, porta 133
    Saint-Antoine, porte 67–8, 103–4, 111, 153–4
    Saint-Bernard, porte 103
    Saint-Denis, porte 51, 101–3, 107–8, 111, 114, 120, 131–2, 134, 153
    Saint-Louis, porte 103
    Saint-Martin, porte 44–5, 102–3, 120
    Septimius Severus, arch of 16, 22, 49, 51–2, 119, 126, 133
    Titus, arch of 16, 22, 43, 52, 102, 111, 119, 126, 133, 138
    Trajan, arch of (Benevento) 127
    Triomphe de l'Étoile, arc de 6, 15, 36, 38–47, 55–6, 62, 65, 67–70, 98, 115, 120, 150, 152–3, 160, 165–6
Arles, Roman theatres 17
auctoritas 92
Augustus / Augustan Rome 3, 17, 27, 127, 156
    association with Apollo 106–7
    and the star 152
    Principate, formation of 25
    reception under Charles V and in Renaissance Europe 133, 135–6, 165
    reception under Napoleon 3, 17–18, 25, 27–8, 53–4, 94, 96, 99, 129, 135–6, 149, 155–6, 162–3, 165–6

reception under the French Republic 25
Res Gestae Augusti 27 *see also adventus*;
    Henri IV; Louis XIV
Aurelian 103
Autun, college of 19
Auxonne, artillery school 20
axe historique, Paris 55, 69–70

Bacchus 127
Baltard, L.-P. 27, 121
Barker, R. 94–7, 99
Bartoli, P. S. 58
Bastille 56–7, 59
    place de la 38, 66–8
    storming of 23, 47, 67
    triumphal arch plans 67
baths *see thermae*
battle of
    Actium 53
    Arcole 20, 30, 65, 140
    Auerstaedt 44
    Austerlitz 29–30, 38, 48, 52, 57, 65, 147
    Castiglione 61–2, 140
    Dantzig 65
    Eylau 40, 65
    Friedland 40, 65
    Iéna 44, 65
    Lodi 20, 65
    Marengo 20, 29–30, 61, 65, 117, 135
    Milvian Bridge 52
    Mont-Thabor 65
    Pyramids 65
    Rivoli 56, 65
    Ulm 52, 65, 128
Bausset (de), L. F. J. 16, 62
Bellori, G. P. 58
Bensérade (de), I. 92
Béranger, A. 155
Berger, R. W. 107
Bergeret, P.-N. 29–30
Bernini, G. L. 50, 68, 109
Blondel, N.-F. 93, 102–4, 111, 114, 116, 119
    and map of Paris 103–4
Bluche, F. 91
Bonaparte, J. 21
Boscoreale cup 126–7
Bosio, F. J. 54
Bourbon, palais 8, 31, 50
    as Temple of Hymen 152

Bourrienne (de), L.-A. F. 65
Bralle, F.-J. 65
Briant, B. 129
Brice, G. 100–2, 104–5, 110
Brienne, military school 19
Brosses (de), C. 14
Brutus, Lucius Junius 24–5, 139, 145–6
    bronze bust of 145–6
Brutus, Marcus 24
    marble head of 145
Bryant, L. M. 130, 148
Bullet, P. map of Paris 103–4
Burke, P. 92–6, 105
Byron, F. G. 137

Caesar *see* Julius Caesar
calendar, Republican 23
Caligula 53
Callet, A. F.
    Allegory of the Surrender of Ulm 128–30,
        136, 149, 152
Cambecérès (de), J.-J.-R. 61
Campo-Formio, treaty of 20
Campus Martius see triumph
Canal de l'Ourcq 8, 117
Canova, A. 22
Capitol *see* Napoleonic; triumph
Capitole, jardin du 22, 133
Capitoline *see* triumph
caput mundi
    Napoleonic Paris as 44, 130, 155, 160,
        162
    Rome as 7, 43–4, 130
Caracalla 52
Carrousel
    arch *see* arch(es)
    Grande: Paris 50, 108, 135, 161
    Grande: Versailles 66, 108
    place du 49–50, 58, 60, 62
Carthage / Carthaginian 30, 107
Castiglione
    battle *see* battle of
    rue de 61–2, 70, 160
Cato the Elder 24–5
Cellerier, J. 120
Ceres 127
Césars, palais des 8
Chaillot, visionary palace 121–2
Chalgrin, J.-F. T. 39

Index 231

Chambray (de), R. F. 58, 119
Champagny (de), J.-B. N 41–2
Champs-de-Mars 137, 139
   as Republican 'Capitol' 145–6
Champs-Élysées, avenue des 38–9, 42–4, 46, 55–7, 62, 65, 67, 69–70, 92, 115, 152, 160, 165
Chapelain, J. 93–4
Charlemagne 1, 30
   and Napoleon 1, 27, 31, 59
Charles V 103
Charles V, Holy Roman Emperor 133–6, 165 *see also* Augustus; Caesar; *Forum Romanum*; triumph (post-antique)
Charles X 55
Charlet, N.-T. 32–3
Chateaubriand, F.-R. 13, 67, 112–13
Chatêlet, place du 65
Chaudet, A.-D. 64
Chaumont (de), L. 63
Cicero 24–5
   De re publica 93
   Orations 19
Cimiez (*Cemenelum*) 18
Cincinnatus 108
Cité, palais de la 131, 134, 153
city gate 16, 40–3, 55, 131
Cleary, R. L. 104, 117
Code Napoléon 31–2, 156
coins 5, 30, 103, 125
Colbert, J.-B. 89–95, 101, 105, 115–16, 118–19, 152
Colonna, F. 134
Colonnade *see* Perrault Cl.
Colosseum 22, 43, 52, 71, 141
column(s)
   Aurelian 127
   plans by Cathala, E.-L.-D. 59
   for revolutionary festivals 139, 141
   Trajan's Column 15, 22, 50, 57–60, 70, 114, 127
   Vendôme Column 15, 22, 38, 57–64, 70–1, 116–17, 159–60
   at Wimille 17
Commission des Artistes 56–7
Commune / Communards 42, 64, 71
Concorde, place de la 38, 41, 46, 49, 55–7, 62, 146

Concorde, pont de la 59, 151–2
Conquêtes, place des 92, 101, 108, 110–11, 117
   statue of Louis XIV 58–9, 61, 64, 101–2, 108, 110–11, 117
   visionary complex 117–18 *see* Vendôme
Constantine 52, 126 *see also* arch(es); Louis XIV
Corneille, P. 26–7, 93
Coronation of Napoleon 4, 97–9
   see also David, J.-L.
Corsica 19–20
Cotelle, J. 109
coup of 18–19 *Brumaire* 19
Courbet, G. 64
Couture, L. 89
currus triumphalis see triumph

Dacia(n) 52, 57, 103
damnatio memoriae 54, 64, 71
David, J.-L. 24, 46
   Bonaparte Crossing the St. Bernard Pass 30–1
   Brutus 24
   Coronation of Napoleon 31, 97
   Distribution of the Eagles 31
   Napoleon in his Study 32
   Oath of the Horatii 24
De mirabilibus urbis Romae 14
Delannoy, F. J. 120
Denon, D.-V. (baron de) 53, 58, 94, 116–19
Desaix General 31, 117
Deseine, F. 14
Desgodetz, A. 92, 119, 126
Desjardins, M. 109
Diocletian, palace 121
Dionysius 125
Domitian 39, 53–4
Domus Aurea see Nero
Driault, E. 69
Ducis, L. 55
Durand, J.-N. -L. 119
Dwyer, P. G. 19, 30

'Eaglet' (Napoleon II) 120–1
east-west axis 8–9 ch. 2, 160
École Militaire, Paris 20
Edwards, C. 130
elephant 66, 134 *see also* fountains

Ellis, G. 31
emperors, compartmentalization of 99, 104, 157
enceinte des fermiers généraux 40, 47
Enlightenment 24, 26, 90
entries / *entrées see* triumph (post-antique)
Esquiline hill 120
Etlin, R. A. 5, 37, 41, 46, 137

fasces 24, 31, 140, 145
Fasti Triumphalis 125
Faubourg Saint Antoine, rue du 68
festivals *see* triumph (post-antique)
fleur-de-lys 64, 102, 104
Fontaine, P.-F.-L. 44, 47–8, 51, 54, 65, 94, 119–21
Fontainebleau, château de 91
fora 8, 117–18
 Augustan 53
 Trajanic 22, 57
Forrest, A. 90
Forum Romanum (Roman Forum) 22, 43, 49, 51–2, 69, 118, 122, 125, 141, 162
 as *campo vaccino* 46–7
 clearing of under Charles V 133
 use of under French Republic 141
 see also Romulus
fountains 8, 66–7, 103, 107–8
 elephant fountain 38, 66–7, 134
 Innocents, fontaine des 134
 triumphal arch fountain 109, 121
 Victoire, fontaine de la 38, 65–6, 134
François I 1, 11, 58, 91, 116, 132, 134–5
 see also triumph (post-antique)
French Revolution *see* Republic
Fronde la, 3, 91

gateways *see* city gate
Geta 52, 54
Germanicus 53–4
 Germanicus statue 108
Gibbon, E. 14, 130
Giesey, R. E. 134
Girardon, F. 101–2, 119
Glanum 15
 Mausoleum of the Julii 15
 see also arch(es)
Gondouin, J. 58
Gonzaga family, palace of 135

Goudin, J. 134
Gracchi 24
Grand César, jardin du 21–2
Grand Tour 13–15, 18
Grande Armée 17, 39–40, 44, 57, 59, 60, 62, 117, 147, 159
Greece / Greek 13, 29, 39, 93, 96, 103, 138, 144
Gregory, A. P. 33
Gros, A.-J. *Bonaparte on the Bridge of Arcole* 30

Hadrian: villa at Tivoli 106, 121
Hampton Court, palace of 135
Hannibal 27, 30, 66
Hardouin-Mansart, J. 91, 101, 109
Harvey, D. 64
Hazareesingh, S. 26
Hellenistic *see* Greece / Greek
Hemmerle, O. B 4–5
Henri II 1, 67, 134, 138, 152
 see also triumph (post-antique)
Henri IV 1, 11, 114, 132, 151–2
 and Caesar 135
 equestrian statue of 151
 links with Augustus 3, 91, 135, 151
 reception under Louis XIV 122, 151
 see also triumph (post-antique)
Heracles on Mount Olympus 138
 see also Hercules
Herculaneum 12–14
 and Napoleon 13–14
Hercules 127, 134
 under Louis XIV 103, 107–8
 and monarchy 134, 138
 under Republic (French) 24, 134, 138
Historia Augusta 92
Hitler, A. 3, 69–70, 165–6
Horace 93, 156
Horne, A. 4, 121
horti 22, 109
Horses of Marly 46
Horses of St. Mark's 49–50, 52–4, 70, 145–6, 159
Huet, V. 3, 27
Hugo, V. 157
Hymen *see* Bourbon, palais

Impérial, rue 65–9, 160
Impero, via dell 165

Index

Ingres, J. A. D. *Napoleon on his Imperial Throne* 31
Invalides, hôtel des 92, 106, 166
Italian States 21

Johns, C. M. S. 22
Julius Caesar 27, 127, 130
   assassination 25, 145
   commentarii 28
   Gallic campaigns 7, 28–9
   Lutetia, occupation of 7, 29
   and Napoleon 4, 17–19, 28–30, 54, 66, 116, 135, 162, 165
   reception under Charles V and in Renaissance Europe 133–5, 165
   reception under French Republic 4, 25, 145, 165
   and revolutionary America 25
   Rubicon, crossing of 4, 102
   see also Henri IV; Louis XIV
Juno 127
Jupiter 127–9, 134, 146
   eagle as armour-bearer 128
   links with Louis XIV 107
   and Napoleon 128
   statue of 60, 146
   temple(s) of *see* triumph

Kostof, S. 42–3, 147–8

La Fontaine (de), J. 93
Lahure, J.-B.-A. 56–7
Lalande (de), J. J. 14, 129, 154
Laocoön 12, 116, 145
Las Cases, M.-J.-E.-D. *see Mémorial*
Lassels, R. 14
Latinus 129
laurel
   antique 128, 146
   post-antique 29, 31, 33, 63, 71, 128–9, 132, 144, 146–7, 149
Le Nôtre, A. 46, 56, 93, 108–9, 111, 115
Le Vau, L. 51, 93
Lebrun, C. 93–4, 106–8, 119
   see also Apollo, gallery and salon of
Lebrun, C.-F. 61
Lefebvre, H. 5–6, 37–8, 40–1, 43, 45–6, 55, 59, 63–4, 70–1, 159, 161–4
Legrand, J.-G. and Landon, C.-P. 7, 47, 50, 53, 114–16

Leith, J. A. 37, 46
Lemot, F.-F. 54
Leon, B. 90
Lepère, J.-B. 58
Lescot, P. 134
lictor 24, 126–7, 140
Ligorio, P. 12
Lister, M. 109–11
Livy 19, 93, 125, 145
Locke, J. 109
Louis XIII 114
Louis XIV 34, 45, 56
   affiliation with antique Rome 1, 11, 40–1, 44–5, 50–1, 58–9, 67–8 ch.3, 129, 144, 147–55, 156–66
   and Augustus 3, 25–6, 92–6, 102, 104–5, 106–7, 129, 135–6, 149, 161–3, 165
   and Caesar 50, 96, 102, 107–8, 116, 135, 161
   and Constantine 102
   influence on Napoleon /Napoleonic Paris 1–6, 9, 37–8, 44–6, 58–9, 67–8, 71–2, 89–91, 94–100, 105, 112–23, 129, 135–6, 147–66
   reception under French Republic 4, 58–9, 61, 64, 71, 90, 112–13, 121, 148
   statues of *see* Conquêtes, place des; Victoires, place des *see also* Apollo; Henri IV; Nero
Louis XV 19, 66, 114, 118
Louis XVI 61, 114, 137–8
Louis XVIII 55
Louis-Philippe 54, 64
Louvois (marquis de), F.-M. 91, 101
Louvre, Palais du 8, 31, 38, 42, 46, 48–50, 55–6, 60, 62, 65, 68, 89, 104–5, 106–7, 111, 115, 153–5, 160–1
   as museum / home to *spolia* 8, 48–9, 55–7, 62, 70, 116, 154–6, 160–1
Lowrie, M. 45–6
Lycurgus 32
Lyons, M. 32, 39

Mably (de) G. B. 20
MacDonald, W. L. 5, 16, 42
Machiavelli, N. 14, 124
Madeleine la 8, 15, 50
Maecenas 92–5, 152
Mainardi, P. 48, 140, 143

Maison Carrée, Nîmes 15
Mantegna, A. *Triumphs of Caesar* 5, 134–5
Marcellus 33, 127
Marcus Aurelius 126
  equestrian statue of 101
  see also column(s)
Marie-Louise 35, 40, 120, 148–9, 162
Marie-Thérèse 148–9
Marius 125
Marrinan, M. 37, 46
Mars
  salon of 108
  god 107, 137
Martin, J. 134
Master Gregorius, *Mirabilia Urbis Romae* 14
Maxentius 52
  Basilica of 141
Mazarin (cardinal), J. 91, 148
Mazedier, R. 35
Medici 96
  Catherine de 56
  Lorenzo de 155
  Marie de 66, 132 *see also* triumph (post-antique)
Meissonnier, J.-L.-E. 55
Mémorial 26, 32–3, 113
Ménestrier, C.-F. 108
Mercier, L.-S. 11, 112, 115
Mercury 127
metro line, Paris' first 68
Minerva 127
  under Louis XIV 107–8
  and Napoleon 152, 154
  and Republic (French) 24
Mirrors, hall of 107–8
Misson, F. 14
Mitterrand, F. 68–70, 166
Moitte, J.-B.-P. 66
Moitte, J.-G. 31
Molière, J.-B. P. 93
Montesquieu (baron de), C.-L. 2, 53
Montfaucon (de), B. 92, 126
monuments *see* power
museums
  Capitoline 14, 140
  Pio-Clementino 14 *see also* Louvre
Mussolini, B. 3, 32, 69, 165

Napoléon, rue 62
Napoleon III 28, 56, 63–4, 68, 89
Napoleonic
  'Capitol' (*nouveau Capitole*) 48–9, 55, 62, 70, 116, 155–6, 160–1
  censorship 34–5
  eagle 31, 33, 128, 147
  'forum', Paris 8, 48–54, 55–6, 62, 70, 118, 160–1
  legend 26, 32–3
  myth 26–33
  occupation of Rome 21–3, 48, 126, 155
  voie triomphale 37, 44, 55–7, 65–9, 70–1, 134, 160 *see also* triumph (post-antique)
Nation, place de la 38, 65, 68
National, palais (National Palace) 50, 57
Navona, piazza 120
Nero 49, 53, 112, 121–2
  association with Apollo 112
  Golden House 71, 121
  and links with Louis XIV 112, 122
  and Napoleon 112, 121–2
newspapers, value of 5, 30, 33–6, 97–9, 138–9, 143, 164
  Gazette 34, 119
  Gazette de France 98, 124, 144
  Journal de l'Empire 35–6, 97–8, 148, 151
  Journal de Paris 11, 143, 145–6
  Journal de Paris National 138–9
  Mercure 112
  Mercure Galant 119
  Moniteur 142
  Moniteur Universel 35, 57, 62, 94, 97–9, 120, 147
  Patriote Français 142, 144, 146
Norvins (de) J. 29
Notre-Dame 97, 131, 153
Notre-Dame, pont 134, 151–2
Nouveau Cours 41, 92, 103–4
Numa 32

obelisks 102–3, 109, 134, 150, 152
Observatory 89, 104, 115
Octavian *see* Augustus
Orange (*Arausio*) 15–16, 18
  Augustus 17–18
  theatre 15, 17 *see also* arch(es)
Östenberg, I. 44

ovatio see triumph
Ovid 44, 93
 Metamorphoses 19, 92, 136

Paix, rue de la 62
Palatine 22, 52, 121
 and Palace of Augustus 107
Palladio, A. 12, 92
Panini, G. P. 12
Pantheon 22
Paoli, P. 19, 157
papal processions 132, 138
Papal States 20–1, 130, 139–40
pubblica passaggiata, Rome *see* Capitole, jardin du
Pei, I. M. glass Pyramid 68
Percier, C. 16, 47, 51, 58, 65, 94, 119, 121
Pericles 27, 96, 155
Perosini, S. visionary palace 122
Perrault, Ch. 93–4, 102, 119
 Parallèle 93–6, 106, 109–10
Perrault, Cl. 93–4, 101, 119
 Colonnade 50, 92, 104–5, 106–7, 111, 154, 161
 frontispiece to *Vitruve* 104–5
Petrarch (Francesco Petrarca) 12
 I Trionfi 133
Piganiol de la Force, J.-A. 111–12
Pincio (Pincian hill) 21, 120
Piranesi, G. B. 12
Pliny the Elder 59–60, 66, 121, 125, 128, 152
 Natural History 66
Plutarch 19, 31, 101, 126, 128, 157–8
 Parallel Lives 20, 25, 27–9
  on Aemilius Paullus 142
  on Alexander the Great 27
  on Caesar 28–9
  on Hannibal 27
  on Lycurgus 32
  on Marcellus 33
  on Numa 32
Polybius 126
pomerium 40, 104
Pompeii 12–14
 Mazois, F. 13
 Napoleon 13–14
Pompey the Great 66, 127, 130
Pope Innocenzo XII 132
Pope Pius VII 21
Pope Sixtus V 58
Popolo, piazza del 21
portes du Soleil 67, 103, 114, 154
 see also arch(es)
Poussin, N. 58
power
 of monuments / space 5–6, 15–19, 33–4 ch.2, 100–23, 150–4, 158–66
 staging of 1–2, 33–4, 62–3, 69 ch. 4, 156, 160–1 *see also* triumph
Poyet, B. 46–7, 49–50, 53, 146, 159
Prix de Rome 12, 118–19
Propertius 93
Pure (de), M. 43, 100, 125, 127–9
pyramids 89, 102, 115 *see also* battle of; Pei, I. M.

quadriga 52–4, 55, 102, 105, 138, 159
Quatremère de Quincy, A.-C. 13, 49, 144
Quirinal
 hill 120
Quirinale, palazzo del 122

Racine, J. 93
Remus *see* Romulus
Republic 23–6, 136–47
 and monarchical past 5–6, 11, 23–6, 37–8, 54, 64, 71, 90, 136–9, 143–6, 158–65
 and Napoleon 1, 4–5, 20, 23, 26–7, 30–2, 37–8, 45–6, 50–1, 57, 59, 61, 67, 71–2, 96–100, 112–14, 123, 125, 135–47, 156–65
 occupation of Rome 21, 139–41
 reception of antique Rome 10–11, 23–6, 46, 49–51, 53, 56–7, 66–8, 99–100, 136–47, 157–65 *see also* Augustus; Caesar; Louis XIV; triumph (post-antique)
République, pont de la 140
Revolution, place de la *see* Concorde, place de la
Rivoli
 battle *see* battle of
 rue de 56–7, 60–3, 65, 70, 160
Robespierre, M. 25, 139, 142, 144, 146
Rollin, C. 20
Roman Gaul 15–18

Roman Lutetia 7–8
  cardo and *decumanus* 8, 68, 160
Romulus 40, 104, 127
  and Remus: she-wolf, fig tree and *Forum Romanum* 141
Rousseau, J.-J. 20, 24, 27, 31, 90, 158
Royou, J.-C. 121, 129–30

Sacra via see triumph
Sacré-Coeur 64
Saint-Cloud, palais de 152–3
Saint-Denis
  abbey 131
  porte *see* arch(es)
  rue 131
Saint Empire Romain Germanique 48
St. Helena 27–8, 122, 158
St. Honoré, rue 61
St. Peter's 132–3
Saint-Rémy-de-Provence *see Glanum*
Saint-Simon (duc de) 90, 116
S. Giovanni in Laterano 120, 132
San Pietro, piazza 140
SS. Trinita dei Monti 120
sans-culottes 138
Saunier, P.-M. 135
Sauval, H. 107, 111
Schneider, R. 131–2
Scipio Aemilianus 93, 130, 139
Scipio Africanus 127, 130, 133, 139
Senate 24, 41, 57, 99, 147 *see also* 'SPQR concept'; triumph
Septimius Severus 52 *see also* arch(es)
Serlio, S. 92, 134
Soane (Sir), J. visionary processional route, London 44
Sobre, J.-N. 59
Soja, E. W. 45
song(s) 11, 34, 63, 129, 143–4
space *see* power
Specchi, A. 132
spolia / booty *see* Louvre; triumph; triumph (post-antique)
'SPQR concept' 99–100
Spreckelsen, J. O. (von) 69
Spurius Carvilius 60
Stirling, L. 8
Strabo 8, 101
Strong, R. 131, 133, 149–50

Suetonius 126
  Lives of the Caesars 12
  on Augustan Rome 17
  on Caesar 134
  on Domitian's Rome 39
  on Nero's Rome 121

Tacitus 19, 101
Tarquinius Priscus 127, 145
temple(s) 8, 50, 147, 156
  Antoninus and Faustina 141
  Apollo 107
  de la Gloire *see* Madeleine la
  Fortuna Virile 22
  Janus 64
  Jupiter *see* triumph
  Montmartre, visions for 64
  Vesta 22
Terror, the 25, 34
thermae 8, 118, 147
  Thermes, palais des 7
  Titus, baths of 22
Thévenin, C. 137
Thibaudeau, A.-C. 29, 135
Thiers, A. 4, 157
Thiéry, L.-V. 102, 111
Tiberius 53, 126
Titus 126 *see also* arch(es); *thermae*
Tolentino, treaty of 140
Tollfree, E. 58
Tournon (de), C. 21–2
Trajan 28, 57–60, 103–4, 127, 133
  see also arch(es); column(s)
Tree(s) of Liberty
  atop mound: Festival of the Supreme Being 139
  Bastille 67
  Capitoline 140
  Forum Romanum 141
Trevi, fontana di 109
triumph 2, 9, 33–4 ch. 4
  Campus Martius 43, 137
  Capitoline 22, 49, 52, 101, 120, 122, 126–7, 129–30, 132, 140, 145, 154
  currus triumphalis 128–9, 146, 149
  entrance-*ritus* / power 2, 33–4, 124, 130–1
  impact on human senses 34
  as multi-media event 33–4

ovatio (*minor triumphus*) 128
porta triumphalis 2, 42–3, 127, 131, 143, 160
route(s) 2, 16, 34, 60–1, 65, 129, 160
Sacra via 43, 49, 52, 69, 126, 129, 132, 153
sacro-religious language of 130, 132
Senate / senators 2, 16, 52, 126–7, 131
spolia 34, 48, 126–30, 142
Temple(s) of Jupiter / Capitol 2, 48–9, 60, 69, 127, 129–30, 132, 140–1, 143, 146, 153–5
   as locus of power / religion 130
triumphator 2, 16, 33–4, 42–3, 48, 124, 126–31, 141, 153
triumph (post-antique)
   Entrée of Napoleon and Marie-Louise (1810) 35–6, 40, 62, 97–8, 148–55, 162, 164
   entrée royale tradition 45, 102, 124–5, 130–6, 149, 153, 160
   Entrée triomphale (1660) 68, 99, 124, 138, 148–55
   Entrée triomphale (1798) / entrance of *spolia* 11–12, 50, 53, 140–7, 154–5, 159, 161
   entry of Charles V
      into Bologna (1530) 133, 135–6
      into Florence (1539) 136
      into Rome (1536) 133
   entry of Duke Borso d'Este into Reggio (1453) 132
   François I into Lyon (1515) 132
   Henri II into Paris (1549) 134–5, 138, 152
   Henri IV into Lyon (1595) 132
   Marie de Medici into Avignon (1600) 132
   Festival of the Federation (1790), Paris 137
   Festival of the Federation (1798), Rome 140
   Festival of the Perpetuity of the Republic (1799) 141
   Festival of the Supreme Being (1794) 139
   Festival of Unity and Indivisibility (1793) 138–9
   marriage ceremony of Alfonso d'Este, Rome (1501) 133
Trône, place (barrière) du *see* Nation, place de la

Trophée des Alpes 17–18
Tuileries, jardins des 55–6, 111
Tuileries, palais des 8, 38, 42, 47, 49–51, 60, 68, 115, 161
   as Napoleon's residence / seat of power 8, 42, 48–9, 55–7, 62, 67, 160–1
Tulard, J. 20, 28

Unter den Linden, Berlin 44
Urbs vs *orbis* 40–4, 47, 131, 136, 152–3, 160

Valerius Maximus 126
Van Zanten, D. 60
Varro 126
Vasari, G. 91
Vasi, G. 14
Vaudoyer, A.-L.-T. 119
Vendôme
   column *see* column(s)
   place 57, 61, 63, 71, 92, 101
Ventimiglia (*Albintimilium*) 18
Venus 107
Versailles, palace and gardens 9, 66, 90, 92–3, 105–9, 112, 116, 119, 121–2, 161
Vertron (de), C.-C. 92
Vespasian 104, 126, 133
Victoires, place des 92, 109–11, 114–15, 117
   statue of Louis XIV 109–11, 114–15, 117
Victory, goddess of 52, 103, 109–10
Villeloin (abbé de), M. 92
Vincennes
   Château de 51, 68, 153
   Cours de 68, 92
Virgil 93
   Aeneid 19, 92, 129, 136
virtus 25, 139
Vitruvius 46, 93–4, 101, 104–5, 161
   De architectura 94, 134
voie Julia 18
Voltaire 90, 96, 140, 163
Voyage d'Italie see Grand Tour
Vuillaume, M. 71

Werner, J.
   Triumph of King Louis XIV 129–30, 136, 152
Winckelmann, J.J. 13
Wintjes, J. 28
Wisch, B. 150

Printed in Great Britain
by Amazon.co.uk, Ltd.,
Marston Gate.